Growth and Variability
in State Tax Revenue

Growth and Variability in State Tax Revenue

An Anatomy of State Fiscal Crises

Randall G. Holcombe
and Russell S. Sobel

Contributions in Economics and Economic History
Number 189

Greenwood Press
Westport, Connecticut • London

For Terri and Reagan
R.S.S.

For Lora, Ross, Mark, and Connor
R.G.H.

Library of Congress Cataloging-in-Publication Data

Holcombe, Randall G.
    Growth and variability in state tax revenue : an anatomy of state
fiscal crises / Randall G. Holcombe and Russell S. Sobel.
        p. cm.—(Contributions in economics and economic history,
ISSN 0084–9235 ; no. 189)
    Includes bibliographical references and index.
    ISBN 0-313-30423-8 (alk. paper)
    1. Revenue—United States—States. 2. Taxation—United States—
States. 3. United States—Appropriations and expenditures, State.
I. Sobel, Russell S., 1968- . II. Title. III. Series.
HJ2385.H65 1997
336.2'01373—dc21   97–5597

British Library Cataloguing in Publication Data is available.

Library of Congress Catalog Card Number: 97–5597
ISBN: 0-313-30423-8
ISSN: 0084–9235

First published in 1997

Greenwood Press, 88 Post Road West, Westport, CT 06881
An imprint of Greenwood Publishing Group, Inc.

Printed in the United States of America

The paper used in this book complies with the
Permanent Paper Standard issued by the National
Information Standards Organization (Z39.48–1984).

10 9 8 7 6 5 4 3 2 1

Contents

Illustrations

TABLES

Preface

Our work on this book originated in 1991, when a recession had a negative impact on state government revenues and pushed many states into what was often described as a fiscal crisis. Both of us were living in Tallahassee at the time, and Florida was feeling the impact of the recession along with the rest of the nation. Our interest in the subject originally was Florida-specific. Florida has no state income tax, and a number of state policy-makers argued that an income tax would be beneficial because it would reduce the negative impact of recessions on the state's finances. We heard this claim repeated by economic analysts within the state government, and by the popular press in Florida. On the surface, this claim made little sense to us. Why would having a state income tax help cushion the effect of a recession on the state's finances? Thus, we set out to investigate.

One obvious possible reason why an income tax might help mitigate Florida's fiscal crisis is that the fiscal crisis is not recession-specific, but rather is caused by an overall lack of revenues to meet the state's needs. We take this claim seriously, and deal with it in the first three chapters, but conclude that while states do face many fiscal challenges, the periodic fiscal crises that states face are the results of revenue downturns during recessions. Thus, fiscal crises are caused by cyclical variability in state revenues, and adding an income tax in those states without one would be helpful only if it would serve to stabilize revenues over the business cycle.

At first glance, there is no reason to think that adding a state income tax would reduce the cyclical variability of revenues in a state that relies mainly on general sales taxes for revenue. Both tax bases are pro-cyclical, but because consumption is more stable over the business cycle than income, it would appear that adding an income tax to a state without one would increase the cyclical variability of the tax base, and actually worsen recession-induced fiscal crises. However, the general sales tax is not exactly a consumption tax. Many consumption items are not taxed, and many non-consumption items are. Similarly, personal income does not exactly correspond to the personal income tax base. Thus, we approached the issue of whether state income taxes are more cyclically variable than state sales taxes is an empirical question, and deal directly with that question in Chapter 7.

The previous literature on the subject of cyclical variability of taxes has used a variety to methodologies, and part of our work has been to analyze those methodologies to decide on the appropriate way to measure cyclical variability. Our approach has benefited from recent advances in time series econometrics, but also has been guided by our conclusion that for purposes of evaluating state fiscal crises, it is important to measure variability related to the business cycle, rather than variability in general. Having developed our methodology, we applied it more broadly to look at different types of taxes, and to compare cyclical variability of revenues across states. For purposes of public policy, we conclude that while there are a few policy changes that could reduce cyclical variability of revenue to a degree (such as adding food to the sales tax base in those states that currently exempt food), state revenues will always exhibit a substantial amount of cyclical variability. Thus, we recommend that state policy makers accommodate the inevitable cyclical variability in revenues by smoothing expenditures over the business cycle. This led us to analyze state rainy day funds as a method of smoothing expenditures, and our analysis of rainy day funds appears in Chapter 9.

Some of the work in this volume has been published previously, and we thank those journals in which our work appeared for permission to use it in this book. We compared the variability of income and sales taxes in "The Relative Variability of State Income and Sales Taxes over the Revenue Cycle," *Atlantic Economic Journal* (June 1995), and while we have completely redone the empirical work, that paper laid the foundation for Chapter 7. Chapter 5, discussing our methodology, is largely taken from "Measuring the Growth and Variability of Tax Bases Over the Business Cycle," *National Tax Journal* (December 1996), and Chapter 9 is largely taken from "The Impact of State Rainy Day Funds in Easing State Fiscal Crises During the 1990–91 Recession," *Public Budgeting and Finance* (Fall 1996).

A number of people have read parts of the manuscript and provided us with data and valuable comments, and we thank Donald Boudreaux, Stratford Douglas, John Barkoulas, Corina Eckl, Daniel Gropper, Stacy Mazer, Stefan Norrbin, and Kevin Reffett. We are especially grateful to Karen Wells and Rhonna Robbins for preparing the manuscript for publication. Our largest debt of gratitude goes to our families who were supportive throughout this undertaking, and we dedicate the book to them.

RGH
RSS

Chapter 1

Revenues and Expenditures: The Components of Crisis

In the first few years of the 1990s the typical state in the United States was facing serious fiscal problems. Expenditures in a number of areas were increasing at a far faster rate than state incomes, health care being the most prominent area in this regard. The expanding areas in state budgets were crowding out expenditures in areas where states have traditionally spent most of their budgets, such as education and highways. As growing areas of the budget created pressure by claiming larger and larger shares of expenditures, the traditional areas also created pressure as they struggled to maintain their places in state budgets. Meanwhile, revenue sources were being stretched to the limit, partly because of past increases that have consumed states' tax capacities, and partly because of tax limitation movements that have escalated since California's overwhelming passage of Proposition 13 on June 6, 1978. The underlying issues and problems are complex, but the essence of a state fiscal crisis is that the demand for expenditures tends to outstrip the supply of revenues.

Most of the blame for state fiscal crises must be placed on the budgeting practices of state governments. States have tended to spend as much as they possibly could every year, which has meant that during the good years, state government spending has increased rapidly, but during recessions, states had to curtail their spending increases, if not their total spending, significantly. Fiscal crises have arisen not so much because of a lack of revenue growth, but rather due to the cyclical variability of state government revenue streams. The fiscal crises that states saw during the early 1990s were similar to fiscal crises they faced as a result of the 1982 recession, but during the later years of the 1980s and during the mid-1990s, after the recessions, there was little talk of fiscal crises the way there was during both the 1982 and 1991 recessions. States regularly face challenges in their budgeting processes, but crises come during recessions.

Because state government fiscal crises occur during economic downturns, the analysis through most of the book focuses on the cyclical variability in state government revenues. This does not mean that spending pressures have nothing to do with state fiscal crises, or that tax base issues are irrelevant. To the contrary, fiscal crises arise because the demand for expenditures exceeds the supply of revenues. Spending pressures are very important, but when viewed in a larger context, states will always have spending pressures because of the very nature of government spending. Most government programs are provided to their beneficiaries at a price below their cost. This virtually guarantees that the beneficiaries will demand more from the programs than the government can ever be prepared to provide. Thus, in good times or bad, government always must choose which demands to satisfy, as the demands of college students compete against the demands of subsidized health care, which compete against all other interest groups.

Whether these competing demands for government funding are worthwhile is beside the point when considering the nature of state government fiscal crises. The real point is that the demand for government spending always exceeds the supply because government services are priced below cost. Therefore, as a matter of routine, state legislatures must choose which among the many competing demands they will fund.[1] High demands for state government services require that hard choices be made, but by themselves do not cause crises.

Certain types of expenditures are sometimes referred to as uncontrollable. Entitlements such as health-care and welfare programs fit into this category, as do many of the services of courts and law enforcement. Open-ended commitments are indeed more difficult to control than more clearly defined budget items, and these are the types of programs that have been creating the greatest amount of pressure on the demand side. Another difficult problem for states is that often such expenditures can be mandated by the federal government, but without federal funding to pay for the mandated expenditures. These are real problems. No expenditure category can continue to grow faster than income growth forever, however, because eventually it would consume all income. These problems are an indication that tough choices must be made, but what legislation has done it can also undo. If one is seeking solutions to state fiscal problems, one cannot view these problems as out of the control of state legislatures.

Tough budgetary choices will have to be made by state legislatures to control spending growth, to raise revenues to finance that growth, or both. These are more fundamental ongoing problems, but not the central cause of state fiscal crises. In many ways, these fundamental problems present more difficult choices to states than the problems of fiscal crises discussed here. How much involvement do we want our state governments to have in areas such as health care and higher education—two areas in which private alternatives are available? What should be the priorities of state government? These important issues are beyond the scope of what is discussed in this book. However, Chapter 2 does examine some of the financing issues to see the relationship between state fiscal crises and underlying expenditure trends. To get a better idea of the nature of state government fiscal crises, the first step is to examine trends in state government revenues and expenditures.

STATE REVENUE AND EXPENDITURE TRENDS

The most recent periods during which a large number of states faced fiscal crises were the recessions of 1982 and 1991. Although one would not claim that states did not feel some pressure during the latter years of the 1980s, or prior to 1981, the crisis atmosphere was certainly more prevalent during these recessions. Figure 1.1 examines state government revenue and expenditure trends over the period of several decades. In the first half of the 1950s, state government spending averaged around 4 percent of gross domestic product (GDP), but Figure 1.1 shows a steady and substantial increase from the mid-1950s up through the early 1970s, when state spending hovered around 8 percent of GDP. In contrast to the doubling in state government's share of GDP that occurred during the decade and a half from the mid-1950s through the early 1970s, state spending leveled off during the 1970s and early 1980s, hovering just above 8 percent of GDP. An upward trend resumed in the late 1980s, and by 1993, state government spending was more than 10 percent of GDP—an 18 percent increase in its share of GDP compared with a decade earlier.

Figure 1.1
State Government as a Percentage of GDP

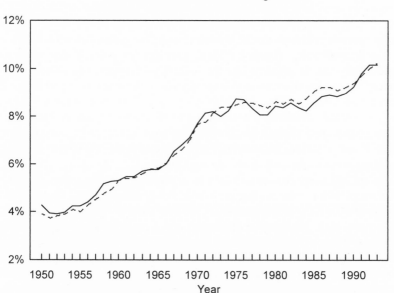

— General Expenditures   - - General Revenue

A similar trend is evident when local expenditures are combined with state expenditures, as illustrated in Figure 1.2. In the early 1950s, state and local government expenditures were less than 8 percent of GDP and increased to more than 14 percent by the mid-1970s. There is a slight decline in state and local expenditures in the later years of the 1970s, but they stabilized and remained around 14 percent of GDP through the mid-1980s. During the late 1980s, spending began rising again, and by 1992 was more than 16 percent of GDP.

Figure 1.2
State and Local Government as a Percentage of GDP

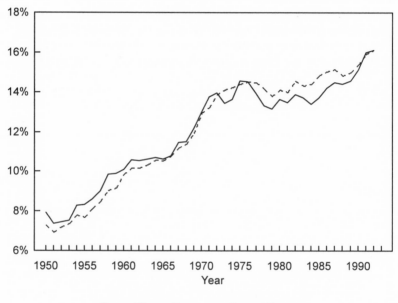

— General Expenditures   - - General Revenue

The big stories in Figures 1.1 and 1.2 are the dramatic changes in the trend rate of growth that happened in the early 1970s and late 1980s. As a percentage of GDP, state government expenditures approximately doubled in the two decades of the 1950s and 1960s, but increased by only slightly in the 1970s and early 1980s. Growth picked up again in the late 1980s, with government expenditures rising as much during the five years from 1988 to 1992 as it did during the entire period from 1970 to 1988. This in itself reveals a great deal about the cause of state fiscal crises. During the early 1980s, the severe fiscal crises were often blamed upon the lack of sufficient revenue growth to support expenditure programs, whereas, ironically, during the early 1990s they were often blamed on the fast revenue growth causing expansions in government programs that could not be continued. The occurrence of state fiscal crises directly following periods of both fast and slow revenue growth is further evidence that the fundamental cause of state fiscal crises is not the long-run rate of expansion in revenues, but rather the short-run fluctuations in revenues caused by recessions.

Figures 1.1 and 1.2 do not fully reveal the amount of new revenues that state governments had to work with during the 1970s and 1980s because, although their growth relative to GDP slowed, continual GDP growth meant that states consistently have had greater revenues to work with. Figure 1.3 shows real state government revenues and expenditures since 1950. These expenditure figures are adjusted for inflation, but not for population growth. As Figure 1.3 reveals, total spending by state governments continually increased over the four-decade period. Although it did slow during the 1970s and early 1980s, it appears as if the upward trend resumed soon after the 1982 recession was over. States had at least six years of rapid revenue growth before the 1991 recession hit. State fiscal crises have not been due to a lack of state government revenue or expenditure growth.

States have also had large increases in expenditures after adjusting for both

Figure 1.3
Size of State Government in Real Dollars

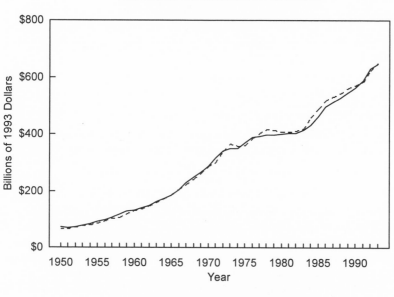

— General Expenditures   - - General Revenue

inflation and population growth. Figure 1.4 shows real per capita state government revenues and expenditures and illustrates that after adjusting for inflation, the amount of state expenditures per person has increased throughout the period. Consistent with the earlier data, state government growth was greater during the 1950s and 1960s than in the 1970s and early 1980s, but resumed its upward trend again in the mid-1980s. Real per capita state government spending grew by 50 percent in the 1950s and by a whopping 80 percent during the 1960s. The early 1970s were characterized by the same rapid growth as the 1960s, but during the period from 1975 to 1983 real per capita state government spending grew by less than 3 percent. Real per capita spending resumed its upward trend, and between 1985 and 1993 grew by 29 percent.

Figure 1.4
Real Per Capita Size of State Government

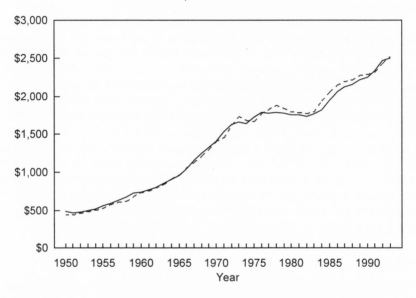

— General Expenditures   - - General Revenue

State government growth has been substantial over all four of these decades, but was considerably greater during the first two decades, and since the 1982 recession, than during the 1970s and early 1980s. This has meant that state governments have experienced recessionary fiscal crises in both slow and fast revenue growth periods. Although the fiscal crises experienced during the recession of the early 1990s were less severe than the ones in the early 1980s, this was due to the differences in the severity of the recessions, not to differences in the long-run revenue growth preceding the recessions.

The occurrence of a fiscal crisis suggests that in some sense there is more demand for government funds than there are funds available. The data in this section suggests, however, that lack of long-run revenue growth is not the underlying problem. Fiscal crises have occurred following periods of both slow and rapid growth of revenue. For purposes of comparison, some of the expenditure figures discussed along with the figures in this section are listed in Table 1.1.

NEW TAXES AND REVENUE GROWTH

The issue of taxes is discussed in detail in Chapter 3, but in the context of the growth of state governments discussed in the previous section, it is worth noting that state governments routinely adopted new tax bases during the 1960s, and this was a major contributor to the rapid growth in state spending during that decade, and to the relative slowdown during the 1970s. From 1960 to 1971 nine states instituted personal income taxes, nine instituted corporation income taxes, and eleven instituted state sales taxes. Since 1971 no states have instituted either a sales or corporation income tax, and only two states, New Jersey in 1976 and Connecticut in 1991, instituted a personal income tax.[2]

When faced with fiscal challenges, states with unused tax bases could tap those tax bases for new sources of revenues. Once those tax bases have been tapped, rates have to be increased to increase spending, and after substantial state and local expenditure growth for decades, taxpayers were resistant to increases in the rates of taxation. This might contribute toward explaining why the relatively large increases in state government as a percentage of income during the 1960s did not continue through the 1970s and early 1980s. From the mid-1980s through the early 1990s, state government growth was fueled by rate increases on existing tax bases rather than the imposition of new taxes, as it was during the 1960s. In fact, the tax increases during the 1990–91 recession were, in dollar amounts, the largest in the history of state government in the United States. Thus, although there appear to be two periods of similar fast revenue growth for state governments, the 1950s and 1960s was a period of the imposition of new taxes, whereas the late 1980s and early 1990s was a period of increased taxation on existing tax bases.

FEDERAL AID TO STATES AND STATE FISCAL CRISES

One factor that might have contributed to the pressure on state government budgets during the early 1980s was the reduction in federal aid to states. Figure 1.5 shows that as a percentage of state and local government expenditures, the federal contribution increased dramatically during the 1960s and early 1970s. This was followed by a dramatic decline in federal aid during the 1980s. It appears that federal aid to states has again begun to rise in the early 1990s. Table 1.2 shows the same numbers to give a better feel for the magnitude of federal aid to state and local governments.

These figures show that throughout the post–World War II period federal funding has been a significant share of state government revenues. At its lowest point, federal funds as a percentage of state revenues fell to around 16 percent in the mid-1950s. Two decades later, in the 1970s, federal funding as a percentage of state revenues rose to around 28 percent. By 1989 the federal contribution to state revenues had fallen to about 23 percent, near the level of the early 1960s. This downward trend appears to have reversed with federal aid rising to just over 27 percent in 1993. A similar picture emerges when federal aid to state and local governments is considered. In percentage terms, state and local governments

Table 1.1
State and Local Government Revenue and Expenditures

Year	State and Local Government (Percentage of GDP)		State Government (Percentage of GDP)		State Government (Millions of 1993 Dollars)		State Government (Per capita, 1993 dollars)	
	Expenditures	Revenue	Expenditures	Revenue	Expenditures	Revenue	Expenditures	Revenue
1950	7.94%	7.29%	4.27%	3.92%	$73,449	$67,525	$482.36	$443.45
1951	7.37%	6.95%	3.93%	3.74%	$72,378	$68,949	$467.32	$445.18
1952	7.46%	7.20%	3.92%	3.84%	$74,687	$73,226	$474.05	$464.77
1953	7.54%	7.38%	3.97%	3.92%	$79,437	$78,533	$495.91	$490.27
1954	8.28%	7.82%	4.26%	4.12%	$84,809	$82,182	$520.22	$504.11
1955	8.34%	7.69%	4.25%	4.01%	$92,609	$87,315	$558.12	$526.21
1956	8.61%	8.13%	4.42%	4.31%	$100,178	$97,692	$593.11	$578.39
1957	9.00%	8.51%	4.70%	4.54%	$108,432	$104,811	$630.47	$609.43
1958	9.86%	9.07%	5.18%	4.79%	$117,685	$108,860	$672.94	$622.48
1959	9.89%	9.17%	5.26%	4.95%	$129,136	$121,400	$726.18	$682.67
1960	10.11%	9.84%	5.30%	5.33%	$132,920	$133,580	$735.70	$739.35
1961	10.57%	10.16%	5.48%	5.40%	$140,721	$138,667	$766.07	$754.89
1962	10.53%	10.19%	5.47%	5.45%	$149,672	$149,079	$802.37	$799.19
1963	10.61%	10.32%	5.70%	5.62%	$162,336	$159,998	$857.82	$845.47
1964	10.69%	10.56%	5.75%	5.81%	$173,829	$175,488	$905.88	$914.53
1965	10.63%	10.53%	5.76%	5.82%	$185,538	$187,758	$954.89	$966.32
1966	10.76%	10.79%	5.99%	6.07%	$205,556	$208,530	$1,045.77	$1,060.90
1967	11.46%	11.20%	6.55%	6.39%	$230,616	$225,277	$1,160.55	$1,133.69
1968	11.52%	11.39%	6.79%	6.65%	$250,778	$245,534	$1,249.48	$1,223.35
1969	12.17%	11.93%	7.09%	7.02%	$267,829	$265,030	$1,321.46	$1,307.64

Year								
1970	12.99%	12.94%	7.68%	7.69%	$289,156	$289,577	$1,410.16	$1,412.21
1971	13.73%	13.21%	8.12%	7.76%	$317,964	$303,625	$1,531.17	$1,462.12
1972	13.96%	13.88%	8.19%	8.17%	$341,580	$340,965	$1,627.38	$1,624.45
1973	13.44%	14.09%	8.01%	8.38%	$351,766	$368,189	$1,659.99	$1,737.48
1974	13.64%	14.24%	8.22%	8.39%	$351,405	$358,545	$1,643.20	$1,676.59
1975	14.55%	14.39%	8.72%	8.49%	$371,464	$361,548	$1,719.96	$1,674.04
1976	14.52%	14.49%	8.69%	8.60%	$390,302	$386,310	$1,790.09	$1,771.78
1977	13.89%	14.44%	8.33%	8.57%	$391,893	$403,279	$1,779.40	$1,831.10
1978	13.30%	14.15%	8.05%	8.47%	$398,488	$419,092	$1,790.27	$1,882.84
1979	13.16%	13.79%	8.06%	8.36%	$399,134	$414,090	$1,773.50	$1,839.95
1980	13.63%	14.12%	8.43%	8.63%	$400,221	$409,636	$1,757.47	$1,798.81
1981	13.44%	13.97%	8.37%	8.52%	$403,223	$410,385	$1,753.40	$1,784.55
1982	13.87%	14.53%	8.56%	8.73%	$403,537	$411,954	$1,737.97	$1,774.23
1983	13.71%	14.30%	8.37%	8.53%	$413,540	$421,429	$1,764.95	$1,798.62
1984	13.39%	14.39%	8.21%	8.77%	$430,823	$459,980	$1,822.83	$1,946.20
1985	13.71%	14.81%	8.55%	9.05%	$463,492	$490,634	$1,943.64	$2,057.46
1986	14.19%	15.03%	8.82%	9.22%	$496,332	$518,806	$2,062.46	$2,155.85
1987	14.47%	15.13%	8.90%	9.23%	$513,813	$533,040	$2,116.16	$2,195.35
1988	14.38%	14.83%	8.82%	9.08%	$527,894	$543,723	$2,154.48	$2,219.09
1989	14.54%	14.99%	8.95%	9.21%	$546,850	$562,526	$2,210.91	$2,274.28
1990	15.12%	15.38%	9.20%	9.38%	$561,951	$572,384	$2,248.63	$2,290.38
1991	15.99%	15.89%	9.77%	9.72%	$588,717	$585,344	$2,330.18	$2,316.84
1992	16.10%	16.11%	10.13%	10.02%	$630,240	$623,455	$2,467.10	$2,440.54
1993			10.14%	10.25%	$646,229	$653,135	$2,502.39	$2,529.13

Source: Tax Foundation, *Facts and Figures on Government Finance,* various years.

9

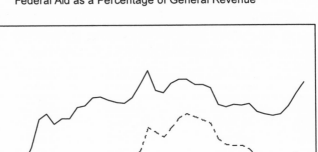

Figure 1.5
Federal Aid as a Percentage of General Revenue

— State Revenue   -· State and Local Revenue

combined rely less on federal financing than state governments alone, but the trend appears similar. In 1956 about 9 percent of state and local revenues came from the federal government, and that figure more than doubled to just over 23 percent in the late 1970s before declining to below 17 percent by the end of the 1980s. This trend has perhaps reversed itself, with federal aid beginning an upward trend again in the early 1990s.

Federal funding makes up a substantial share of state revenues, but that share has varied considerably over the decades. From its height in the 1970s, federal funding as a share of state expenditures had fallen by about five percentage points, which as a percentage of the total is a decline of about 18 percent. Looking at state and local revenues together, the impact is even more dramatic, as the federal share of state and local revenues declined by about 30 percent. Thus, during the late 1970s and early 1980s, as state expenditures were growing more slowly than in the past, federal contributions to states were declining as a percentage of total state spending. Heading into the recession in the early 1980s, federal aid was on the decline. Although this can be viewed as a contributing factor to the severity of state fiscal crises during the early 1980s, it certainly cannot be the entire explanation, as the exact opposite was true for the fiscal crises of the early 1990s. Heading into, and throughout, the recession of 1991, states were receiving more federal aid than during the late 1980s. The last two columns in Table 1.2, and Figure 1.6, show that, even after adjusting for inflation and population, there is a similar pattern.

Table 1.2
Federal Aid to State and Local Governments

Year	Federal Aid (Percentage of General Revenue)		Federal Aid (Per Capita, 1993 Dollars)	
	State	State and Local	State	State and Local
1950	18.57%	10.91%	$89.58	$97.89
1951	18.11%	9.65%	$84.65	$84.65
1952	17.00%	9.83%	$80.61	$88.81
1953	17.51%	10.28%	$86.83	$96.97
1954	16.90%	9.66%	$87.91	$97.73
1955	16.08%	9.28%	$89.75	$101.74
1956	16.05%	9.08%	$95.21	$104.90
1957	16.60%	9.52%	$104.65	$114.91
1958	18.95%	10.85%	$127.54	$139.09
1959	22.64%	13.04%	$164.41	$178.07
1960	23.44%	13.44%	$172.44	$188.44
1961	22.02%	12.69%	$168.70	$187.61
1962	22.72%	13.07%	$182.32	$201.89
1963	22.78%	13.54%	$195.43	$216.17
1964	24.26%	14.43%	$219.74	$242.96
1965	24.41%	14.77%	$233.12	$260.38
1966	25.48%	15.95%	$266.44	$299.82
1967	25.54%	16.46%	$296.45	$334.63
1968	25.21%	16.78%	$315.04	$355.45
1969	24.85%	16.41%	$328.45	$372.08
1970	24.80%	16.64%	$349.66	$396.97
1971	25.53%	17.35%	$390.94	$449.22
1972	27.11%	18.60%	$441.24	$516.20
1973	29.01%	21.65%	$481.64	$602.89
1974	26.38%	21.02%	$433.54	$573.18
1975	26.14%	20.39%	$449.54	$584.92
1976	27.34%	21.65%	$489.34	$647.47
1977	27.92%	22.82%	$496.84	$677.49
1978	27.92%	23.43%	$499.84	$692.92
1979	27.20%	22.95%	$482.42	$664.74
1980	27.12%	22.50%	$476.61	$639.38
1981	26.76%	22.16%	$469.14	$624.16
1982	24.50%	19.98%	$425.81	$562.89
1983	24.20%	19.28%	$427.15	$557.31
1984	24.58%	19.22%	$448.04	$571.09
1985	24.47%	19.17%	$475.69	$597.84
1986	24.62%	18.67%	$507.68	$619.62
1987	23.63%	17.50%	$500.11	$602.44
1988	23.25%	16.68%	$500.81	$586.27
1989	23.06%	16.50%	$509.94	$592.80
1990	23.28%	16.39%	$523.59	$605.21
1991	24.32%	16.97%	$566.59	$647.10
1992	25.99%	18.44%	$641.21	$722.42
1993	27.48%		$687.56	

Source: Tax Foundation, *Facts and Figures on Government Finance*, various years.

The growth in federal aid to state governments closely follows the trend in state government spending. From the middle 1950s up through the early 1970s, federal grants to states increased substantially. Federal aid showed essentially no trend during the rest of the 1970s and early 1980s, and began rising again in the mid-1980s. The new upward trend in federal aid to states appears to have started earlier, perhaps as early as 1982, when the data is corrected for inflation and population, as it is in Figure 1.6. Again, the data show that state fiscal crises have happened following periods of both slow and rapid growth of federal aid to the states. One would be hard-pressed to place the blame for state fiscal crises on the federal government.

Figure 1.6
Real Per Capita Federal Aid

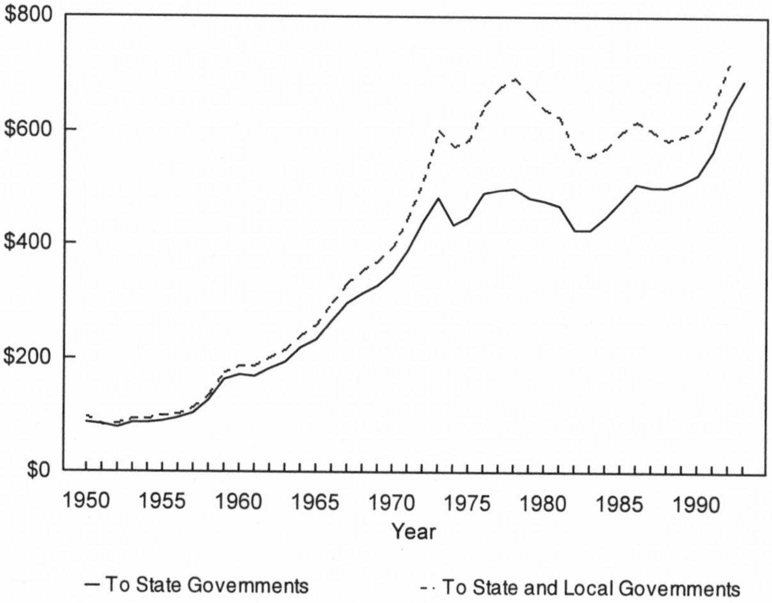

— To State Governments   -- To State and Local Governments

RECESSIONS AND CRISIS

A review of the history of state government finances from 1950 to 1993 shows that there are two, and possibly three, distinctly different regimes that state governments have operated under. The first is the period from 1950 through the early 1970s. During this time, states enjoyed growing revenues and expenditures. States enhanced their revenues by implementing new tax bases. Many states adopted their first income and sales taxes during this period. Federal aid grew in almost every year from 1952 to 1973, augmenting states' fiscal capacity.

The latter 1970s and early 1980s showed sharply lower rates of growth in state revenues and expenditures, and virtually no growth in federal aid to states. Thus, one would expect states to encounter more difficult fiscal situations. However, the slowdown in the rate of growth of state government spending should not obscure the fact that state spending still continued to increase over the decades. In real per capita terms, state government spending increased by 50 percent in the 1950s, by 80 percent in the 1960s, by 26 percent in the 1970s, and by 26 percent in the 1980s. The slowdown in the rate of growth of state government spending is apparent, but at the same time state government spending still increased significantly in each decade, both in real dollar terms and as a percentage of GDP.

Beginning again in the mid-1980s, state government revenues and expenditures began rising. Fueled by a healthy economy and increasing reliance on existing tax bases, states were able to expand their expenditures despite cuts in federal aid. After almost a decade of strong economic growth, the economy once again slipped into a recession in the early 1990s. Despite the healthy fiscal times of the mid and late 1980s, and the resumed increases in federal aid, states again found themselves experiencing severe fiscal crises during the recession. The mid-1990s saw continued growth in state government as the economy came out of the recession, and the tax increases instituted during the recession provided even greater revenues as the economy expanded.

The negative impact of recessions on state governments is what has led to state government fiscal crises. Along with the recession in 1982 came the perception that state governments faced severe fiscal crises, but concerns along these lines subsided until the recession of 1991, when similar discussions of fiscal crisis were heard.[3] States always have greater demand for their services than they have resources to supply, simply because they give output to constituents below cost. That in itself does not create a crisis. However, the slowdowns in revenues due to recessions have precipitated crises, because states are unable to keep the commitments they have made under the prerecession regime. This is true regardless of whether expenditure programs were increasing or remaining steady prior to the recession. As long as states continue to spend all available revenues during the nonrecession years, cyclically declining revenues will cause fiscal crises.

THE PROBLEM IN CONTEXT

The fundamental problem that leads to state government fiscal crises is cyclical variability in the revenue stream. The preceding analysis suggests that as long as revenues show stable growth from year to year, fiscal crises do not appear, but slowdowns in revenue growth produce a widespread crisis atmosphere. Thus, the problem that needs to be analyzed is cyclical variability of state government revenues.

Some clarification is in order before pursuing the analysis of cyclical variability. Although the issue of cyclical variability in the revenue stream is fundamental to understanding fiscal crises, this does not imply that this variability is the most significant fiscal problem that states face, and it certainly does not imply that if the problem of cyclical variability in the revenue stream can be overcome, that states' fiscal problems will be solved. States raise revenues and undertake expenditures programs to meet the demands of their constituents. The burden of taxes on states' taxpayers and the degree to which state expenditures actually satisfy the demands of states' constituents both loom as more important issues than the cyclical variability of the revenue stream.

Placed in context, the issue of cyclical variability is only a small part of the overall fiscal picture of state governments. Yet it is important to separate the ongoing problems states face when determining their budgetary priorities from the short-run crises that they face due to revenue downturns. Steven Gold argues, "There were many causes of the state fiscal crisis. Any simple explanation of its roots is inadequate."[4] Gold's statement is true, but he takes a much broader view of fiscal crisis than is taken here. He lists as underlying causes growing Medicaid expenditures, federal mandates, and dysfunctional tax systems, to name a few. In the mid-1990s, these problems remain in much the same form as during the 1991 recession, yet after the recession, the crisis atmosphere went away. Gold considers some significant ongoing fiscal problems that states face, but crises appear when revenue growth slows due to recessions, and this volume focuses specifically on the crises caused by revenue variability rather than on a broader list of state fiscal challenges.

Although the issue of cyclical variability is only a small part of the total picture, it is an important issue nonetheless, because it relates directly to more important issues. Demands for state government services tend to be countercyclical, whereas the revenue stream is procyclical, so the issue of cyclical variability relates directly to the ability of state governments to satisfy their constituents' demands. Furthermore, government programs are sure to be less effective when they run into severe budget constraints, when they tend to be needed the most. Rather than being concerned about how to deliver services, the attention of those working in the government becomes diverted to how to weather the fiscal crisis. A smoothing of the cyclical variability of revenues can assist in delivering better services. Although other fiscal issues may appear to be more important in the overall scheme of state government finance, the issue of cyclical variability in state revenues relates directly to those other more important issues.

CYCLICAL VARIABILITY: THE FUNDAMENTAL PROBLEM

Not surprisingly, economists have given considerable attention to the issue of revenue variability. Chapter 4 discusses the issues faced by state policy makers in dealing with revenue streams that fluctuate over the business cycle. Chapter 5 examines some of the attempts to quantify and analyze the problem, but the analysis undertaken here departs from most earlier work in that it emphasizes short-run cyclical variability, rather than long-run growth or general revenue variability. There are two common ways of analyzing revenue variability. The first is to find the trend rate of growth of revenue and then use a measure of deviation from the trend as the measure of variability. This measure is undoubtedly useful for some purposes, but it fails to capture the essence of the problem because it is not variability in general, but rather variability correlated with business cycles that is associated with fiscal crises. A degree of fluctuation from year to year may have some negative consequences for state governments, but fluctuations associated with business cycles create more substantial fiscal problems. The second common way that cyclical variability is measured is to use a linear regression of the tax base (or its revenues) on income, specified in logarithmic form. As discussed in Chapter 5, this regression method measures only the long-run growth potential of the tax, and not the short-run fluctuations over the business cycle. Thus, the analysis here departs from earlier work in emphasizing the short-run cyclical component of revenue variability

Any attempt to quantify revenue variability with a numerical measure is a simplification in the sense that it attempts to summarize with one number a complex intertemporal phenomenon. In one sense, there can be no single correct measure of cyclical variability, because any summary is sure to leave out some component of revenue variability. Because of this, revenue variability is considered relative to a number of different indicators to come up with different measures. Chapter 5 gives measures of cyclical variability for each major state tax base when compared to the national economy. Chapter 6 does this analysis on a state-by-state basis using the revenues derived from taxes, giving measures of variability when compared to the revenue cycle of all states, to the state's own income, and to the national economy. Each of these measures has a different interpretation. At this point, the key thing to understand is that cyclical variability is different from deviation around a trend, and is different from long-run growth. Any appropriate measure of cyclical variability should capture the movements in state government revenues associated specifically with business cycles. The measures presented here attempt to capture and quantify the cyclical component of revenue variability.

FISCAL CRISES: THE KEY FACTORS

As the prior discussion makes clear, cyclical variability is the primary focus of analysis in examining the underlying causes of state fiscal crises. Before directly examining cyclical variability, however, Chapters 2 and 3 look in more detail at state government revenues and expenditures. Despite the cyclical nature of the problem, it is after all the excess of demands for spending over the supply of revenues that underlies the problem. Chapter 2, which looks at state government spending, finds that there have been important changes in the structure of state government spending over the decades that have created additional demand pressure on state governments. The relevance of these factors is considered in some detail. Likewise, the evolution of state government revenues has contributed to the fiscal pressure felt by state governments, primarily, as noted above, due to the slowdown in overall revenue growth in the 1970s and early 1980s when compared to the previous two decades. Chapter 3 looks at state revenues in more detail.

Despite the importance of those details considered in Chapters 2 and 3, a key point of this introductory chapter is that the demands for state government spending always exceed the supply of funds because the government distributes its output below cost. Thus, there will always be pressure for more spending, but this by itself does not create a crisis. Cyclical downturns in revenue create crises. Chapter 4 discusses the applied policy side of the difficult issues involved in managing a portfolio of state taxes, each having different cyclical variability. Chapter 5 examines methodological issues involved in analyzing cyclical variability of the state government revenue stream, and Chapter 6 is the first of several chapters that measure cyclical variability on an individual level for states. Chapter 6 develops measures that compare the cyclical variability of the states to see which states exhibit the most cyclical variability. Chapter 7 looks specifically at the cyclical variability of the two largest revenue sources of state governments: income taxes and sales taxes. Chapter 8 examines the potential trade-off between stability and revenue growth. Chapter 9 discusses the potential for state rainy day funds to help states ease the fiscal pressure associated with future recessions.

The final chapter presents a summary of the analysis and recommendations. Ultimately, this analysis concludes that, although there are some state policy changes that could be used to limit the cyclical variability of a state's revenue stream, the most important step that states can take is to establish a properly structured rainy day fund. Some measures that might have some impact on revenue variability, such as removing the exemption for food from a state sales tax, might be faulted on equity grounds, but in any event, such changes have the potential for only minimal impact on the overall cyclical variability of state revenues. However, because cyclical variability can be forecast to some degree, the best strategy states could pursue to cope with the problem is to set aside some revenues during the good years to minimize the negative impact of revenue downturns during the bad years.

NOTES

1. There is an extensive literature on the way in which legislatures deal with interest groups to determine which programs will be funded, and to what degree. Models of legislative politics along these lines are found in Randall G. Holcombe, *An Economic Analysis of Democracy* (Carbondale: Southern Illinois University Press, 1985) and in Barry R. Weingast, Kenneth A. Shepsle, and Christopher Johnsen, "The Political Economy of Benefits and Costs: A Neoclassical Approach to Distributive Politics," *Journal of Political Economy* 89, no. 4 (August 1981): 642–64. For insightful discussions dealing with the trade-offs among interest groups, see Gary S. Becker, "A Theory of Competition among Pressure Groups for Political Influence," *Quarterly Journal of Economics* 98 (August 1983): 371–400, and Sam Peltzman, "Toward a More General Theory of Regulation," *Journal of Law & Economics* 19 (August 1976): 211–40.

2. One state, Alaska in 1979, repealed its personal income tax during this period. Connecticut originally adopted its personal income tax in 1969, but only taxed capital gains, interest, and dividends. In 1991, Connecticut began taxing salaries and wages.

3. See, for examples, James A. Papke, "The Response of State-Local Government Taxation to Fiscal Crisis," *National Tax Journal* 36, no. 3 (September 1983): 401–5, and Steven D. Gold, "State Tax Increases of 1983: Prelude to Another Tax Revolt?" *National Tax Journal* 37, no. 1 (March 1984): 9–22, for discussions of fiscal crisis during the 1982 recession and Richard H. Matoon and William A. Testa, "State and Local Governments'

Reaction to Recession," *Economic Perspectives* (March/April 1992): 19–27 (Federal Reserve Bank of Chicago) for a discussion relevant to the 1991 recession.

    4. Steven D. Gold, "State Fiscal Problems and Policies," in *The Fiscal Crisis of the States: Lessons for the Future*. Steven D. Gold, ed. (Washington, D.C.: Georgetown University Press, 1995), 12.

Chapter 2

State Government Spending

Although the fundamental problem that causes state fiscal crises is cyclical in nature, the underlying demands for state government spending are what keep pressure on state governments to spend as much as they can year after year. Thus, state government spending is an underlying factor behind state fiscal crises. The major expenditure items for state governments historically have been education and highways, but recently highway spending has declined in relative importance while other expenditure categories have been rising. By the early 1970s welfare expenditures were a larger component of state government spending than highways. This chapter takes a detailed look at the expenditure side of state government budgets to see why expenditure demand keeps pressure on states to spend more.

It is worth emphasizing that pressures for more spending will continue year in and year out, regardless of how much revenue state governments raise. This is so because governments usually give away their output, as is typical with state-financed health care, or charge less than the cost of the output, as with education, which virtually guarantees that the demand for government programs will always exceed their supply. Thus, in the final analysis, it cannot be demand factors alone that cause fiscal crises. The demand for government output will always exceed the supply as long as government does not charge the full cost of its output, regardless of the level of funding. Fiscal crises are not the result of the demand for spending exceeding available funds, because that condition will always exist. Rather, fiscal crises arise when the state's financial commitment to its programs exceeds its revenues. This chapter provides some background to show where those pressures come from, but also examines how the composition of state government expenditures has changed over the years.

One thing that makes state government finance interesting to study is that every state is different, creating what David Osborne called laboratories of democracy.[1] Because some states rely much more heavily on local governments than others, it is worth looking at state and local government expenditures together for many purposes. Much of this chapter examines the individual components of state government spending, but first the breakdown between state and local government expenditures is examined.

STATE VERSUS LOCAL GOVERNMENT SPENDING

Traditionally, local governments have produced elementary and secondary schools, parks, fire and police protection, and infrastructure, leaving states to produce higher education, state roads that connect localities, and environmental amenities such as state parks and ecosystem protection designed to serve more than just a local constituency. In recent decades, the importance of state government has been expanding relative to local, however. Partly, this is because the mix of goods is tilting more toward those produced by state governments, but in addition, states have seen increased revenues relative to local governments. In addition to growing state spending, another consequence of growing state revenues is an increased reliance on state funds by local governments. State aid to local governments now accounts for about 30 percent of all local revenue.

Figure 2.1 shows the growth in the state component of state and local government expenditures over the four decades from 1950 to 1992. In the 1950s and early 1960s state governments spent about as much as local governments.

Figure 2.1
State General Expenditures

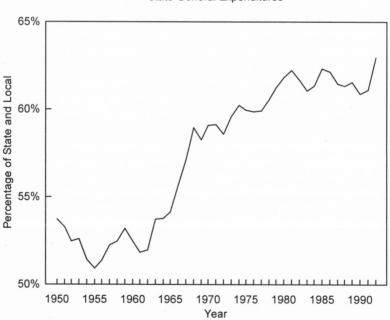

Throughout the 1950s and through 1965, states did not spend more than 55 percent of total state and local spending. That relationship began changing rapidly in the late 1960s so that by the early 1970s, states spent about 60 percent of total state and local government expenditures. The greatest change took place in only a few years, from 1965 through 1970, but then through the end of the 1980s, the state share of state and local expenditures remained roughly constant at around 62 percent.

A number of factors might have contributed to this dramatic change. On the revenue side, Chapter 1 explained how state governments greatly expanded their tax bases during the 1960s as many state added sales or income taxes, but the major tax base expansions of state governments ended after 1971. Another contributing factor was the increase in transfer programs that occurred around that time, which is discussed in more detail later in this chapter. Still another factor has been the desire to use state funding to equalize the level of expenditures on local services across the state's population. This period was one of relative optimism regarding the potential benefits of increased government, creating a bias among many policy makers favoring larger government.[2] Yet another factor is the increase in federal grants to state and local governments during this period. Finally, recall that the era of rapidly increasing state and local spending ended around this time, which might have contributed to a more stable split between state and local spending. Looking at aggregate figures conceals a great deal of variety among the states. Table 2.1 illustrates this variation by listing the state share of state and local spending by state for 1960, before the big movement toward centralization, and in 1992.

In 1960 the fraction of state and local expenditures comprised of state expenditures ranged from a high of 77 percent to a low of 33 percent. Hawaii was at the high end of the scale, and might be considered a special case, but five other states had state expenditures exceeding 70 percent of state and local expenditures, including Alabama at 70 percent, Delaware at 75 percent, Louisiana at 75 percent, and New Mexico and South Carolina, each at 72 percent. At the opposite end of the scale, New Jersey, with 33 percent, was the only state with state expenditures below 40 percent of total state and local expenditures, but Illinois was at 42 percent and Nebraska and New York both were at 44 percent.

By 1992 no state had its state share of state and local government expenditures below 50 percent. The lowest state was Colorado, where just over half of state and local government expenditures were spent by the state, followed by Florida at 53 percent and Texas at 55 percent. At the high end in 1992, Hawaii remained the most centralized state, with the state government spending 81 percent of the total. Alaska was just barely below Hawaii, also around 81 percent. New Mexico was the only other state spending above 80 percent of total state and local expenditures. In 1992 fifteen states had state expenditures exceeding 70 percent of total state and local expenditures, up from six states in 1960. By 1992 only two states had a state share of state and local expenditures below 55 percent, compared with 20 states in 1960.

Growth and Variability in State Tax Revenue

Table 2.1
State General Expenditures as a Percentage of State and Local General
Expenditures

	1960	1992		1960	1992
Alabama	70.10%	68.31%	Montana	56.00%	72.02%
Alaska	63.29%	81.05%	Nebraska	44.07%	63.89%
Arizona	42.65%	61.24%	Nevada	56.32%	55.63%
Arkansas	69.73%	76.69%	New Hampshire	55.53%	60.04%
California	50.59%	63.03%	New Jersey	32.96%	65.78%
Colorado	50.94%	50.56%	New Mexico	71.58%	80.24%
Connecticut	49.14%	66.10%	New York	44.02%	59.28%
Delaware	74.90%	76.53%	North Carolina	67.73%	68.99%
Florida	51.20%	52.74%	North Dakota	62.41%	73.97%
Georgia	60.35%	57.18%	Ohio	46.78%	64.31%
Hawaii	76.83%	81.08%	Oklahoma	66.19%	70.09%
Idaho	58.77%	70.90%	Oregon	59.23%	58.05%
Illinois	41.84%	58.62%	Pennsylvania	55.06%	66.68%
Indiana	50.90%	64.71%	Rhode Island	58.02%	75.50%
Iowa	53.07%	65.16%	South Carolina	71.96%	68.37%
Kansas	49.27%	59.04%	South Dakota	55.94%	65.90%
Kentucky	67.43%	77.25%	Tennessee	59.30%	63.78%
Louisiana	74.65%	67.70%	Texas	51.74%	55.27%
Maine	58.09%	69.45%	Utah	60.44%	69.87%
Maryland	51.71%	61.36%	Vermont	63.68%	72.40%
Massachusetts	51.35%	71.70%	Virginia	53.59%	60.12%
Michigan	56.68%	61.27%	Washington	65.21%	68.00%
Minnesota	51.47%	61.20%	West Virginia	68.89%	75.50%
Mississippi	66.66%	69.55%	Wisconsin	51.96%	61.42%
Missouri	51.81%	63.52%	Wyoming	63.88%	70.09%

Source: ACIR, *Significant Features of Fiscal Federalism*, various years.

There has been a clear movement toward centralization of state and local government expenditures, with most of the centralization coming in the late 1960s. Only seven states became less centralized between 1960 and 1992, and most of them only slightly. In 1960 the average state government accounted for 57.7 percent of all state and local spending, whereas in 1992 this figure had risen to 66.4 percent. There remains, however, a great deal of variation among states in the split of spending between state and local governments.

CHANGES IN THE COMPONENTS OF STATE GOVERNMENT SPENDING

The components of state government spending have changed dramatically in the past several decades. Table 2.2 shows expenditures in five major spending areas as a percentage of total state government spending. This section discusses some relative changes in the components, with following sections looking specifically at each spending area.

Spending on education grew during the 1950s and 1960s, peaking at around 40 percent of state expenditures in the late 1960s and early 1970s. Since 1975 education spending has declined slightly in relative importance. Much of this reflects higher education, which is almost exclusively the province of state governments. If state and local expenditures were considered, the trend would not be much different, however. The dramatic increase in the 1950s is not as noticeable, but there is still a slight decline in the 1980s.

The most dramatic change in the overall priorities of state expenditures is with highways. In the late 1950s and early 1960s between 25 and 30 percent of state expenditures went toward roads, but by the early 1990s that had fallen to below 8 percent. Part of the growth in state government expenditures has been in the health and welfare areas, but this growth has not been as great as the decline in highway expenditures. Welfare spending declined throughout the 1950s but began rising again in the 1960s so that by 1970 it was about 17 percent of state expenditures. Welfare had risen to about 26 percent by 1993, which is a bit of an increase, but not as dramatic as the decline in highway expenditures. Similarly, health care expenditures were at their peak in terms of the percent of state spending in the 1950s, and fell through the 1960s, only to start a gradual increase again through the 1970s and 1980s. In looking at the data, one should note that Medicaid, a rapidly rising component of state budgets, is classified as a component of welfare, not health.

Looking through the percentages conceals the growth in overall spending that has already been documented. Table 2.3 looks at the same spending categories as Table 2.2, but this time lists them as a percentage of GDP. Seen this way, the dramatic growth in education expenditures becomes more apparent. From the early 1950s through the middle 1970s education as a percentage of GDP roughly tripled, and then remained about constant for the next decade and a half. However, this latter period was after the baby-boom generation had passed through school, so per pupil expenditures continued rising.

The decrease in highway spending is apparent when viewed as a percentage of GDP, as is the increase in welfare expenditures. State welfare expenditures as a percentage of GDP roughly doubled from the early 1950s to the late 1970s, but remained relatively stable until the early 1990s when they began to rise again. Roughly the same is true of health expenditures.

When the mix of state government expenditures is examined, the most dramatic change is the large decline in state funding of highways. The other categories

Table 2.2
Components of State General Expenditures (Percentage of Total)

Year	Education	Highways	Public Welfare	Health & Hospitals	Corrections
1950	21.33%	19.56%	17.91%	7.73%	1.50%
1951	28.97%	22.90%	18.36%	8.70%	1.62%
1952	29.38%	24.02%	17.42%	9.31%	1.63%
1953	29.85%	24.42%	17.06%	8.95%	1.62%
1954	29.48%	26.13%	16.17%	8.89%	1.58%
1955	29.66%	28.14%	15.49%	8.56%	1.57%
1956	30.23%	28.98%	14.24%	8.52%	1.57%
1957	31.08%	28.24%	13.14%	9.03%	1.56%
1958	31.12%	28.36%	12.54%	9.24%	1.57%
1959	30.96%	29.28%	12.40%	8.97%	1.59%
1960	31.79%	26.87%	13.62%	7.66%	1.56%
1961	33.51%	25.75%	13.45%	7.67%	1.64%
1962	34.33%	25.46%	13.70%	7.52%	1.63%
1963	34.75%	25.55%	13.47%	7.39%	1.56%
1964	35.91%	25.17%	13.17%	7.24%	1.57%
1965	36.06%	24.43%	13.49%	7.29%	1.57%
1966	38.58%	22.32%	13.09%	7.05%	1.44%
1967	39.95%	21.27%	13.51%	6.88%	1.41%
1968	40.21%	19.62%	14.32%	6.96%	1.39%
1969	39.92%	18.40%	15.97%	6.92%	1.34%
1970	39.75%	17.36%	17.01%	6.90%	1.42%
1971	39.38%	16.63%	18.27%	6.90%	1.41%
1972	38.81%	15.48%	19.36%	7.05%	1.41%
1973	38.45%	13.80%	20.04%	6.80%	1.44%
1974	39.09%	13.14%	18.80%	7.04%	1.51%
1975	39.13%	12.63%	18.49%	7.35%	1.59%
1976	38.80%	11.78%	19.28%	7.23%	1.61%
1977	38.58%	10.55%	19.75%	7.59%	1.74%
1978	38.77%	10.39%	19.90%	7.73%	1.82%
1979	38.76%	10.59%	19.39%	7.74%	1.88%
1980	38.53%	10.98%	19.38%	8.04%	1.95%
1981	38.21%	10.03%	20.29%	8.12%	2.01%
1982	38.21%	9.32%	20.50%	7.97%	2.19%
1983	37.78%	9.27%	20.19%	8.39%	2.37%
1984	37.48%	9.34%	20.26%	8.42%	2.50%
1985	37.68%	9.87%	19.58%	7.96%	2.69%
1986	37.23%	9.87%	18.98%	7.87%	2.86%
1987	37.11%	9.58%	19.13%	7.82%	2.90%
1988	36.91%	9.54%	19.18%	7.91%	3.08%
1989	36.89%	9.10%	19.42%	8.04%	3.20%
1990	36.38%	8.71%	20.65%	8.39%	3.40%
1991	34.26%	8.48%	22.43%	8.27%	3.47%
1992	34.56%	8.00%	25.32%	8.11%	3.28%
1993	35.44%	7.94%	26.07%	8.23%	3.20%

Source: U.S. Census Bureau, *State Government Finances in* ... , various years.

Table 2.3
Components of State General Expenditures (Percentage of GDP)

Year	Education	Highways	Public Welfare	Health & Hospitals	Corrections
1950	0.91%	0.83%	0.76%	0.33%	0.06%
1951	1.14%	0.90%	0.72%	0.34%	0.06%
1952	1.15%	0.94%	0.68%	0.36%	0.06%
1953	1.18%	0.97%	0.68%	0.36%	0.06%
1954	1.25%	1.11%	0.69%	0.38%	0.07%
1955	1.26%	1.20%	0.66%	0.36%	0.07%
1956	1.34%	1.28%	0.63%	0.38%	0.07%
1957	1.46%	1.33%	0.62%	0.42%	0.07%
1958	1.61%	1.47%	0.65%	0.48%	0.08%
1959	1.63%	1.54%	0.65%	0.47%	0.08%
1960	1.69%	1.43%	0.72%	0.41%	0.08%
1961	1.83%	1.41%	0.74%	0.42%	0.09%
1962	1.88%	1.39%	0.75%	0.41%	0.09%
1963	1.98%	1.46%	0.77%	0.42%	0.09%
1964	2.07%	1.45%	0.76%	0.42%	0.09%
1965	2.08%	1.41%	0.78%	0.42%	0.09%
1966	2.31%	1.34%	0.78%	0.42%	0.09%
1967	2.62%	1.39%	0.88%	0.45%	0.09%
1968	2.73%	1.33%	0.97%	0.47%	0.09%
1969	2.83%	1.30%	1.13%	0.49%	0.10%
1970	3.05%	1.33%	1.31%	0.53%	0.11%
1971	3.20%	1.35%	1.48%	0.56%	0.11%
1972	3.18%	1.27%	1.59%	0.58%	0.12%
1973	3.08%	1.11%	1.60%	0.54%	0.11%
1974	3.21%	1.08%	1.55%	0.58%	0.12%
1975	3.41%	1.10%	1.61%	0.64%	0.14%
1976	3.37%	1.02%	1.68%	0.63%	0.14%
1977	3.21%	0.88%	1.64%	0.63%	0.14%
1978	3.12%	0.84%	1.60%	0.62%	0.15%
1979	3.12%	0.85%	1.56%	0.62%	0.15%
1980	3.25%	0.93%	1.63%	0.68%	0.16%
1981	3.20%	0.84%	1.70%	0.68%	0.17%
1982	3.27%	0.80%	1.75%	0.68%	0.19%
1983	3.16%	0.78%	1.69%	0.70%	0.20%
1984	3.08%	0.77%	1.66%	0.69%	0.21%
1985	3.22%	0.84%	1.67%	0.68%	0.23%
1986	3.28%	0.87%	1.67%	0.69%	0.25%
1987	3.30%	0.85%	1.70%	0.70%	0.26%
1988	3.26%	0.84%	1.69%	0.70%	0.27%
1989	3.30%	0.81%	1.74%	0.72%	0.29%
1990	3.35%	0.80%	1.90%	0.77%	0.31%
1991	3.35%	0.83%	2.19%	0.81%	0.34%
1992	3.50%	0.81%	2.57%	0.82%	0.33%
1993	3.59%	0.80%	2.64%	0.83%	0.32%

Source: U.S. Census Bureau, *State Government Finances in* ... , various years.

showed less dramatic changes, and the biggest changes tended to be before 1980. This reinforces the idea that fiscal crises are the result of cyclical variability in state revenues, rather than the result of any dramatic changes in the demand for state spending. This section has provided a summary of the major spending areas of state governments. The next several sections considers the individual components in more detail.

EDUCATION

Education has always been one of the major priorities of state governments. As Table 2.2 indicates, state education spending as a percent of total state spending increased substantially from the early 1950s, when it was about 30 percent of total state spending, through the late 1960s when it rose to over 40 percent. Since that time, education spending as a percentage of total state spending has declined slightly but steadily, and by 1993 was just above 35 percent of total state expenditures. A substantial part of that growth up through the late 1960s was the increase in higher education expenditures as state universities grew. However, this growth in higher education leveled off after 1970.

In 1950 higher education expenditures were 16.7 percent of total state and local educational expenditures, and rose slightly to 17.4 percent by 1960. The decade of the 1960s saw tremendous growth in higher education, and by 1970 higher education was 25.7 percent of state and local educational expenditures. Higher education's share increased only slightly to 26.7 percent by 1980, and remained at 26.7 percent in 1990. In the context of state fiscal crises, the large increases in higher education occurred in the 1960s, before substantial fiscal crises, and during the period of rapid overall state government growth. Fiscal crises appeared only after the educational system had stabilized—at least in terms of higher education's share—so this is unlikely to be a contributing factor to recent crises.

Elementary and secondary education is a local government responsibility, albeit with heavy state involvement both in funding and oversight, whereas higher education is almost entirely a state government function. Thus, it is interesting to note that although higher education's share of the educational budget has been stable since 1970, the state's share of educational expenditures has continued to rise, reflecting increased state funding of elementary and secondary education. Figure 2.2 shows state educational expenditures as a percentage of state and local educational expenditures and shows the continued increase. The increase is rapid in the 1960s, going from about 46 percent in 1960 to about 59 percent in 1970, during the period when higher education received an increased emphasis. But that growth has continued, and by 1993 state government expenditures on education were almost 65 percent of total state and local expenditures on education. The additional state share of educational expenditures is one of the demands on state budgets, but this growth has slowed through the 1980s and early 1990s, as Figure 2.2 shows, and cannot be held responsible for state fiscal crises.

Figure 2.2
State Education Expenditures

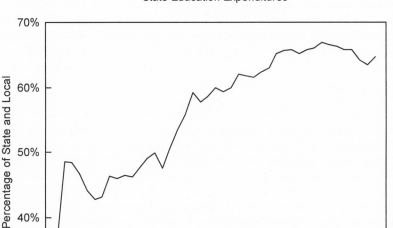

An examination of the evolution of state educational expenditures shows that although education has been becoming increasingly more state funded and less locally funded, education as a share of state budgets has been slowly declining. In percentage terms, educational expenditures have been crowded out by other budgetary areas, although overall growth in state expenditures has meant increasing funding overall. Surely demands for education have put pressure on state governments, but in a manner similar to other government programs where recipients of the expenditure pay less than the total cost of the service. Thus, there is no good argument that the demands for educational expenditures have caused fiscal crises in state governments.

WELFARE

The latter half of the twentieth century has seen an increasing involvement by government in welfare services, and this involvement has included state governments along with the federal government. Table 2.2 shows that welfare as a percentage of state government expenditures has increased substantially since the mid-1960s, after declining through the 1950s. In the 1950s, when state government expenditures were lower in total, welfare composed more than 15 percent of state expenditures, but that dropped to between 13 and 14 percent from the mid-1950s through 1966 as state government expenditures grew more rapidly in other areas.

From that point, a rapid increase pushed welfare expenditures up to more than 20 percent of state expenditures in 1973, and in 1993 welfare expenditures were more than 26 percent of state government expenditures.

Because state government expenditures had been growing as a percentage of GDP, looking at welfare as a percentage of state expenditures conceals some growth relative to GDP. In the early 1960s, state welfare expenditures were around 0.75 percent of GDP, and were as low as 0.62 percent in 1957. From that point, steady growth pushed state welfare expenditures above 1 percent of GDP by 1969, and above 1.5 percent of GDP by 1972. By 1993, state welfare expenditures exceeded 2.6 percent of GDP.

At the same time, federal government welfare expenditures have grown rapidly as well. Table 2.4 shows public welfare expenditures as a percentage of federal, state, and local expenditures. Between 1965 and 1975 public welfare expenditures more than tripled as a percentage of the federal budget. Since 1975, however, their relative importance in the federal budget has changed little. The importance of public welfare in local government budgets actually declined throughout this period. Public welfare expenditures comprised about 8 percent of local government budgets in 1970, but fell to about 5 percent by 1992. State government expenditures on public welfare grew from 13.4 percent of total expenditures in 1965 to 19.4 percent in 1980. From 1980 to 1990 there was relatively little growth in public welfare expenditures as a percentage of state budgets, but beginning in the early 1990s they have risen somewhat. The combined expenditures of all levels of government show a similar trend, rising rapidly until 1975, stabilizing throughout the 1980s, and rising again in the early 1990s. Nonetheless, as a percentage of total government spending, public welfare has tripled in importance since 1965. The table shows that welfare expenditures have put more pressure on state budgets than on either the federal or local budgets.

Table 2.4
Federal, State, and Local Public Welfare Expenditures

| Year | As a Percent of Total General Expenditures | | | |
	Federal	State	Local	Total
1965	2.9%	13.4%	6.8%	3.7%
1970	6.2%	17.0%	7.8%	6.4%
1975	10.5%	18.5%	7.4%	9.1%
1980	10.7%	19.4%	6.2%	9.0%
1985	9.1%	22.4%	5.1%	7.9%
1990	9.4%	20.7%	4.8%	8.3%
1991	11.2%	22.4%	5.0%	9.3%
1992	13.3%	25.3%	5.0%	10.9%

Note: Total excludes duplicative intergovernmental transfers.
Source: ACIR, *Significant Features of Fiscal Federalism*, 1994.

The major contributor to these increases in welfare expenditures has been the Medicaid program. When looking at state budgetary data, Medicaid is usually included under welfare rather than health, because Medicaid involves a payment from the state for medical care on behalf of the recipient, so is a vendor payment rather than a state expenditure on a health-care program or facility. Medicaid is by far the largest component of the welfare budget of states, comprising about 75 percent of state welfare expenditures. Thus, any discussion of the increase in state welfare expenditures is essentially a discussion of the increase in Medicaid.

Medicaid was established in 1965, and by 1970 cost states more than $6 billion. By 1993, state government expenditures on Medicaid exceeded $115 billion. Some of this growth was due to inflation, but even after adjusting for inflation, state Medicaid expenditures increased by over 400 percent from 1970 to 1993. The federal government contributes between 50 and 79 percent of the cost of Medicaid, depending on the income of the state, leaving states to finance a significant portion of the Medicaid program. Although the Medicaid program is state run, it must follow federal guidelines, which sometimes leaves states with less discretion than they would like. For example, one restriction is that all recipients of Aid to Families with Dependent Children (AFDC) must also be eligible for Medicaid.

Table 2.5 shows public assistance medical payments, which mostly is Medicaid, as a percentage of state welfare expenditures for selected years since 1970. Even in 1970 Medicaid comprised almost half of state welfare expenditures, and by 1980 the figure had risen to more than 63 percent. Table 2.5 shows a steady increase from 66.3 percent in 1985 to 75 percent in the early 1990s. Medicaid is one of the major causes of the resumed growth of state government in the 1990s. If any budgetary area can lay claim to being a contributory factor to state fiscal crises, Medicaid would be that area.

As Table 2.3 showed, welfare expenditures as a percentage of GDP rose from about 1.7 percent in 1980 to about 2.6 percent in 1993, and Table 2.2 shows that as a percentage of state budgets, welfare increased from 19.4 percent to 26.1 percent during that same time period. Fueled by Medicaid increases, welfare expenditures have been putting pressure on state spending, but this upward pressure has been consistent through relatively prosperous years, when states did not have fiscal crises, and during economic downturns when states did have fiscal crises. Surely measures must be taken to curb these increases in Medicaid expenditures that have been driving the increases in state welfare expenditures. There is pressure here, but not only in crisis years. Getting Medicaid expenditures under control would help the financial situation of states trying to weather fiscal crises, but these crises would not have been avoided if Medicaid expenditures had risen less rapidly.

Table 2.5
Public Assistance Medical Payments as a Percentage of State Public Welfare Expenditures

Year	Percent
1970	47.8%
1975	54.0%
1980	63.3%
1985	66.3%
1986	66.6%
1987	68.7%
1988	69.1%
1989	71.1%
1990	75.6%
1992	73.4%
1993	74.4%

Source: Tax Foundation, *Facts and Figures on Government Finance*, various years.

HEALTH CARE

State governments have long been involved in providing health care both directly through state hospitals and through public health programs. Although health-care costs have been rising significantly, state expenditures on health care have remained relatively stable as a share of state budgets, ranging from about 7 to 9 percent. As Table 2.2 shows, in the late 1950s health care expenditures rose to slightly above 9 percent of state government expenditures. After falling to below 7 percent of state expenditures in the early 1970s, health expenditures of state governments rose to above 8 percent by the late 1980s.

As Table 2.3 indicates, health expenditures of state governments have been steadily rising as a percentage of GDP since 1950. They made up only 0.33 percent in 1950, and were up to 0.53 percent in 1970, and further increased to 0.83 percent in 1993. Although health expenditures have been rising steadily, they remain a small part of the total budgets of states, so cannot be blamed for periodic fiscal crises. The more alarming trend in the health area is the rise in Medicaid expenditures by states, which falls into the budgetary category of welfare, as opposed to health. State government expenditures on health could be analyzed in more detail, but this overview indicates that health expenditures are not significant enough to push states to fiscal crises, particularly when Medicaid is not categorized as a health expenditure.

CORRECTIONS

One of the basic services state governments provide is law enforcement, which includes courts, prisons, and some law enforcement through state troopers and other law enforcement agencies. State expenditures on corrections, which primarily consists of the costs of state prisons, have risen alarmingly over the decades, and that increase has accelerated since the late 1970s. In the early 1950s corrections expenditures composed about 1.6 percent of state government budgets, as shown in Table 2.2, and the percentage actually dropped to below 1.4 percent in the late 1960s, although as a result of rising expenditures in other areas. As a percent of GDP, Table 2.3 shows corrections slowly rising from 0.06 percent in 1950 to 0.11 percent in 1970.

From the early 1970s corrections expenditures began rising more rapidly, to 0.16 percentage of GDP by 1980, and to 0.34 percent by 1991. Figure 2.3 illustrates the rise in correctional expenditures as a percent of GDP. The increases in correctional expenditures are substantial and rising, and show that this is a policy area that deserves attention. Much of the increase in the 1980s was related to the war on drugs that, by some indications, has slowed down since 1989. In 1980, for example, there were 256 arrests on drug charges per 100,000 population, and this steadily increased to a peak of 527 arrests for drugs by 1989. In 1991 drug arrests declined to 401 per 100,000.

Figure 2.3
State Correction Expenditures

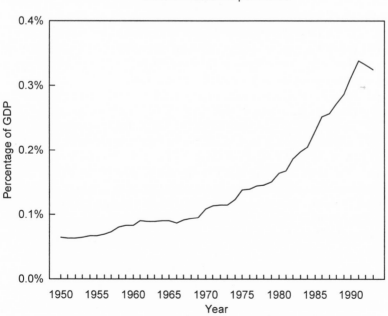

The whole criminal justice system raises a number of interesting and important policy questions, especially in light of rapid increases in correctional expenditures by states. However, in a broader context these expenditures were only 3.2 percent of total state expenditures in 1993, so could not have a large impact in overall state budgets in the context of looking for causes to state fiscal crises. Like all expenditure areas, the correctional budget puts strain on the budget at the margin, but the corrections budget is small enough relative to other expenditure areas that it cannot be viewed as a causal factor behind state fiscal crises.

HIGHWAYS

State governments have devoted a considerable fraction of their budgets to highways, but this fraction has fallen dramatically over the past few decades. Figure 2.4 shows state highway expenditures as a percentage of total state expenditures. In 1950 states were spending about 20 percent of their budgets on highways, and this figure continued to increase until in 1959 states were devoting more than 29 percent of their expenditures to highways. From this peak, the share of state budgets devoted to highways continued to fall so that by 1970 states were spending 17.4 percent of their budgets in highways, by 1980 they were spending 11 percent, and by 1993 expenditures on highways were less than 8 percent of state government expenditures.

Figure 2.4
State Highway Expenditures

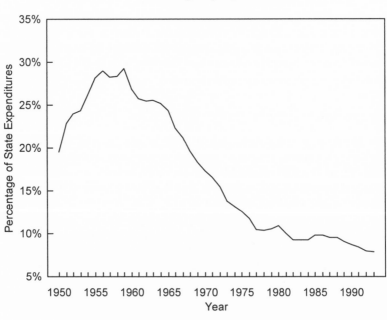

This dramatic decline in state highway expenditures is mirrored in the figures showing highway expenditures as a percentage of GDP. State highway expenditures were more than 1.5 percent of GDP in 1959, and had fallen to around 0.8 percent of GDP by the mid-1980s. Surely a contributing factor to increased traffic congestion is the reduction in the percentage of income spent on roads.

A number of factors have contributed to the decline in the importance of highway expenditures. One is that highways tend to be financed from earmarked gasoline taxes that are not indexed to inflation. Legislators are always reluctant to raise taxes, and during inflationary periods taxes that are not indexed, like the gas tax, tend to decline in importance relative to those that, like general sales taxes, are indexed. The tax factors are discussed at greater length in Chapter 3, which deals with the revenue side of state government budgets, and Chapter 4, which discusses earmarked revenues within the context of state budgeting. Another contributing factor to the decline in highway expenditures has been a change in emphasis in government budgets at all levels. The 1960s ushered in an era where citizens began expecting their governments to provide more direct human assistance through transfer programs, which may have contributed to crowding out some public goods like roads. Yet another contributing factor is that roads are durable goods, so road construction in any one year will have a small impact on the total amount of roadways available. This may make it easier to postpone highway construction in favor of more urgent demands for public spending.

Whatever the reasons, this decline in the share of state expenditures devoted to highways is certainly the most dramatic change in state government expenditures that has occurred over the four decades reviewed in this chapter. The decline in highway expenditures may have contributed to fiscal pressure on states in that in many areas it represents postponed construction that is taking on more of a sense of urgency, meaning that there is more pressure on legislatures to fund highway improvements. However, this would normally be accomplished by increasing the earmarked taxes designated to finance roads, and should not be a major contributor to the periodic fiscal crises that states have seen.

CONCLUSION

The purpose of this chapter has been to present a brief history of state government expenditures to see to what extent demands for expenditures might have contributed to state fiscal crises. In one sense, expenditures must be behind the fiscal crises that states have periodically experienced, because the fiscal crises are caused by the demand for state expenditures exceeding the state revenues available to finance those demands. However, these demands are constant, whereas fiscal crises appear periodically, and are associated with recessions. Are there any particular areas of state government budgets that might be held more responsible for fiscal crises than others?

One area that stands out is welfare expenditures, and the largest and fastest-growing component of welfare expenditures is Medicaid. Because federal regulations require that anyone eligible for AFDC is also eligible for Medicaid, the

Medicaid system is closely intertwined with welfare programs in a more general sense. Because the demand for welfare programs is countercyclical, unusually high demands will coincide with periods with unusually slow revenue growth. There is little that one can do to modify the countercyclical nature of welfare programs, but the longer-run growth of Medicaid will have to be dealt with either by increasing revenues available to fund the program, by cutting back benefits, or some combination. However, the tremendous growth rates in the Medicaid program cannot be sustained indefinitely. From 1980 to 1985 Medicaid expenditures, adjusted for inflation, grew 21 percent, from 1985 to 1990 they grew 47 percent, and from 1990 to 1993 they grew by 70 percent.

This long-run growth has not led to fiscal crises, however. It has strained state budgets, but fiscal crises have been associated with recessions, and the counter-cyclical nature of welfare demands are likely to be more associated with fiscal crises. This naturally turns one's attention to the revenue side of the budget, which is discussed in the following chapter.

Outside of Medicaid, other programs cannot lay much claim to being causal factors in state fiscal crises. Corrections expenditures have increased substantially, but still compose less than 3.5 percent of total state expenditures. Other areas have not seen substantial growth, and highway expenditures have seen substantial declines. After analyzing state government expenditures, one must conclude that although there will always be political pressure for more expenditures in every area, expenditures do not produce crises. Rather, downturns in state revenues leave states unable to meet the expectations of constituents during recessions. Thus, the next chapter examines the structure of state government revenues to see how they might contribute to state fiscal crises.

NOTES

1. David Osborne, *Laboratories of Democracy* (Boston: Harvard Business School Press, 1988).

2. This idea is considered in Edward M. Gramlich, "Alternative Federal Policies for Stimulating State and Local Expenditures: A Comparison of Their Effects," *National Tax Journal* 21, no. 2 (June 1968): 119–29. In the 1990s, by comparison, people are looking for ways to limit the expenditures of governments at all levels, a phenomenon that is most visible in citizen initiatives to create constitutional limits on spending.

Chapter 3

State Government Taxes

State fiscal crises arise when states' spending commitments exceed the revenues they have available to meet those commitments. As the previous chapter has suggested, spending pressures will always be present. Crises have appeared when, due to recessions, revenue growth has slowed. The cyclical nature of state government revenues is examined in detail in the following chapters. This chapter lays a foundation by examining the components of state government revenue.

THE STATE TAX BASE

The largest components of state government revenues have traditionally been sales taxes, personal and corporation income taxes, excise taxes on alcohol and tobacco products, and excise taxes on motor fuels. Table 3.1 illustrates how those revenue sources have changed in importance over the years. As the table shows, sales and personal income taxes have been rising over the period from 1950 to 1993, with personal income taxes increasing much more than sales taxes. In 1950 sales taxes accounted for just over 20 percent of state government tax revenues and remained relatively stable up through the early 1960s. Sales tax revenues then crept up to their present level of around 33 percent of state tax revenues. State personal income taxes, by contrast, have shown faster growth over the period, starting from just over 9 percent of state tax revenues and rising to more than 31 percent. Personal income taxes now account for about as much state government tax revenue as general sales taxes.

A striking feature of the table is the sharp decline in taxes on motor fuels, which goes hand in hand with the sharp decline in highway spending that was discussed in the previous chapter. As income tax revenues have risen over the decades, motor fuels taxes have declined. A big difference between the two sources of revenues is that motor fuels revenues tend to be earmarked for transportation, whereas personal income tax revenues go into general revenue. This limits funding for roads, while

Table 3.1
Composition of State Tax Revenues

Year	Personal Income	General Sales	Corporation Income	Motor Fuels	Alcohol & Tobacco
1950	9.13%	21.06%	7.39%	19.47%	11.49%
1951	9.01%	22.39%	7.69%	19.14%	10.93%
1952	9.26%	22.61%	8.50%	18.97%	9.82%
1953	9.18%	23.06%	7.68%	19.13%	9.60%
1954	9.05%	22.91%	6.96%	20.00%	9.07%
1955	9.43%	22.74%	6.36%	20.29%	8.70%
1956	10.27%	22.70%	6.65%	20.09%	8.52%
1957	10.76%	23.21%	6.77%	19.46%	8.30%
1958	10.35%	23.51%	6.82%	19.57%	8.47%
1959	11.13%	23.33%	6.32%	19.30%	8.58%
1960	12.25%	23.85%	6.54%	18.49%	9.19%
1961	12.36%	23.67%	6.64%	18.00%	9.31%
1962	13.27%	24.86%	6.36%	17.83%	8.83%
1963	13.37%	25.04%	6.80%	17.41%	9.07%
1964	14.09%	25.10%	6.99%	16.74%	9.01%
1965	14.00%	25.69%	7.38%	16.46%	8.93%
1966	14.59%	26.80%	6.94%	15.75%	9.06%
1967	15.38%	27.95%	6.98%	15.15%	8.76%
1968	17.12%	28.68%	6.92%	14.23%	8.70%
1969	17.95%	29.67%	7.58%	13.46%	8.19%
1970	19.15%	29.56%	7.79%	13.10%	8.02%
1971	19.70%	30.02%	6.64%	12.86%	8.12%
1972	21.71%	29.43%	7.38%	12.05%	7.77%
1973	22.91%	29.08%	7.97%	11.84%	7.45%
1974	23.01%	30.47%	8.11%	11.06%	7.14%
1975	23.48%	30.92%	8.29%	10.30%	6.73%
1976	24.03%	30.62%	8.15%	9.70%	6.36%
1977	25.22%	30.56%	9.08%	8.99%	5.73%
1978	25.70%	31.15%	9.48%	8.39%	5.39%
1979	26.11%	31.61%	9.71%	7.99%	4.98%
1980	27.06%	31.49%	9.72%	7.09%	4.67%
1981	27.31%	31.00%	9.45%	6.50%	4.49%
1982	28.08%	30.97%	8.61%	6.44%	4.24%
1983	29.04%	31.29%	7.67%	6.30%	4.06%
1984	29.98%	31.79%	7.88%	6.30%	3.61%
1985	29.68%	32.34%	8.19%	6.20%	3.62%
1986	29.58%	32.80%	8.05%	6.18%	3.40%
1987	30.85%	32.38%	8.41%	6.35%	3.22%
1988	30.34%	32.94%	8.21%	6.51%	3.12%
1989	31.18%	32.84%	8.39%	6.34%	2.96%
1990	31.97%	33.18%	7.24%	6.45%	2.99%
1991	31.97%	33.22%	6.55%	6.65%	3.10%
1992	31.85%	32.82%	6.58%	6.77%	3.01%
1993	31.86%	32.52%	6.85%	6.67%	2.86%

Source: U.S. Census Bureau, State Government Finances in..., various years.

at the same time providing more discretion to state legislatures regarding their spending. Alcohol and tobacco taxes, like motor fuels taxes, have declined in importance for state governments. In 1950 alcohol and tobacco taxes accounted for over 11 percent of state tax revenue. After falling to just under 9 percent of tax revenues by the mid-1950s, they remained fairly constant through the late 1960s. Beginning in the 1970s, alcohol and tobacco taxes rapidly declined as a source of revenue, and by 1993 accounted for just under 3 percent of total tax revenues. Much of this decline has been due to preferences for healthier lifestyles causing reductions in consumption of these items.

In contrast to the big changes in general sales, motor fuels, alcohol and tobacco, and personal income taxes, corporate income tax collections as a percentage of state revenues have remained relatively constant over the decades. Around 1950, corporate income taxes were responsible for only a little less revenue than personal income taxes, and both were minor elements in state government revenues. In fact, alcohol and tobacco taxes in 1950 accounted for a larger share of tax revenues than either personal or corporation income taxes. By the late 1970s, with motor fuels and alcohol and tobacco taxes continually falling, corporate income tax revenues moved up to become the third most important source of tax revenues for state governments. The four largest sources of revenues detailed in Table 3.1 are also illustrated in Figure 3.1, which graphically shows the trends in those state tax revenue sources.

Figure 3.1
Sources of State Government Revenues

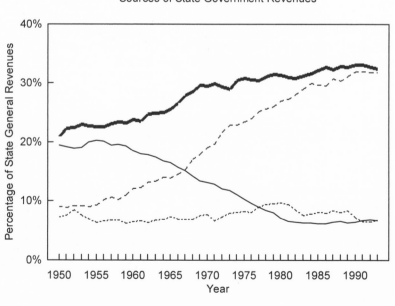

-- Personal Inc.　■ General Sales　... Corporate Inc.　— Motor Fuels

The trends shown in Figure 3.1 reveal that states have increasingly come to rely on general sales taxes, and especially personal income taxes, while de-emphasizing motor fuel taxes as a revenue source. This goes hand in hand with the de-emphasis on state government highway expenditures discussed in the previous chapter. With this overview of state tax revenues, the remainder of the chapter looks at individual revenue sources in greater detail.

STATE SALES TAXES

Since 1950 state sales taxes have been the largest source of state government revenues, and this remains true through the 1990s although personal income taxes have almost gained parity with sales taxes. As the previous section has shown, sales taxes have risen from 21.1 percent of state government tax revenues in 1950 to 32.5 percent in 1993. Because state government budgets have also grown over this period, the percentage of people's incomes devoted to state sales taxes has increased even more, from 0.58 percent in 1950 to 1.80 percent in 1993. Figure 3.2 shows the growth of state sales taxes as a percentage of GDP.

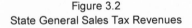

Figure 3.2
State General Sales Tax Revenues

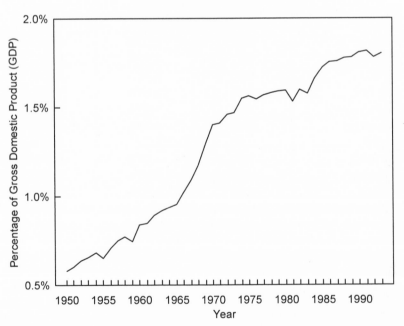

The continual increase shown in Figure 3.2 is a result of two main factors. States with sales taxes have continued to raise their rates over the years, and sixteen states that did not have sales taxes in 1950 have added them since. Table 3.2 lists those states establishing sales taxes since 1950, along with the initial sales tax rate and the rate as of 1994. Most of the states instituting sales taxes did so in the 1960s, and the last state to institute a sales tax was Vermont, which established its sales tax in 1969. Recall from Chapter 1 the substantial decline in the growth rate of state governments between the 1960s and the 1970s. One reason for substantial growth in the 1960s was the establishment of new taxes such as the sales tax in eleven states.

Table 3.2
States Establishing General Sales Taxes, 1950 to 1994

State	Year Established	Initial Rate	Rate in 1994
Georgia	1951	3.00%	6.00%
Maine	1951	3.00%	6.00%
South Carolina	1951	2.00%	5.00%
Pennsylvania	1953	3.00%	6.00%
Nevada	1955	2.00%	7.00%
Kentucky	1960	3.00%	6.00%
Texas	1961	2.00%	6.25%
Wisconsin	1961	3.00%	5.00%
Idaho	1965	3.00%	5.00%
New York	1965	2.00%	4.00%
Massachusetts	1966	3.00%	5.00%
New Jersey	1966	3.00%	6.00%
Virginia	1966	2.00%	3.50%
Minnesota	1967	3.00%	6.50%
Nebraska	1967	2.50%	5.00%
Vermont	1969	3.00%	5.00%

Sources: Tax Foundation, *Facts and Figures on Government Finance*, 1994, and ACIR, *Significant Features of Fiscal Federalism*, 1994.

An efficiently designed sales tax will tax all retail sales once, but only once. In practice, state sales taxes fall short of this ideal in two ways. They tax some sales twice by taxing intermediate goods, and they do not apply the tax to other sales at all. According to one estimate, the percentage of the state general sales tax levied on retail sales varies from 35 percent to 82 percent, depending on the state, with an average of 59 percent.[1] The remainder of the general sales tax is double-taxation levied primarily on producers' goods. Many services are exempt from taxation throughout the states, construction contracts are often exempt, and twenty-five of the states with sales taxes exempt food from the sales tax.[2] Exemptions are sometimes made to lessen the burden on the poor by not taxing necessities like food and prescription drugs, and practical considerations are often a part of the decision on what to cover with the tax. Those sales that are easy for the state to count and keep track of make good targets for taxation, whereas those transactions that can easily be kept hidden may not be taxed simply because of the difficulty of enforcing the tax law.

Many services, ranging from lawn care to painting to child care, are performed by individuals with no fixed business location who could easily evade taxes, for example, and so often are not required to pay tax. In an interesting case study, Florida extended its general sales tax to services in 1987, including many nonretail services provided by larger businesses, such as advertising and legal services. The tax was repealed the next year due to intense opposition from these larger businesses, and the advertising industry in particular. Although it is easy to see that it was special interests who were behind the repealing of the tax, it is also interesting to note that the bulk of the services tax would have fallen on nonretail services, creating inefficient double-taxation.[3] Efficiency considerations do count for something in developing tax policy, but the Florida services tax illustrates that often taxes are extended to large bases that are easy to monitor without much consideration of efficiency.

As Table 3.2 shows, there have been substantial rate increases in many of the states that established sales taxes, and these rate increases are representative of the other states with longer-standing sales taxes. All of the states in the table have had rate increases, and many have had sales tax rates double. Sales tax rates in Nevada and Texas have more than tripled since they were originally enacted. It is often easier to raise the rate on the existing tax base than to expand the tax base. State sales taxes have risen along with state government expenditures, but as Figure 3.1 shows, sales taxes have become an increasing percentage of state government revenues as well.

The sales tax is primarily a state tax, but thirty-one states have local option sales taxes that allow local governments to add to the state tax rate.[4] In these cases, the sales tax paid by taxpayers exceeds the state sales tax rate. While giving localities another tax base, the local option sales tax also enables localities to use the state government to collect taxes for it, thus reducing some local administrative costs associated with tax collection.[5]

STATE INCOME TAXES

Personal income taxes are the second-largest tax revenue source for state governments, and if added to corporate income taxes, become the largest source of revenue. In 1990 all but ten states had a personal income tax, and of those ten, Tennessee, New Hampshire, and Connecticut taxed nonwage income. In 1991 Connecticut passed a more comprehensive income tax, thus placing it among those states with income taxes. The last state before Connecticut to institute an income tax was New Jersey, in 1976.

Personal income taxes have grown substantially in importance as a state revenue source since 1950. Figure 3.1 shows how personal income tax collections have increased as a component of state government tax revenues. State income tax collections have grown even more substantially when looked at as a percentage of income. Figure 3.3 illustrates this growth. In 1950 state personal income taxes comprised 0.25 percent of GDP, and the percentage has steadily increased so that by 1993 state personal income taxes were 1.77 percent of GDP. As with the sales tax, this growth is partly a result of increasing income tax rates and partly due to the adoption of personal income taxation by states that did not previously tax income.

Figure 3.3
State Personal Income Tax Revenues

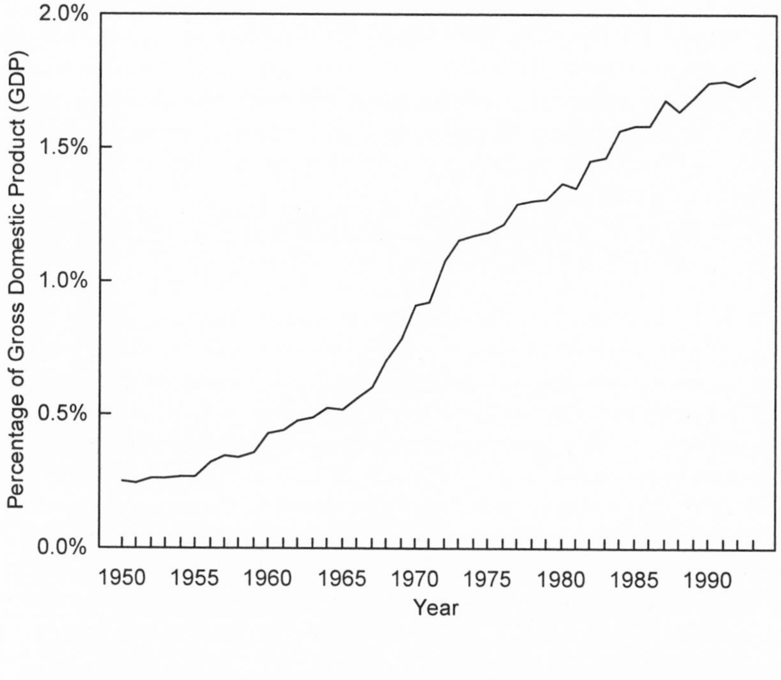

Since 1950 eleven states introduced personal income taxes. Except for New Jersey and Connecticut, all of the states introducing a personal income tax did so in the decade between 1961 and 1971. Table 3.3 lists those states along with the year in which the income tax was introduced. One must be struck by the similarity in the time frame during which income taxes were introduced and during which sales taxes were introduced, as reported in Table 3.2. The 1960s were the decade in which state tax bases expanded rapidly to enable rapid state government growth.

Table 3.3
States Establishing Personal Income Taxes, 1950 to 1994

| | Year | Top Marginal | Top Marginal |
State	Established	Rate Initially	Rate in 1994
West Virginia	1961	5.50%	6.50%
Indiana	1963	2.00%	3.40%
Michigan	1967	2.60%	4.60%
Nebraska	1967	7.70%	6.99%
Illinois	1969	2.50%	3.00%
Maine	1969	6.00%	8.50%
Ohio	1971	3.50%	7.50%
Pennsylvania	1971	2.30%	2.95%
Rhode Island	1971	10.50%	11.78%
New Jersey	1976	2.50%	7.00%
Connecticut	1991(a)	4.50%	4.50%

Repealed:
Alaska   1979

Note: (a) Limited tax on capital gains, interest, and dividends prior to this date.
Source: ACIR, *Significant Features of Fiscal Federalism,* 1994.

Another similarity between income taxes and sales taxes is the increase in the tax rates after the introduction of the tax. The two columns to the right of the table show the highest marginal tax rate with the initial income tax and the highest tax rate in 1994. Most of the states listed in the table increased their rates, although in percentage terms by less than the typical increase in sales tax rates. Nebraska's top rate could be characterized as falling to its current 6.99 percent because when instituted, Nebraska taxed 10 percent of the taxpayer's federal tax burden. Since the top federal tax rate in 1967 was 77 percent, the top Nebraska rate would have been 7.70 percent.[6] Personal income tax collections have become a more significant revenue source for state governments because states not previously taxing personal income instituted the tax—although this was the case primarily in the 1960s—and because of rising tax rates.

The corporate income tax, in contrast, has remained relatively constant as a percentage of state government revenues, as shown in Figure 3.1, despite the fact that it was also instituted in a number of states during the 1960s. Table 3.4 lists the states establishing corporate income taxes along with their years of adoption. More states began using corporate income as a tax base during the 1950–1994 period than either personal income or general sales. Of the eleven states that began taxing corporate income, six began taxing personal income at the same time. As with sales and personal income taxation, the period during which corporate income taxes were established corresponds with the high-growth years in state government spending.

Table 3.4
States Establishing Corporate Income Taxes, 1950 to 1994

State	Year Established
Delaware	1957
New Jersey	1958
Indiana	1963(a)*
Michigan	1967(b)*
Nebraska	1967*
West Virginia	1967
Illinois	1969*
Maine	1969*
New Hampshire	1970
Florida	1971
Ohio	1971*

Notes: (a) Gross income tax; (b) Replaced by a single business tax in 1976.
 * Established personal income tax at the same time.
Source: ACIR, *Significant Features of Fiscal Federalism*, 1994.

Although corporate income taxation has not grown substantially in percentage terms as a revenue source for state governments, it has approximately doubled from 1950 to 1993 as a percentage of GDP, as shown in Figure 3.4. In 1950 state corporate income taxes were about 0.2 percent of GDP, and remained at about that level through the late 1950s. Corporate income tax revenues had substantial growth through the 1960s and 1970s, however, and peaked at 0.49 percent of GDP in 1980. They declined somewhat through the 1980s and early 1990s, so that by 1993 they were 0.38 percent of GDP.

During the same period, federal government reliance on corporate income tax revenues has declined substantially, so the slow growth in corporate income tax collections when compared to personal income tax collections follows the federal trend of relying more heavily on personal income. The slower growth of corporate income tax revenues is particularly interesting in light of the fact that more states adopted corporate income taxes than personal income taxes during the period when personal income tax revenues grew faster. Personal income tax collections were only slightly greater than corporate income tax collections in 1950, but were more than four times as great by 1993. One of the noteworthy developments in state public finance since 1950 is the increased reliance on personal income tax revenues by state governments.

Figure 3.4
State Corporation Income Tax Revenues

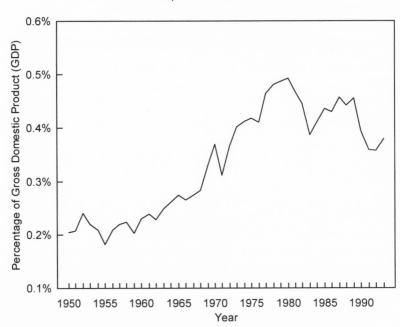

ARE STATE INCOME AND SALES TAXES NECESSARY?

Personal income taxes and general sales taxes are the largest two revenue sources for state governments, although two other revenue sources—charges and fees and federal grants—come close. However, twelve states do not utilize one or the other of these tax bases, including Alaska, which has neither personal income taxes nor general sales taxes. Alaska is in a unique situation with substantial revenues from severance taxes on oil, but four other states do not have sales taxes and eight other states do not have personal income taxes. Six states do not have corporate income taxes, including Michigan, which repealed its tax in 1976 and replaced it with a modified value-added tax. States that do not have one of these three types of taxes in 1995 are listed in Table 3.5.

As this listing of states makes clear, states can rely on sales or personal income taxes without utilizing both. Some of the states utilize related tax bases. Tennessee and New Hampshire, for example, tax interest and dividend income, but not labor earnings. Alaska, Florida, New Hampshire, and Tennessee have corporate but not personal income taxes. Florida, which has a constitutional prohibition against taxing personal income, also has an intangible property tax that taxes individual and business holdings of stocks, bonds, accounts receivable, and other intangible

Table 3.5
States with No Personal or Corporate Income or Sales Tax, 1995

State	Personal Income Tax	Corporation Income Tax	General Sales Tax
Alaska	No(a)		No
Delaware			No
Florida	No		
Michigan		No(c)	
Montana			No
Nevada	No	No	
New Hampshire	(b)		No
Oregon			No
South Dakota	No	No	
Tennessee	(b)		
Texas	No	No	
Washington	No	No	
Wyoming	No	No	

Notes: (a) Established 1949, repealed 1979, (b) limited income tax (interest and dividends only), (c) repealed in 1976 and replaced with single business tax.
Source: ACIR, *Significant Features of Fiscal Federalism*, 1994.

financial assets. States can get by without both a personal income tax and a general sales tax, as this listing of twelve states illustrates. Whether it is desirable to tax both tax bases is discussed in later chapters.

TAXES ON MOTOR FUELS

Whereas income and sales taxes tend to be used as a general revenue source for states, taxes on motor fuels tend to be earmarked for transportation. Chapter 2 noted how there has been a substantial decline in the percentage of state government expenditures devoted to highways, and that decline is reflected in the decline in the percentage of state revenues collected as motor fuel taxes, which is illustrated in Figure 3.1. Figure 3.5 shows the decline in motor fuels taxes as a percentage of GDP.

In a growing economy, a decline as a percentage of GDP in some revenue areas need not signify an absolute decline in revenues, but during the 1970s inflation-adjusted revenues raised from motor fuel taxes fell, meaning that gas taxes were raising less spending power for state governments in 1980 than they were in 1970.

Figure 3.5
State Motor Fuel Tax Revenues

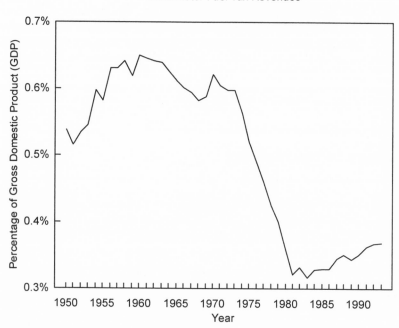

Over the entire period from 1950 to 1993 inflation-adjusted motor fuel tax revenues rose on average 3.6 percent per year. However, in the 1970s they fell on average 2.7 percent per year, and between 1980 and 1990, rose by only 2.6 percent per year. This decline in revenues from a tax base normally earmarked for roads goes a long way toward explaining why state expenditures on highways have fallen so much as a percentage of state budgets, as described in the previous chapter.

How could a tax base that at one time was so important to state governments decline so substantially? One reason is that gas taxes tend not to be indexed to inflation, and legislators are reluctant to explicitly raise tax rates. During the 1970s, when inflation doubled the price level in ten years, gas taxes did not keep up. Inflation automatically raises the dollar level of retail sales and of income, so income and sales taxes automatically adjust for inflation. The gas tax, which does not, was not increased enough to compensate for inflation, so revenues from gas taxes continued to be eroded. It appears that at least partly, the de-emphasis on highways in state budgets was the result of legislative inaction in the face of inflation rather than any conscious policy choice.

SEVERANCE TAXES

Severance taxes are taxes placed on the extraction or use of natural resources within a state. Examples include oil, coal, natural gas, fish, and timber. The use of severance taxes varies greatly across states because states have such varied tax bases. Table 3.6 provides some detail on severance taxes for states that rely relatively heavily on them. Alaska is the most extreme example of reliance on severance taxes, with 71.8 percent of state tax revenues coming from them in 1992. This figure is exaggerated by the fact that Alaska does not have either a personal income or general sales tax. As a proportion of Alaska's total general revenue,

Table 3.6
Severance Tax Revenues, 1992

State	Revenue (in Millions)	Percent of Tax Revenue
Alaska	$1,150.6	71.8%
Kansas	$88.8	3.2%
Kentucky	$203.3	4.0%
Louisiana	$487.9	11.5%
Montana	$123.8	13.0%
New Mexico	$228.9	10.2%
North Dakota	$83.3	11.0%
Oklahoma	$355.0	9.2%
Oregon	$63.8	1.9%
Texas	$1,013.8	6.0%
West Virginia	$180.8	7.7%
Wyoming	$249.4	38.6%
U.S. Total	$4,647.5	1.4%

Source: Tax Foundation, *Facts and Figures on Government Finance*, 1994.

severance taxes account for 21.5 percent, which is still substantial. Other states with relatively heavy reliance on severance taxes are Wyoming, with 38.6 percent of state tax revenues from severance taxes, Montana with 13 percent, Louisiana with 11.5 percent, North Dakota with 11.0 percent, and New Mexico with 10.2 percent. Public finance in Alaska is substantially different from that in the other states listed in the table, with Wyoming being the most similar because it also does not have a personal income tax.

Total severance taxes collected by states in 1992 totaled $4.6 billion, and the top two states, Alaska and Texas, accounted for almost half of that total. Severance taxes in total are a small part of state finance, accounting for just over 1 percent of total state tax collections. They also have fallen from recently higher levels. In 1982 total severance taxes peaked at $7.8 billion. Even as late as 1985, total severance taxes provided above $7 billion in revenue for state governments. Although several states do rely on severance taxes for a substantial amount of revenue, severance taxes are a minor part of most state budgets.

OTHER REVENUE SOURCES

States receive a substantial amount of revenue from other sources. An important source of state revenues is grants from the federal government, which are discussed later in this chapter. Another important source of state revenues is charges and fees. This includes tuition charged at state universities and community colleges, payments for treatment at state hospitals, as well as minor revenue sources like admission to parks and tolls on toll roads. Additionally, a category often referred to as miscellaneous revenue is also becoming a larger share of state government revenue. This miscellaneous revenue includes interest earnings, net lottery revenues, and fines. Figure 3.6 shows that charges and miscellaneous revenue are becoming an increasingly important source of state government revenues. The growth parallels that of personal income tax collections, except that the more rapid growth happens in the late 1970s, rather than the early 1970s as it did for personal income taxes.

Figure 3.6
State Charges and Miscellaneous Revenues

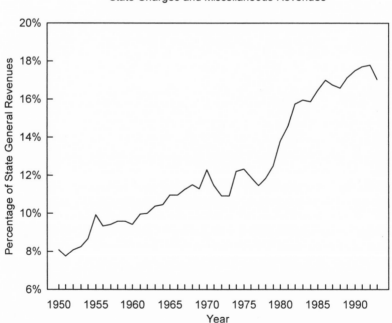

In 1950 charges and miscellaneous revenue made up 8 percent of state government revenues, as compared to 6.2 percent for personal income tax collections. Charges and miscellaneous revenue exhibited steady growth, and made up 17.0 percent of state revenues in 1993, compared to 17.2 percent for personal income taxes. The increased reliance on charges can enhance government efficiency if consumers of government services have to volunteer to pay for the services government provides. Governments must become more entrepreneurial to attract consumer dollars, following one line of reasoning.[7] The incentives for efficiency are weakened to the extent that the state combines tax dollars with charges to subsidize public sector consumption. State universities, for example, subsidize tuition with tax dollars creating a competitive advantage over private universities. Still, there are some incentives for efficiency as long as consumers are asked to pay something, and more significantly, as long as they have private sector alternatives.

Table 3.7 provides a detailed breakdown of the sources of charges and miscellaneous revenue in 1993. The division of revenues between the two categories is about even, with charges revenues accounting for slightly over 51 percent of the total. Within the category of charges, higher education accounts for the largest share, most of it coming from tuition. Payments for treatment at state hospitals is the second largest source of charges revenue, accounting for 12.6 percent of total charges revenue. All of the other sources of charges revenue are substantially smaller than these two, but highway toll charges and charges for usage of state-owned natural resources both provide over $1 billion in revenues for state governments. The category of miscellaneous revenue is also highly concentrated in just a few sources. The largest components are interest earnings and net lottery revenues. Lottery revenues are a growing area for state governments, but still remain a small part of the overall revenue picture. In 1993 states raised $10 billion from lotteries, but this is only about half of the amount raised from tuition charges for higher education.

Other tax sources contribute to state government coffers as well. Two that are noteworthy are motor vehicle and operators' licenses and alcoholic beverage and tobacco taxes. Although these revenue sources contribute a relatively small amount to state revenues, it is interesting to note that, like motor fuels taxes, they had negative growth in the 1970s after adjusting for inflation. Over the period from 1950 to 1993 motor vehicle and operators' license revenues averaged an annual inflation-adjusted growth rate of 4.1 percent, but from 1970 to 1980 had a growth rate of negative 0.8 percent. Between 1980 and 1990 these revenues again had a positive growth rate of 2.6 percent per year. Taxes on alcohol and tobacco grew at an average of 2.0 percent per year over the entire period, but had a negative growth rate of −2.2 percent during the 1970–1980 period. They also had negative growth from 1980–90 of −1.1 percent.

Perhaps the negative growth in alcoholic beverage and tobacco tax revenues can partly be attributed to reduced consumption of those goods. Liquor store sales declined during the 1980s, for example, although not during the 1970s when growth in revenues was even more negative than in the 1980s. However, both of these tax sources have in common with motor fuels taxes that they tend not to be indexed to inflation, meaning that unless legislators explicitly raise the rates, real revenues

Table 3.7
Sources of Charges and Miscellaneous Revenue, 1993

	Revenue (in Millions)	Percentage of Total	Percentage of Category
Charges revenue			
Air transportation	$725.8	0.65%	1.26%
Misc. commercial activities	$241.6	0.22%	0.42%
Elementary & secondary ed.			
School lunches	$13.1	0.01%	0.02%
School tuition	$3.0	0.00%	0.01%
Other	$6.7	0.01%	0.01%
Total	$22.8	0.02%	0.04%
Higher education			
Auxiliary	$9,052.9	8.14%	15.78%
Tuition	$21,808.2	19.62%	38.01%
Other	$385.7	0.35%	0.67%
Total	$31,246.9	28.11%	54.45%
Hospital	$13,953.2	12.55%	24.32%
Regular highway	$225.4	0.20%	0.39%
Toll highway	$2,835.7	2.55%	4.94%
Housing & community Dev.	$253.4	0.23%	0.44%
Natural resources			
Agriculture	$578.5	0.52%	1.01%
Forestry	$333.0	0.30%	0.58%
Other	$618.6	0.56%	1.08%
Total	$1,530.0	1.38%	2.67%
Parks & recreation	$867.2	0.78%	1.51%
Sewerage	$28.5	0.03%	0.05%
Solid waste	$318.1	0.29%	0.55%
Water transportation & terminal	$409.3	0.37%	0.71%
All other	$4,723.4	4.25%	8.23%
Total charges	$57,381.2	51.61%	100.00%
Miscellaneous revenue			
Special assessments	$151.7	0.14%	0.285%
Property sale other	$199.6	0.18%	0.375%
Interest earnings	$25,288.8	22.75%	47.01%
Fines & foreits	$1.961.4	1.76%	3.65%
Rents	$559.3	0.50%	1.04%
Royalties	$1,650.9	1.48%	3.07%
Donations from private sources	$4,769.8	4.31%	8.92%
Net lottery revenue	$10,179.0	9.16%	18.92%
All other	$9,008.3	8.10%	16.75%
Total miscellaneous	$53,795.8	48.39%	100.00%
Total Charges and Miscellaneous	$111,177.0	100.00%	

Source: U.S. Census Bureau, State Government Finances in 1993.

from these tax sources will fall with inflation. During the 1970s, the decade with the greatest amount of inflation in the United States, revenues from all of these nonindexed tax sources fell. The evidence suggests that revenue sources that do not automatically adjust for inflation will tend to fall behind those that do, because of a reluctance on the part of state legislatures to explicitly raise rates.[8]

STATE VERSUS LOCAL TAXES

One factor that could affect the cyclical variability of taxes is the reliance on state versus local revenue sources. Table 3.8 gives a breakdown of revenue sources for state and local governments for each decade from 1960 to 1990. The table shows the increasing reliance on both general sales and individual income taxes, as previously noted. In 1990 general sales taxes composed more than 33 percent of state taxes, with individual income taxes running a close second at almost 32 percent. Both of those revenue sources have shown an increasing trend over the decades. Meanwhile, motor fuels taxes have plummeted from about 18.5 percent of state taxes to about 6.5 percent. Along with declines in other sales and gross receipts taxes, the overall category of sales and gross receipts taxes makes up significantly less as a percentage of total tax revenues in 1990 than it did in 1960. Most of the decline came in the decade of the 1970s.

One might conjecture that the tax bases relied on by states would tend to fluctuate along with fluctuations in income. This will obviously be true for income taxes, and will be true for sales taxes to the extent that consumption varies with income. Local government revenues, on the other hand, are heavily dependent on property taxes, and the assessed value of property is likely to fluctuate relatively little in response to fluctuations in income. Given assessment practices, the assessed value of property is undoubtedly more stable than even the market value of property. Thus, local government revenues are likely to be more stable than state government revenues, and this conjecture is demonstrated to be true later in this volume.

If much of the stability in local government revenues is due to the stability of property tax revenues, Table 3.8 reveals that local government's dependence on property taxes has been declining over the decades. In 1960 local governments received more than 87 percent of their tax revenue from property taxes, and that had fallen to just over 72 percent by 1990. Again, the largest change occurred in the 1970s. The greatest change in the other direction has been increased reliance on sales and gross receipts taxes, which have more than doubled from 7.4 percent of tax revenues in 1960 to 15.3 percent in 1990. Still, with heavy reliance on the property tax, local governments have a more stable revenue source than state governments, which goes some distance toward explaining why fiscal crises have been much more prominent at the state level than at the local level. If the trend away from local reliance on property taxes continues, however, local governments may not be as insulated from recessionary fiscal crises in the future.

Table 3.8
Sources of State and Local Tax Revenue, 1960 to 1990

	1960	1970	1980	1990
State governments				
Sales and gross receipts	58.27%	56.82%	49.50%	48.94%
General sales	23.85%	29.56%	31.49%	33.18%
Motor fuels	18.49%	13.10%	7.09%	6.45%
Alcohol & tobacco	8.72%	7.77%	4.53%	2.91%
Other sales	7.21%	6.39%	6.38%	6.41%
Individual income	12.25%	19.15%	27.06%	31.97%
Corporate income	6.54%	7.79%	9.72%	7.24%
Vehicle operator licenses	8.72%	6.16%	3.88%	3.55%
Other taxes	14.22%	10.07%	9.84%	8.29%
Local governments				
Individual income	1.40%	4.20%	5.78%	5.66%
Sales and gross receipts	7.40%	7.90%	13.97%	15.32%
Property	87.36%	84.88%	73.13%	72.06%
Other taxes	3.83%	3.02%	7.12%	6.96%

Source: U.S. Census Bureau, *Statistical Abstract of the United States*, various years.

DIFFERENCES AMONG THE STATES

State tax structures vary widely. As Table 3.5 noted, nine states have no personal income tax, and five states have no general sales tax. This is noteworthy because each of those tax sources makes up more than 30 percent of state tax collections as a whole. States also differ dramatically in their degrees of decentralization, as shown in Table 3.9. At the decentralized end of the spectrum, New Hampshire collects less than 30 percent of its state and local taxes at the state level. The next closest states, New York, Colorado, South Dakota, and Oregon, collect close to 50 percent of their state and local taxes at the state level, and New York's inclusion on that list is due to the large tax collections made by the city of New York. At the other end of the spectrum are Delaware and Hawaii collect in excess of 80 percent of state and local taxes at the state level.

The substantial differences among states mean that although one can look at averages of all the states, as is frequently done in this volume, those averages might also conceal interesting differences among the states. Thus, it is worthwhile examining issues on a state-by-state basis as well as looking at averages among the states. Whereas state fiscal crises can be widespread among the states, some states weather tough periods better than others, and a state-by-state examination can help uncover some of the reasons that some states are more successful than others.

Table 3.9
State Taxes as a Percentage of State and Local Taxes, 1991

State	Percent	State	Percentage
Alabama	70.7%	Montana	64.5%
Alaska	71.8%	Nebraska	56.7%
Arizona	62.7%	Nevada	67.5%
Arkansas	74.6%	New Hampshire	29.6%
California	64.7%	New Jersey	54.0%
Colorado	48.6%	New Mexico	78.3%
Connecticut	56.8%	New York	47.0%
Delaware	82.4%	North Carolina	69.7%
Florida	56.7%	North Dakota	68.6%
Georgia	60.2%	Ohio	57.0%
Hawaii	81.1%	Oklahoma	72.8%
Idaho	72.3%	Oregon	51.4%
Illinois	54.0%	Pennsylvania	57.7%
Indiana	63.4%	Rhode Island	58.7%
Iowa	63.3%	South Carolina	70.8%
Kansas	58.1%	South Dakota	50.5%
Kentucky	78.6%	Tennessee	61.7%
Louisiana	61.3%	Texas	52.5%
Maine	62.1%	Utah	65.7%
Maryland	57.7%	Vermont	57.0%
Massachusetts	65.4%	Virginia	55.6%
Michigan	56.3%	Washington	71.2%
Minnesota	67.8%	West Virginia	79.3%
Mississippi	72.9%	Wisconsin	63.6%
Missouri	60.7%	Wyoming	61.5%

Source: Tax Foundation, *Facts and Figures on Government Finance*, 1994.

REVENUES FROM THE FEDERAL GOVERNMENT

Federal grants to state governments provide a significant source of funds, and one that is not as much under state control as the revenue sources considered so far in this chapter. Table 3.10 shows that federal grants to states, and to states and localities, have been a substantial source of funding for decades. In 1950 the federal government contributed 18.6 percent of state government revenues, and through the mid-1950s this figure fell to around 16 percent. The next decade and a half saw a substantial rise to a height of almost 28 percent in the late 1970s, followed by a decline in the 1980s to 23 percent. The early 1990s have seen a reversal of this downward trend as federal grants grew to more than 27 percent of state revenues by 1993. The vast proportion of this recent growth can be attributed

Table 3.10
Federal Aid to State and Local Governments

| Year | Federal Aid (Percent of General Revenue) | |
	State	State and Local
1950	18.57%	10.91%
1951	18.11%	9.65%
1952	17.00%	9.83%
1953	17.51%	10.28%
1954	16.90%	9.66%
1955	16.08%	9.28%
1956	16.05%	9.08%
1957	16.60%	9.52%
1958	18.95%	10.85%
1959	22.64%	13.04%
1960	23.44%	13.44%
1961	22.02%	12.69%
1962	22.72%	13.07%
1963	22.78%	13.54%
1964	24.26%	14.43%
1965	24.41%	14.77%
1966	25.48%	15.95%
1967	25.54%	16.46%
1968	25.21%	16.78%
1969	24.85%	16.41%
1970	24.80%	16.64%
1971	25.53%	17.35%
1972	27.11%	18.60%
1973	29.01%	21.65%
1974	26.38%	21.02%
1975	26.14%	20.39%
1976	27.34%	21.65%
1977	27.92%	22.82%
1978	27.92%	23.43%
1979	27.20%	22.95%
1980	27.12%	22.50%
1981	26.76%	22.16%
1982	24.50%	19.98%
1983	24.20%	19.28%
1984	24.58%	19.22%
1985	24.47%	19.17%
1986	24.62%	18.67%
1987	23.63%	17.50%
1988	23.25%	16.68%
1989	23.06%	16.50%
1990	23.28%	16.39%
1991	24.32%	16.97%
1992	25.99%	18.44%
1993	27.48%	

Source: Tax Foundation, Facts and Figures on
Government Finance, various years.

to increased federal Medicaid expenditures, but other welfare programs such as supplemental feeding programs, grants for family support payments, and subsidized housing programs have also contributed to this growth. As of 1994, over 40 percent of federal grants were for Medicaid , compared with just under 20 percent in 1970.

The pattern of federal revenues going to states provides an interesting backdrop to an analysis of state government finance, because there is an upward trend from the middle 1950s up through the early 1970s, followed by a downward trend until 1990. This feature of the data can help separate out trends that are associated with time from the effects of federal grants.

A similar pattern exists for federal grants to state and local governments, also shown in Table 3.10, but note that although the directions of the trends are the same, grants to state and local governments have increased much more as a percentage of total revenues than grants to state governments alone, indicating a growing trend of federal grants directly to localities. Still, grants to state and local governments are never as large as a percentage of total revenues as grants to states alone, showing that federal grants remain a more important source of revenues to state governments than to local governments.

There is a surprising amount of variation among the states in the percentage of state and local revenue funded by federal grants. Table 3.11 shows federal grants as a percentage of state and local revenue in 1991. Alaska and Florida are at the bottom of the list as the only states below 13 percent, but Virginia, Nevada, and New Jersey are close to that level. At the high end of the scale, Mississippi, South Dakota, and Montana all get more than 25 percent of their state revenues in the form of federal grants, but North Dakota and Wyoming are close to that level as well.

The figures in Table 3.11 indicate that, as noted above, there is substantial variation among states that could be masked by aggregating all states and that federal government policy has the potential to exert a substantial impact on states and localities on the revenue side of the budget, in addition to the expenditure side through policies such as matching grants and federal mandates.

STATE TAXES OVER THE REVENUE CYCLE

The purpose of this chapter has been to give an overview of state government revenues to provide better understanding of how revenue factors might underlie state fiscal crises. In an important way, state fiscal crises are entirely revenue-driven, because there will always be a greater demand for state government expenditures than the government can supply. Thus, state legislatures must decide how to allocate available funds to potentially unlimited demands. When states overcommit, revenue crises occur.

Figure 3.7 shows the annual percentage change in state government revenues, after adjusting for inflation, from 1950 to 1993. After substantial growth in the 1950s and 1960s, revenue growth slowed in the 1970s and 1980s. This is highlighted in the figure by the solid lines showing the average rate of growth in the two periods. Prior to the early 1970s, state government revenues were averaging

Table 3.11
Federal Aid as a Percentage of State and Local Revenue, 1991

State	Percent	State	Percent
Alabama	21.6%	Montana	25.5%
Alaska	11.3%	Nebraska	15.7%
Arizona	14.6%	Nevada	13.7%
Arkansas	21.8%	New Hampshire	14.3%
California	16.3%	New Jersey	13.9%
Colorado	15.0%	New Mexico	18.7%
Connecticut	17.1%	New York	17.3%
Delaware	14.9%	North Carolina	17.9%
Florida	12.6%	North Dakota	24.5%
Georgia	17.9%	Ohio	18.3%
Hawaii	15.1%	Oklahoma	17.4%
Idaho	19.2%	Oregon	20.0%
Illinois	15.2%	Pennsylvania	17.2%
Indiana	16.3%	Rhode Island	22.6%
Iowa	16.7%	South Carolina	21.0%
Kansas	14.7%	South Dakota	25.5%
Kentucky	20.7%	Tennessee	22.4%
Louisiana	21.6%	Texas	16.1%
Maine	19.5%	Utah	20.2%
Maryland	15.1%	Vermont	21.9%
Massachusetts	18.9%	Virginia	13.4%
Michigan	16.8%	Washington	16.4%
Minnesota	15.8%	West Virginia	20.9%
Mississippi	27.2%	Wisconsin	16.0%
Missouri	18.3%	Wyoming	23.5%

Source: Tax Foundation, *Facts and Figures on Government Finance*, 1994.

7.7 percent annual growth in real terms. Since that time, the average annual growth has been substantially lower, approximately 3.2 percent. This fundamental change in the nature of state government revenues between the periods before and after 1970 is an important consideration throughout this analysis. The slower revenue growth present since the 1970s has meant that states have been less able to keep commitments made in previous years. In this environment, downturns like those that occurred in 1980 and 1991 have led to fiscal crises. Not only does it appear that there was a fundamental change in the long-run rate of growth in state revenues around 1970, but perhaps also a change in the degree of variability around the trend growth line. The impact of economic fluctuations on state government revenues appears to be larger after 1970 than before. This chapter suggests that changes made in state tax structures could have contributed to creating an environment susceptible to fiscal crisis.

Figure 3.7
Annual Change in Real State General Revenue

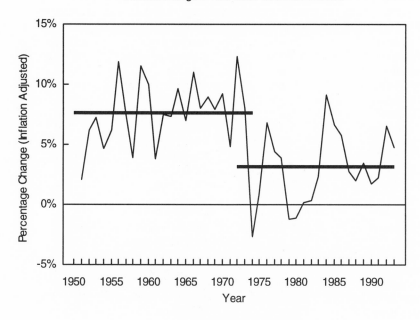

▬ Long-Run Average Growth

In the 1960s, states undertook massive tax increases, partly increasing existing tax rates, but also introducing new taxes. From 1960 to 1969 eleven states introduced general sales taxes, and from 1961 to 1971 nine states introduced personal income taxes. No states introduced personal income taxes in either the 1950s or the 1980s, and no state has introduced a general sales tax since 1969. These new taxes, coupled with strong economic growth during the 1960s, helped to cushion any fiscal blows that might have been felt by states, but after exploiting new tax bases through the 1960s, there was less opportunity to look for new taxes in the following decades to continue the growth of the 1950s and 1960s. Thus, states became more vulnerable.

Other factors making states more vulnerable to fiscal downturns are the increased reliance on general sales and personal income taxes, which tend to fluctuate over the business cycle, and a move toward centralization, which is a move away from more stable local tax bases. These factors raise a number of questions. Could states adjust their tax bases to reduce their vulnerability to cyclical fluctuations? Are some taxes more cyclically variable than others? Might a portfolio of tax bases work better to dampen cyclical fluctuations than heavy reliance on a single tax? The next several chapters examine some of these questions.

Regardless of these underlying changes in state tax structures, over a period of decades state taxes have continued to take a larger and larger share of state income. Figure 3.8 shows the trend in state taxes as a percent of GDP from 1950 to 1993.

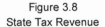

Figure 3.8
State Tax Revenue

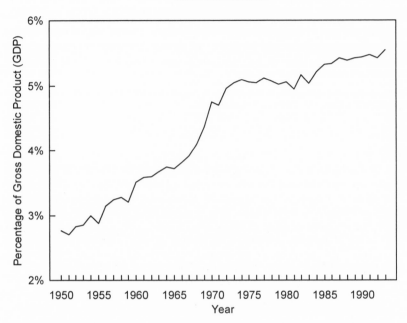

In 1950 state taxes were about 2.8 percentage of GDP and, after dipping in the early 1950s had risen to 3.5 percent by 1960. The 1960s saw tremendous growth, and by 1970 state taxes were 4.7 percent of GDP. There was only slight growth in the 1970s, leaving state taxes at 5.0 percent of GDP by 1980. By 1993 state taxes were 5.5 percent of GDP. Thus, there has been steady tax revenue growth over the decades, and since 1980 the share of GDP made up by state taxes has increased by 10 percent (from 5.0 to 5.5 percent). Since income has also grown through the decades, one cannot blame state fiscal crises on a lack of revenue growth.

For purposes of laying a foundation for an empirical examination of the cyclical variability that has contributed to state fiscal crises, the material in this chapter has shown that the decades of the 1950s and 1960s were different in some important ways from the following decades. Most notably, there was a substantial slowdown in revenue growth in the early 1970s when compared to earlier decades. Furthermore, states undertook major changes in their tax bases through the 1960s, and through the early 1970s, mostly by adding sales and income taxes as new tax bases. Tax systems were changing much more before the 1970s than after. Thus, from an empirical standpoint, the 1950s and 1960s could be expected to have some significant differences from the decades that followed.

There have been substantial changes in state taxes over the decades, but the underlying tax structure does not appear to be the direct cause of state fiscal crises.[9] State tax revenues have continued to increase, both in real dollar terms and as a percentage of GDP, for decades. Although state tax structures have been able to deliver increasing revenues to states over longer periods of time, cyclical downturns have had a negative impact, and it is those cyclical fluctuations that are the focus of most of the rest of this study. With this background, the next several chapters consider the issue of cyclical variability of state government revenues in detail. Chapter 4 discusses some of the state policy considerations involved in choosing a portfolio of taxes to reduce revenue variability. Chapter 5 explores theoretical issues related to cyclical variability, and Chapters 6 through 9 look more directly at empirical issues.

NOTES

1.   Raymond J. Ring, Jr., "The Proportion of Consumers' and Producers' Goods in the General Sales Tax," *National Tax Journal* 42, No. 2 (June 1989), pp. 167–79.

2.   Because five states have no sales tax, this leaves twenty states that tax food. In addition, the District of Columbia also exempts food and drugs. Only two states, Illinois and New Mexico, tax prescription drugs under the sales tax.

3.   Walter Hellerstein, "Florida's Sales Tax on Services," *National Tax Journal* 41, No. 1 (March 1988), pp. 1–18, for a discussion of Florida's ill-fated tax on services. The issue has continued to resurface in Florida since the repeal of the tax.

4.   In contrast, Alaska has no state sales tax but has local sales taxes.

5.   In a situation where two levels of government share a common tax base there is the possibility that the combined tax rate of the two governments will exceed the optimal tax rate. See Marilyn R. Flowers, "Shared Tax Sources in a Leviathan Model of Federalism," *Public Finance Quarterly* 16, No. 1 (January 1988), pp. 67–77, Charles B. Wagoner, "Local Fiscal Competition: An Intraregional Perspective," *Public Finance Quarterly* 23, No. 1 (January 1995), pp. 95–114, and Russell S. Sobel, "Optimal Taxation in a Federal System of Governments," *Southern Economic Journal* (October 1997), forthcoming.

6.   Both the initial and 1994 top marginal tax rates for Rhode Island are calculated in a similar manner because they still base their tax on the taxpayer's federal tax liability.

7.   See David Osborne and Ted Gaebler, *Reinventing Government: How the Entrepreneurial Spirit is Transforming the Public Sector* (Reading, Mass.: Addison-Wesley, 1992) for this argument.

8.   This tendency may become even more pronounced if other states follow the lead of Oklahoma and Colorado, which have amended their constitutions to require that any new taxes or increases in existing tax rates be approved by the voters.

9.   One factor that might have contributed to problems is poor revenue forecasts that leave states with inadequate revenues to fund budgeted expenditures. See Daniel R. Feenberg, William Gentry, David Gilroy, and Harvey S. Rosen, "Testing the Rationality of State Revenue Forecasts," *Review of Economics and Statistics* 71, No. 2 (May 1989), pp. 300–308, and William M. Gentry, "Do State Revenue Forecasters Utilize Available Information?" *National Tax Journal* 42, No. 4 (December 1989), pp. 429–39. John L. Mikesell, "Election Periods and State Tax Policy Cycles," *Public Choice* 33, No. 3 (1978), pp. 99–106, suggests that politics might contribute to the instability of tax revenue flows.

Chapter 4

Budgeting for Stability: Some Principles

The degree to which a state's tax revenues fluctuate with the economy is one of its more important budgetary considerations. A state whose revenues are very unstable over the business cycle must take more precautions to prevent major fiscal crises from happening during recessions. From this standpoint, designing a state tax structure that reduces revenue variability is desirable. The complete elimination of revenue variability is impossible, however, because all revenue sources are influenced by the economy. If a state wishes to reduce the budgetary pressures experienced during recessions, it must first design a tax structure that increases the stability of revenues. Then, it must plan for how it will cope with the recessionary revenue losses it can expect given its tax structure.

Most states have established rainy day funds to aid in coping with the predictable losses of tax revenue associated with economic recessions. In fact, most states that have this type of fund created it soon after a recession.[1] Although protecting against a recession is not the only reason for establishing a fund, it is undoubtedly the most important. Revenues systematically fluctuate with the state economy, and a rainy day fund can be used to smooth revenues over the business cycle. In this manner, states can ease the fiscal stress associated with recessionary times. Chapter 9 deals more specifically with the issue of state rainy day funds and how successful they were in helping states ease the fiscal pressure felt during the 1990–1991 recession.

The previous chapters focused on the trends in state government revenues and expenditures over the past four decades. This chapter analyzes the state budgetary process, which is the link between the revenue and expenditure sides of public finance. The way in which a state's budget is organized, through a system of funds, has important implications for how susceptible it is to fiscal crises. Through the use of funds, a state can manage its portfolio of tax sources to minimize the impact of recessionary declines in revenues. After discussing this issue, the fundamental logic behind the analysis of tax variability is developed. In Chapter 3, overall trends in taxes were presented. In this chapter, each major state tax source is discussed in terms of its stability over the business cycle. The logic presented in this chapter serves as the foundation for the empirical analysis that follows.

STATE FUND STRUCTURES

As was seen in the previous chapter, state government revenues come from many different sources such as federal grants, roadway tolls, school tuition payments, lottery proceeds, and a variety of taxes. States dedicate each source of revenue to a certain fund, and these funds are categorized by the types of expenditure programs that they can finance. Although the structure of funds tends to differ quite substantially across states, one fund that is common to all states is the general fund. For most states, this is the most important fund, because it is the only one not earmarked for a specific purpose. The general fund represents the resources of the state available for appropriation by the legislature. A state road fund would, on the other hand, be earmarked for spending on state roads; and federal grants for things such as Medicaid would generally be kept in a conglomerate category called federal funds. The defining characteristic is whether or not the money can be discretionarily allocated by the legislature, or whether it is dedicated for spending on a particular item.

The general revenue and expenditure data used throughout this book are consistent with the U.S. Census Bureau definitions and are not the same as state general fund revenue and expenditure. General revenues and expenditures, as defined by the Census Bureau, are inclusive of all state activities except state-run utilities and liquor stores and state-funded insurance trusts (such as state employee retirement programs and unemployment compensation). In contrast, general fund revenues and expenditures refer only to those moneys not dedicated for a specific purpose. As an example, many states earmark the revenue from their motor fuels tax for spending on roads through a state road fund. This would be included in the calculation of general revenue, but not in general fund revenue. Additionally, federal grants to states that are earmarked for specific purposes are not included in state general fund revenues, but are included in general revenues as defined by the Census Bureau. This distinction is important because in 1993, general fund revenues and expenditures were only about 48 percent of general revenues and expenditures for all U.S. states combined. This means that approximately 52 percent of all state revenues are earmarked for specific purposes. This figure varies quite substantially across states, however, as is shown in Table 4.1.

Table 4.1 shows the percentage breakdown of state government expenditures by fund source. The first column shows the percentage of expenditures that are finance from the general fund. The second column shows the percentage of state expenditures financed from earmarked federal funds, and the third column shows the percentage of expenditures financed from other earmarked funds. The final column shows the percentage of own source funded expenditures (excluding federal) that are financed through earmarked funds. Excluding federal funds gives a more accurate picture of the percentage of the state's own money that is earmarked for specific purposes. At the top end of the list, Montana, Wyoming, Oregon, and Florida have over half of their own source revenues going into earmarked funds.

Table 4.1
State Expenditures by Fund Source, 1993

State	General Fund	Federal Funds	Other State Funds	Earmarked Own Source
Alabama	35%	58%	7%	17%
Alaska	59%	19%	22%	27%
Arizona	49%	30%	19%	28%
Arkansas	32%	28%	39%	55%
California	47%	34%	14%	23%
Colorado	44%	28%	28%	39%
Connecticut	61%	15%	13%	18%
Delaware	45%	18%	31%	41%
Florida	34%	21%	40%	54%
Georgia	56%	27%	13%	19%
Hawaii	49%	13%	24%	33%
Idaho	44%	32%	23%	34%
Illinois	44%	21%	32%	42%
Indiana	55%	32%	12%	18%
Iowa	42%	22%	36%	46%
Kansas	44%	27%	28%	39%
Kentucky	42%	32%	26%	38%
Louisiana	36%	33%	30%	45%
Maine	42%	29%	27%	39%
Maryland	53%	20%	23%	30%
Massachusetts	73%	21%	6%	8%
Michigan	38%	30%	32%	46%
Minnesota	63%	21%	15%	19%
Mississippi	34%	41%	25%	42%
Missouri	44%	27%	28%	39%
Montana	23%	29%	48%	68%
Nebraska	44%	23%	32%	42%
Nevada	43%	23%	33%	43%
New Hampshire	35%	34%	28%	44%
New Jersey	65%	20%	13%	17%
New Mexico	49%	22%	26%	35%
New York	53%	28%	16%	23%
North Carolina	56%	25%	19%	25%
North Dakota	36%	33%	31%	46%
Ohio	41%	24%	32%	44%
Oklahoma	45%	26%	28%	38%
Oregon	32%	16%	52%	62%
Pennsylvania	50%	27%	22%	31%

Table 4.1 (continued)

State	General Fund	Federal Funds	Other State Funds	Earmarked Own Source
Rhode Island	52%	31%	15%	22%
South Carolina	38%	30%	30%	44%
South Dakota	37%	39%	25%	40%
Tennessee	40%	35%	23%	37%
Texas	55%	27%	16%	23%
Utah	49%	23%	26%	35%
Vermont	42%	33%	21%	33%
Virginia	45%	17%	37%	45%
Washington	52%	21%	23%	31%
West Virginia	40%	34%	23%	37%
Wisconsin	52%	23%	25%	32%
Wyoming	28%	24%	47%	63%

Year	All U.S. States Combined			
1987	53%	22%	24%	31%
1988	53%	22%	23%	31%
1989	53%	22%	23%	30%
1990	53%	23%	22%	29%
1991	52%	23%	22%	30%
1992	49%	26%	24%	33%
1993	48%	27%	23%	32%

Note: New Mexico is for 1992 and Nevada for 1989 (latest available).
Source: U.S. Census Bureau, *Statistical Abstract of the U.S.*, various years.

This implies that these states have the least legislative discretion in their spending when compared to other states. Interestingly, all of these states have a general sales or personal income tax, but not both. Because these tax sources usually go into the general fund, it is easy to see why these states might be at the top of the list. At the lower end of the list, Massachusetts has the least degree of earmarking with only 8 percent of own source revenues not going into the general fund. Alabama, New Jersey, Connecticut, Indiana, Georgia, and Minnesota follow as the other states having less than 20 percent of own source funds earmarked. This group of states has the most legislative discretion in their spending, because a higher percentage of their tax revenue flows into the general fund.

Looking at the total for all states combined, it appears that the percentage of expenditures accounted for by the general fund has been falling. This is due, however, not to an increase in the earmarking of state tax revenues, but rather to the increase in federal grants during the early 1990s. When federal money is excluded, the percentage of own source revenues that are earmarked has remained fairly stable over the years listed here.

Because each of a state's funds have different revenue sources, each will have a different degree of variability over the business cycle. A fund that receives revenues from a stable tax source will be more stable over the business cycle than a fund that receives revenues from an unstable tax. A state may use this knowledge to its advantage by earmarking the revenue sources that are most unstable over the business cycle with the expenditure programs that have more flexibility to be cut during recessions. The most important expenditure programs should be funded with the most stable sources of revenue. A state would not, for example, want to fund welfare programs with highly cyclical tax sources. Generally the expenditure demands placed on welfare programs rise during recessions and fall during economic booms. If a state were to fund one of these programs with a tax source that fell substantially during recessions it would create a major budgetary problem. The state would systematically have to increase the tax rate during recessions to generate enough money to fund the program. This does not mean that a state should totally avoid tax sources with high variability, but rather that it must pay attention to where it designates the revenues.

Because the general fund represents a conglomeration of revenue sources, none of which are earmarked, this makes it is possible for a state to diversify its general fund in a way that allows for reliance on more unstable tax sources. A highly variable tax will not cause as many problems when pooled in the general fund with other more stable taxes. Expenditure programs financed from the general fund are dependent on the variability of the entire pool of general fund revenues, not just the variability of a particular revenue source. Revenues within the general fund are substitutable, so a general fund expenditure program can be financed with different proportions of taxes at different stages of the business cycle. During a recession a very procyclical revenue source will provide much less in revenues, but this can be partially offset by heavier reliance on other, more stable, general fund revenue sources. The key to stabilizing the general fund is diversification so that more stable revenue sources can allow the state to tax unstable revenue sources also. A state would not want to rely too heavily on any one unstable revenue source for its general fund revenues.

The focus of this book is on the fluctuations in revenue due to the business cycle, rather than fluctuations due to other factors. The reason for this focus is that state fiscal crises are associated with revenue declines during business cycle downturns, rather than revenue fluctuations in general. The major difference between these two types of variability is that dealing with noncyclical variance is much easier than dealing with systematic cyclical variability. If a state has five sources of revenue, some will be higher than usual and others will be lower than usual in any given year. The combined revenues from all sources should be more stable than the revenues from any one individual tax. This is the principle of diversification that many investors use when choosing a portfolio of stocks. Having just one tax with high random variance as the only source of funding for a specific program would not be desirable. When used jointly with relatively stable taxes to fund a program, taxes with high random variance cause fewer budgetary problems.[2]

Cyclical variability, on the other hand, cannot be so easily avoided. Even the portfolio of a diversified investor will fluctuate with the overall market. For a state that has many revenue sources, the random fluctuations will partially offset each other, but a recession will still cause the state's total revenues to fall. The problem is that all major sources of tax revenue fluctuate with the business cycle. Fortunately, states may take advantage of the fact that different taxes have differing degrees of cyclical variability.[3]

An important thing to remember is that changes in tax laws and tax rates also influence tax revenues. When looking at tax revenues, observed variations may be due to either changing economic conditions or legislated changes. To isolate only those movements caused by economic fluctuations, it is preferable to look at movements in the tax base, rather than in tax revenues. Looking only at movements in the tax base, however, abstracts from the revenue stabilizing potential of legislative action. If one tax base is more unstable over the business cycle, but the applicable tax laws can be more easily changed by legislative action, that tax may actually be a more stable source of revenue over the business cycle. Thus, both the cyclical variability of the tax base and the cyclical variability of tax revenues are important.

THE STABILITY OF MAJOR STATE TAX SOURCES

With knowledge of the variability of alternative revenue sources, a state can more easily adjust its portfolio of taxes as to reduce the budgetary problems it faces during recessions. Chapter 3 examined the structure and history of the major state government tax bases. The remaining portion of this chapter explores the susceptibility of each major state government tax source to economic fluctuations.

The Consumer Sales Tax

As was seen in Chapter 3, the consumer sales tax is the largest source of tax revenue for states. Because the tax is based on consumer purchases, the responsiveness of sales tax revenues to economic fluctuations will be dependent on how consumers' purchases vary with changes in their income. One economic theory is that current consumption is determined by expected lifetime income, rather than current income, suggesting that consumption should be more stable over the business cycle than income.[4] Regardless of overall consumption patterns, consumers' purchases of some items are much more sensitive to income changes than other items. This means that an important feature of a state sales tax is which goods are exempted from the tax. Comparing the forty-six states that currently have a sales tax, the most commonly exempted items are prescription drugs, food, gasoline, liquor, and clothing. The justification for exempting these items from taxation is that they are necessities, and that by taxing them the tax burden falls more heavily on families with lower incomes. When compared to total retail sales, however, purchases of these types of items are relatively stable over the business cycle, so exempting such items from the sales tax base makes the revenues from the tax less stable over the business cycle. Another characteristic of the sales tax that varies across states is the taxation of services. Following the logic above, it is possible that the inclusion of certain services in the sales tax base may change the variability of a state's tax revenues. Cyclical variability in the sales tax is due primarily to changes in consumption over the business cycle, but exactly what is included in the tax base can also have an effect on the cyclical variability of sales tax revenues. There is considerable variation among state in the structure of sales taxes.

Figure 4.1 shows how the combined sales tax revenues of all states fluctuates with the national economy. It is apparent that there is close correlation between national income and consumption. Throughout both the economic recessions and booms, sales tax revenues tended to change in a pattern very similar to gross domestic product. During the recessionary periods of 1974–1975, 1980–1982, and 1990–1991, state sales tax revenues tended to fall by slightly less than GDP. In

Figure 4.1
State General Sales Tax Revenue and the Economy

— Gross Domestic Product   - · General Sales Tax Revenue

contrast, during the more healthy economic times of the late 1970s and 1980s, sales tax revenues tended to grow slightly faster than the economy. Obtaining a more precise, quantifiable measure of this relationship between a tax and the economy is the main focus of the next several chapters of this book.

Selective Excise Taxes

Selective excise taxes are sales taxes on certain specific items. The most common type of selective excise tax is a sin tax, such as one levied on alcohol, tobacco, or gambling. Taxes on privilege or luxury items, however, are also common. The logic behind the analysis of selective excise taxes is quite similar to the logic presented above regarding the sales tax. Consumers' purchases of items such as tobacco and liquor are very stable over the business cycle because they do not fluctuate very much when income fluctuates. As consumers are becoming more conscious about their health, however, the revenues from these taxes are declining. Additionally, the revenues from these taxes do not automatically increase with inflation because they are usually levied on a per unit basis. They are not good sources of long-term revenue growth for a state, but they are fairly stable sources of revenues during economic recessions. Figure 4.2 shows the relationship between

Figure 4.2
State Alcohol and Tobacco Tax Revenue and the Economy

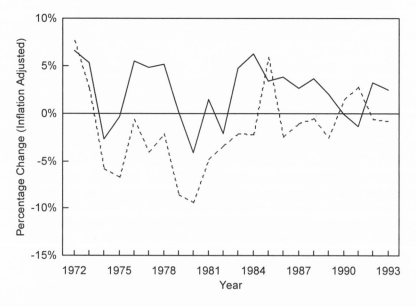

— Gross Domestic Product   -- Alcohol and Tobacco Tax Revenue

state alcohol and tobacco tax revenues and the economy. The most interesting feature to notice in the figure is the revenue changes that occurred during the 1990–1991 recession. When GDP was falling, revenues from this tax were actually rising. In fact, two of the only three years of positive growth in the revenues from this tax between 1974 and 1993 occurred during the 1990–1991 recession. Certainly the revenues from this tax were a stabilizing influence on state finances during the 1990–1991 recession. During the 1980–1982 recession, revenues from this tax did decline, and by a larger percentage than would have been expected given the data from the 1990–1991 recession.

Selective excise taxes are also placed on luxury-type goods. Taxes on privilege-type items place a larger burden on those individuals with higher incomes. However, following the same logic as above, purchases of these items are very responsive to income and employment levels, and will fluctuate highly over the business cycle. Some states, for example, exempt automobile purchases from the consumer sales tax and tax them under a distinct privilege tax. This exemption increases the stability of the consumers' sales tax by taking one of the more cyclically variable items out of the sales tax base. Standing alone, however, a motor vehicles privilege tax is a very unstable source of revenues.

Motor Fuels Taxes

As was seen in Chapter 3, taxes on motor fuels have been falling in importance for state governments in recent history. They are, however, fairly stable over the business cycle, because consumers' purchases of motor fuels are not very sensitive to income fluctuations. Figure 4.3 shows how state motor fuels tax revenues fluctuate with the economy. Particularly interesting is the stability of the revenues from this tax from 1982 forward. During the 1990–1991 recession, revenues from this tax barely moved at all. Looking back at earlier recessions might lead to a different conclusion, but one might argue that the period immediately following the energy crisis of the 1970s was different. The negative growth during the 1974–1981 period is not so much associated with the business cycle, but is due to the structural changes caused by the energy crisis. Because motor fuels taxes are levied on a per gallon basis, and not as a percentage of the price, the revenues form this tax depend on units of fuel consumption, rather than on the amount spent on motor fuel. With the substantial inflation of the 1970s, state legislatures did not adjust the tax rate enough to keep up with inflation. The slowdown in motor fuel tax revenues continued through the early 1980s until inflation was brought under control.

The Personal Income Tax

The personal income tax is the second largest source of revenues for state governments. Although one might be tempted to associate personal income with the overall performance of the economy, there is an important difference. State personal income taxes are based on taxable income, which differs substantially from

Figure 4.3
State Motor Fuels Tax Revenue and the Economy

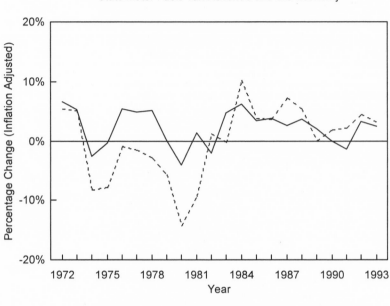

— Gross Domestic Product   - - Motor Fuels Tax Revenue

total national income as measured by GDP. In 1991, total federal taxable income
(which most states use as the basis for their tax) for the entire United States was
around 41 percent of GDP. Total federal adjusted gross income, on the other hand,
was approximately 62 percent of GDP, showing the large difference that deductions
and exemptions have on the tax base. Of the sources of adjusted gross income,
salaries and wages accounted for almost 77 percent of the total.

Figure 4.4 shows how state personal income tax revenues fluctuate with the
national economy. Like sales tax revenues, personal income tax revenues tend to
have a close correlation with the national economy. While the revenues tend to
have more yearly ups and downs than GDP, the overall fluctuations are similar.
During 1991, personal income tax collections were down almost 1 percent from the
previous year after adjusting for inflation. Tax collections from this source were
actually hit harder during 1991 than during the 1980–82 recession.

Figure 4.4
State Personal Income Tax Revenue and the Economy

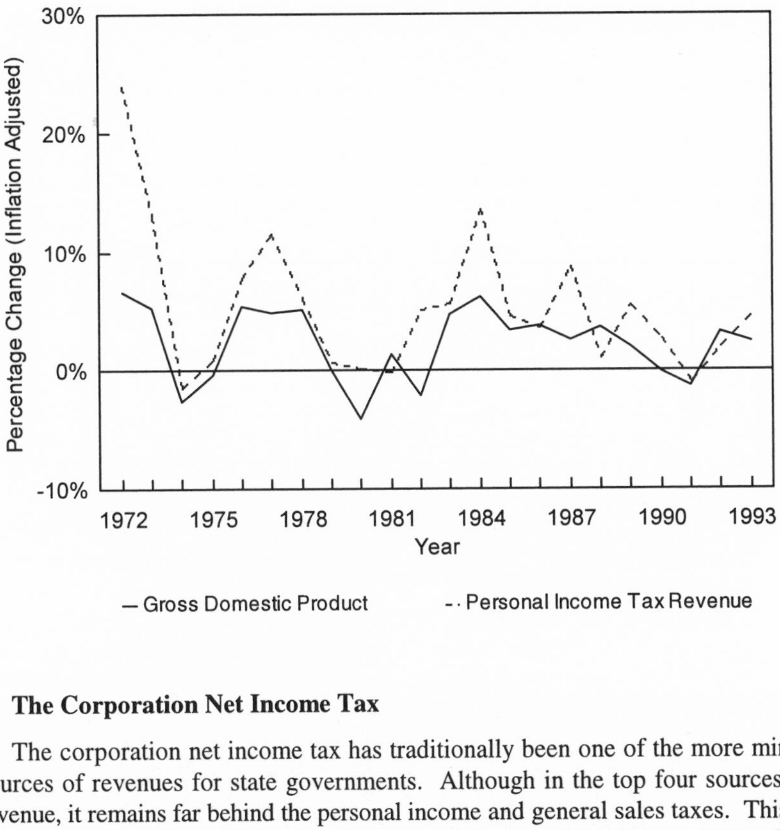

— Gross Domestic Product   -- Personal Income Tax Revenue

The Corporation Net Income Tax

The corporation net income tax has traditionally been one of the more minor sources of revenues for state governments. Although in the top four sources of revenue, it remains far behind the personal income and general sales taxes. This is fortunate because the corporate net income tax is one of the most variable of all sources of tax revenue. Figure 4.5 shows how state corporate income tax revenues fluctuate with the economy. As can be seen in the figure, corporate net income declines quite drastically during recessions and expands rapidly during economic booms. In 1990 alone, state corporate income tax collections fell by a whopping 13.5 percent. Combined with the decline of 10 percent in 1991, the revenues from this tax certainly put fiscal pressure on state finances during the 1990–1991 recession. Corporation income tax revenues actually fell by more during the 1990–1991 recession than they did in either of the two previous recessions (1974–1975 and 1980–1982). Recessions have a major impact on the revenues from this tax, and it is currently the most unstable of the four largest source of revenues for state governments.

Figure 4.5
State Corporation Income Tax Revenue and the Economy

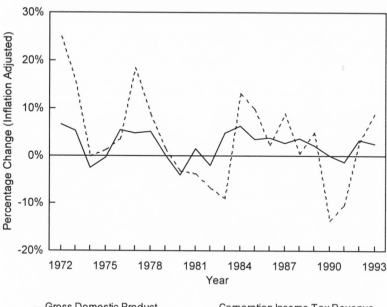

— Gross Domestic Product   -- Corporation Income Tax Revenue

A COMPARISON

The figures presented earlier show how each tax fluctuated with the economy. Of most interest is the relative variability among the taxes. Figure 4.6 shows personal income, corporate income, and general sales tax revenues to provide a better understanding of which is more stable. It is clear in the figure that the corporate income tax is the most unstable of the three revenue sources, but whether the personal income or general sales is more stable is unclear. During the 1974–1975 recession it appears that personal income tax revenues fell more, whereas during the 1980–1982 recession it appears that general sales revenues fell more. During the 1990–1991 recession, they fell approximately equally.

Because the difference between the long-run growth of a tax and its cyclical variability is of major importance in this analysis, Figure 4.7 shows some data to help make this distinction. In the figure, the same taxes as were graphed in Figure 4.6 are shown, but here in levels rather than annual growth rates. To help make the data comparable, all are measured as a percentage of the 1972 revenue amounts. Adjusting the data in this way makes it easier to see which taxes have had more long-run growth over the period. In the figure, it is apparent that personal income tax revenues exhibited higher long-run growth than did general sales tax revenues over the 1972–1993 period. Inflation-adjusted personal income tax collections in

Figure 4.6
A Comparison of Cyclical Variability

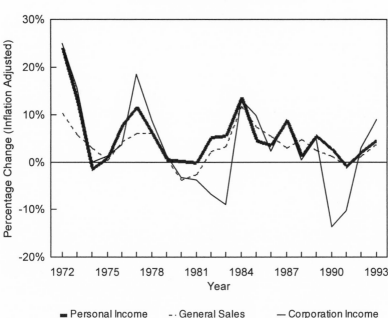

1993 were just over 250 percent, or 2.5 times, the 1972 collections, whereas the same figure for sales tax collections was 188 percent. The long-run growth of the corporate income tax revenues is harder to discern, but appears to be somewhat less than general sales. In 1993 tax collections from this source were 159 percent of the 1972 amount, but this was actually lower than the peak of 182 percent in 1989. The 1993 collections were approximately equal to the 1979 amount. Thus, just looking from 1972 to 1979, the corporate income tax has the highest growth, but from that point on it has the lowest growth. The data in Figure 4.7 highlight the distinction between long-run growth and cyclical variability. Over the 1972–1993 period, corporate income taxes clearly have higher cyclical variability, but also have lower long-run growth than personal income taxes. Thus, it is important to measure cyclical variability independently of long-run growth.

The next chapter describes the empirical problems associated with measuring cyclical variability independently from other factors. Empirical methods previously used by other researchers are reviewed, and the chapter utilizes a more modern time series econometric technique, which yields better estimates than earlier methods. Most important empirically are the distinctions between random variance, long-run growth, and cyclical variability. The empirical model developed in Chapter 5 is used in subsequent chapters to directly estimate the cyclical variability of each major tax source by state.

Figure 4.7
A Comparison of Long-Run Growth

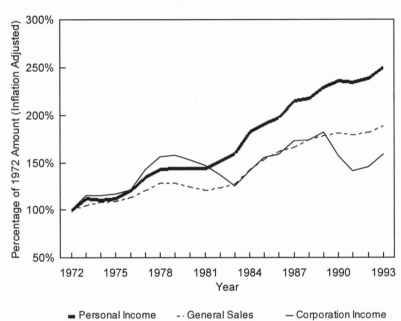

■ Personal Income   - · General Sales   — Corporation Income

NOTES

1.   Steven D. Gold, *Preparing for the Next Recession: Rainy Day Funds and Other Tools for the States*, Legislative Finance Paper no. 41 (Denver: National Conference of State Legislatures, 1983).

2.   For a good discussion of this portfolio approach to state tax management see Jack P. Suyderhoud, "State-Local Revenue Diversification, Balance, and Fiscal Performance," *Public Finance Quarterly* 22, no. 2 (April 1994): 168–94.

3.   If certain taxes lagged behind the business cycle, and others ran slightly ahead, this would also create an opportunity to smooth revenues. Unfortunately, most taxes do not have significant timing differences, as is shown later in this volume.

4.   Milton Friedman, *A Theory of the Consumption Function* (Princeton, N.J.: Princeton University Press, 1957).

Chapter 5

Measuring Cyclical Variability

The budgetary pressures felt by state governments have their origins in the fact that the demand for state spending always exceeds the revenues brought in by the state. This situation is changes little from year to year, largely because the state charges the consumers of state output less than the output costs to produce. However, state fiscal crises tend to appear along with economic downturns, and the periodic nature of fiscal crises indicates that they are not due to constant budgetary pressures, but rather to cyclical problems that arise along with the business cycle.

The demand for government expenditures tends to be countercyclical. Demands placed on government-funded health and welfare programs, unemployment compensation, job training, and even college enrollments will tend to increase during economic downturns. Government revenue, in contrast, will tend to be procyclical, with revenues falling off during recessions. If governments were able to foresee these cyclical impacts on revenues and expenditures, they could plan to avoid the negative consequences by building up reserves during prosperous years and spending them down during recessions. Such planning would require that governments be able to predict variations in their revenues from year to year. This chapter looks at methodological issues related to the variability of state government revenues to see how they might be measured. This lays a foundation for the following chapters to empirically examine how state government revenues vary over the business cycle.[1]

Ironically, the financial problems facing many states in the early 1990s have sometimes been blamed on the lengthy prosperity of the 1980s. After recovering from the recession that bottomed out in 1982, the U.S. economy went through the rest of the decade without another recession. State government revenues generated by prosperous economies were then committed to spending programs that could not be sustained through the recession of 1990–1991, creating financial hardship.[2] One explanation for the problem is purely political: governments are shortsighted, and will spend as much as they can in the short run without fully accounting for the long-run consequences. There is certainly some truth in this explanation, but greater cyclical variability will make states more vulnerable to changes in revenue streams over the business cycle.[3]

THE INCOME ELASTICITY OF TAX BASES OVER THE BUSINESS CYCLE

The income elasticity of state and local government taxes has been used as an indicator of both the short-run cyclical stability and long-run growth potential of various tax bases for decades. In their seminal contribution, Groves and Kahn argued that more income-elastic tax bases had more growth potential over time because as income grew, income-elastic tax bases would grow more rapidly than income.[4] At the same time, fluctuations in income would cause more income-elastic tax bases to be more unstable over the business cycle. Following this logic, there is an inherent trade-off between growth and stability in tax bases, with more income-elastic bases both growing faster and being less stable over the business cycle. Although some authors have questioned whether this trade-off automatically exists, it is often accepted in the literature without much question.[5]

Estimates of the income elasticity of various taxes have commonly been obtained by regressing the log level of tax revenues on the log level of income.[6] There is reason, however, to question the adequacy of these estimates, in terms of their ability to measure both long-run growth potential and short-run cyclical variability, because of the econometric properties of the regression. First, because both income and tax revenues drift systematically upward through time (i.e., they are nonstationary), regressing tax revenues on income provides information only about the long-run relationship between the tax and income.[7] Beginning with Groves and Kahn, many authors have assumed that this elasticity estimate, which is a measure of the long-run growth potential, also measures short-run variability.[8] This may not be correct because two taxes that have the same long-run growth rate will not necessarily vary by the same amount around that growth rate. Thus, one number cannot be used to proxy both the growth and variability of a tax. To avoid this problem, some researchers have proxied variability by measuring the deviation around trend growth, but this method also has problems. A second problem with the standard regression is that the elasticity estimates from these regressions will be asymptotically biased, and the estimates will have inconsistent standard errors, which make standard hypothesis testing inaccurate. These regressions will also produce artificially high R^2s.[9]

This chapter begins with a brief discussion of the model traditionally used to estimate the income elasticity of taxes. It then analyzes the time series properties of income and taxes to identify the potential problems with the traditional methods of estimation. After finding that these problems can be important, better time-series econometric techniques are used to provide asymptotically unbiased estimates of the long-run growth potential (the long-run elasticity) of all major state tax bases. Then a different model is used to measure the cyclical variability (the short-run elasticity) of the tax bases. These results are then compared with several other measures that are found in the literature. The chapter concludes by examining the stability of the estimated long-run and short-run elasticities over the past four decades, to determine whether the current estimates might be useful for designing future tax policy aimed at reducing revenue variability and increasing long-run revenue growth.

STANDARD MODEL OF TAX REVENUE

The standard model that has been widely used to estimate the income elasticity of tax revenue is

$$\ln (B_t) = \alpha + \beta \ln (Y_t) + \epsilon_t, \tag{5.1}$$

where B_t represents the level of the tax base during period t and Y_t is the level of aggregate income during the period.[10] The coefficient from this levels regression represents the income elasticity of revenues from this tax base.[11] Following Groves and Kahn the income elasticity, β, serves as a proxy for both the long-run growth and the short-run variability of the tax. This chapter examines some of the properties of the model of variability of tax revenues implied in equation (5.1), using data on aggregate national tax bases and national income for estimation. Using the actual tax base eliminates any problems with measuring tax rates and their changes, and because the data are aggregated across states, it eliminates any problems of state business cycles differing from the national cycle. This provides a reasonable and tractable data set on which to explore the econometric issues involved in estimating tax revenue elasticity.

The data used here represent all of the major tax bases used by state governments. Two proxies are examined for the state personal income tax base. Personal taxable income from the Internal Revenue Service's *Statistics of Income* series, and adjusted gross income, from the same source, are examined. Most states use something close to federal adjusted gross income as the base for state income taxes, so this measure closely approximates the state income tax base. Empirical results presented later in the chapter do show some interesting differences between these two measures. Corporate taxable income, also from *Statistics of Income*, are used as the measure of the corporate income tax base. Total retail sales and non-food retail sales, both from the *Statistical Abstract of the United States*, will be used as the measure of the sales tax base, without and with a food exemption, respectively.[12] Total motor fuel consumption, in gallons, from the *Statistical Abstract*, are used as a measure of the motor fuels tax base. Finally, total liquor store sales, also from the *Statistical Abstract*, will be used as the measure of the alcohol "sin" tax base. Although this is perhaps the least accurate of all of the tax base measures, it at least provides a consistent measure of the tax base through time. Gross domestic product (GDP) is used to measure aggregate income. All of the variables are converted to constant dollars using the GDP deflator, and their natural logs are used in the regressions. The data set covers the period from 1951 to 1991, with the exceptions that corporate taxable income was only available from 1960 to 1989 and that personal taxable income and fuel consumption were only available up through 1990.

THE STATIONARITY OF TAX BASES AND INCOME

Depending on the econometric properties of the variables in equation (5.1), the estimate of β may be subject to several problems. One important characteristic of the variables is whether they are stationary. A stationary variable is one that tends to return to some mean value through time. Any variable that has an upward trend will not be stationary (i.e., it will be nonstationary), as it will continue to move upward through time, with no inherent tendency to return downward. The test that is commonly used to determine whether a variable is stationary is the augmented Dickey-Fuller (ADF) test.[13] The results of this test for all of the tax bases and gross domestic product are given in Part A of Table 5.1. A significant *t*-statistic indicates that the variable is stationary in its level form, whereas an insignificant *t*-statistic indicates that the variable is nonstationary.[14]

In Part A of Table 5.1 all of the *t*-statistics are insignificant, which means that the variables are all nonstationary in their regular or levels form. Because both income and the tax base in equation (5.1) are nonstationary, two problems will result. The first and most important of these problems is that it becomes necessary to separately estimate the long-run and short-run relationship between the variables by using two different regression equations. The levels regression given in equation (5.1) between the two nonstationary variables provides the long-run relationship, whereas a second regression, using stationary versions of the variables, must be used to obtain the short-run relationship. To gain a better understanding of why this is the case, consider the data plotted in Figure 5.1(a).

Figure 5.1(a) shows two hypothetical tax bases and national income. Both tax bases have the same long-run rate of growth, which in this example is two times the growth rate of GDP. The two tax bases differ, however, in how much they vary over the business cycle. Tax base 1 has more variability over the business cycle (a larger decline during recessions and more growth during booms) than does tax base 2. Figure 5.1(b) shows the regression plots of both tax bases. The dashed line shows that the least-squares regression lines are identical for the two tax bases. The slope of this dashed line is the elasticity estimate that would be obtained from equation (5.1), so equation (5.1) would produce identical elasticity estimates for both tax bases. The estimate for both is 2.0, which shows that over the long run, a 1 percent growth in national income is associated with a 2 percent growth in both of the tax bases. The most important point is that this estimate is insensitive to changes in how much the tax base fluctuates around that trend growth. In fact, a tax base that grew in a straight line (or even one that moved counter to the business cycle) would still receive an estimate of 2.0 from equation (5.1) as long as it trended upward at the same long-run rate of growth as the tax bases given in Figure 5.1(a). Thus, the estimate from equation (5.1) measures only the long-run relationship between the tax base and income.

Table 5.1
Stationarity Tests

Variable		*t*-statistic
Part A:	Test for Stationarity in Levels	
GDP		-1.01
PINC		-1.07
AGI		-0.83
CINC		-2.21
SALES		-0.92
NFSALES		-0.79
FUEL		-2.24
LIQUOR		-1.93
Part B:	Test for Trend Stationary	
GDP		-1.63
PINC		-1.65
AGI		-1.99
CINC		-2.46
SALES		-2.62
NFSALES		-3.01
FUEL		-0.75
LIQUOR		-0.16
Part C:	Test for Difference Stationary	
ΔGDP		-4.20**
ΔPINC		-4.14**
ΔAGI		-4.44**
ΔCINC		-3.06*
ΔSALES		-4.26**
ΔNFSALES		-4.50**
ΔFUEL		-3.00*
ΔLIQUOR		-3.04*

Notes: For definitions of the variables see Table 5.2. * Indicates rejection of the null hypothesis (that is nonstationary) at a 5% level, and ** at a 1% level. Thus a significant value indicates that the variable is stationary.

To obtain an estimate of the short-run variability of the tax, the variables must be transformed into stationary form. The exact transformation necessary to make the variables stationary depends on the nature of the variable. A nonstationary variable may be either trend stationary or difference stationary. A trend stationary variable can be rendered stationary by removing a linear time trend from the variable, whereas a difference stationary variable can be rendered stationary only

Figure 5.1(a)
Hypothetical GDP and Tax Bases in Levels

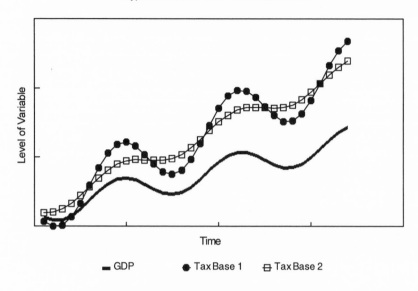

Figure 5.1(b)
Regression Plot of GDP and Tax Bases in Levels

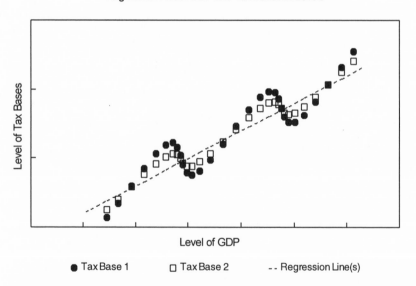

Note that the same regression line fits both tax bases. This common regression line has a slope of 2.0 which are the long-run relationships. The short-run relationships (which are the vertical distances between the regression line and the observations) are not reflected in the estimated slope coefficient (the elasticity estimates).

by taking the first difference of, or change in, the variable. The "random walk" that is familiar to economists is an example of a nonstationary variable that is difference stationary. Within the present context, the change form is simply the annual growth rate of the variable. Which of these types of nonstationary, if any, is present here is of great importance not only because it will have to be used to determine which transformation needs to be done to estimate the short-run elasticity of the tax, but also because several previous authors attempted to measure cyclical variability by regressing the log level of the tax on a trend line and then computing the deviation of the regression residuals. If, in fact, the variables are difference stationary rather than trend stationary, then this alternative regression will also have econometric problems because it is misspecified.[15]

The results in Part B of Table 5.1 show the tests of whether the variables are stationary after adjusting for a constant trend. All of the t-statistics suggest that the variables are still nonstationary, implying that the trend does not remove the nonstationarity. The results in Part C of the table test whether the variables are stationary in their change, or first difference form, denoted by a delta (Δ) before the variable. All of the t-statistics are now significant, suggesting that all of the variables are stationary in their change form. Thus, the correct version of the regression to obtain the short run income elasticity is given by

$$\Delta \ln(B_t) = \alpha + \beta \Delta \ln(Y_t) + \varepsilon. \tag{5.2}$$

To gain a better understanding of what is being estimated by equation (5.2), consider the data given in Figure 5.2(a). The tax bases in Figure 5.2(a) are the same data from Figure 5.1(a), but in their change (or difference) form. In Figure 5.2(a) it becomes easier to see that tax base 1 has more pronounced ups and downs over the business cycle than does GDP, but that tax base 2 has a smoother cycle than GDP. Figure 5.2(b) shows the regression plot, and the slope of the dashed lines are the coefficients that would be estimated by equation (5.2). Because both variables in the regression are stationary, the coefficient estimates from the regression are not subject to any bias or inconsistency.

The estimates for the data in Figure 5.2(b) are 1.5 for tax base 1 and 0.5 for tax base 2. These short-run income elasticities are the percentage change in the tax base associated with a 1 percent change in national income. They measure how pronounced the cyclical ups and downs in the tax base are with respect to GDP. Just like the estimates from equation (5.1) measure the long-run relationship (and are insensitive to the short-run relationship), these estimates measure the short-run relationship (and are insensitive to the long-run relationship). Thus, to identify both the long-run growth potential and short-run cyclical variability of a tax base it is necessary to estimate both equations. This is done in the next section of this chapter.

The second problem that the nonstationarity creates with the estimation of equation (5.1) is that the coefficient estimate obtained from the regression (which is the long-run elasticity) will be asymptotically biased and its standard error will be inconsistently estimated. To better understand why this problem exists, return to the data in Figure 5.1(b), which showed the regression plot for a hypothetical

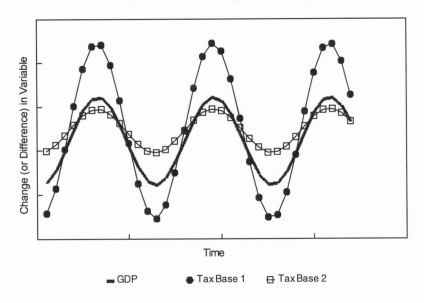

Figure 5.2(a)
GDP and Tax Bases in Change (or Difference) Form

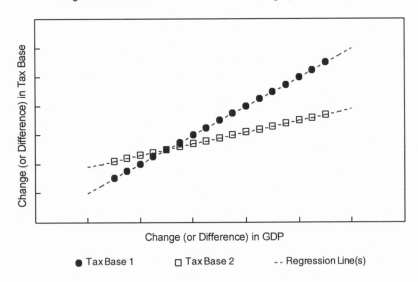

Figure 5.2(b)
Regression Plot of GDP and Tax Bases in Change (or Difference) Form

Note that the slope of the regression line that fits tax base 1 now differs from the slope of the regression line that fits tax base 2. The estimated slope coefficients (the income elasticity estimates) are 1.5 for tax base 1 and 0.5 for tax base 2. These reflect the short-run relationship between the tax bases and GDP. The long-run relationships are not, however, picked up in this regression.

example of the relationship between taxes and income over the long run. For tax base 1, the vertical distance between the data points (the black circles) and the regression line (the dashed line) is the error term in the regression. The error term is clearly correlated through time. This serial correlation in the error term results in the coefficient estimate being biased (the direction of the bias depending on whether there are more upward or downward dips) and also results in an inconsistent estimation of the standard error of the coefficient. This inconsistent standard error could result in faulty conclusions, for example, regarding the difference between the income elasticity of the sales and income taxes. There are two econometric techniques that can be used to correct for these problems. Stock and Watson show that adding leads and lags of the change in the independent variable to the regression will correct for the coefficient bias.[16] This procedure is called dynamic ordinary least squares (DOLS) and is typically performed using five leads and lags.[17] Although DOLS eliminates the coefficient bias, the inconsistency of the standard error must be corrected by using a second procedure, the Newey-West correction.[18] This technique corrects for serial correlation of the standard error by modeling it as a moving average process. The combined use of DOLS and Newey-West can produce better estimates of the long-run elasticity (and its standard error) than have been obtained in the past from the standard levels regression.[19]

Before proceeding to estimate the long and short run income elasticities of the tax bases, it is important to discuss one last potential problem in the estimate of the short-run elasticity from equation (5.2). Two nonstationary variables that have a long-run relationship with one another will tend to move back together whenever they get too far apart. Thus, one may observe one variable moving down in the same period another is moving up simply because the variables deviated from the levels implied by their long-run relationship. This error correction, as it is often called, can cause a bias in the estimate of the short-run elasticity. Engle and Granger show that this bias can be removed by the inclusion of another variable in equation (5.2) that shows how far apart the two variables were from their long-run relationship during the prior time period.[20] This is often called the error correction term and it is simply the estimated error from equation (5.1) in the prior time period. Including the estimated error (lagged once) from the estimation of equation (5.1) as an independent variable in equation (5.2) adjusts for this bias. This revised form of equation (5.2) is called the error correction model.[21]

The next section of this chapter uses all four models just discussed to obtain estimates of both the short and long run elasticities of the tax bases discussed earlier. Both regular OLS and then DOLS will be used to obtain estimates of the long-run income elasticity of the tax bases from equation (5.1) and the regular change and error correction models will be used to obtain estimates of the short-run income elasticity of the tax bases from equation (5.2).

ESTIMATES OF TAX BASE ELASTICITY

In equation (5.1), where the log of income is regressed against the log of a tax base, the β coefficient shows how rapidly a tax base grows when compared to income in the long run. A β greater than 1 indicates that the tax base grows faster than income, whereas a β less than 1 indicates a tax base that grows slower than income. Equation (5.2) uses the change in the logs of the variables rather than the variables themselves, thus the coefficient β in equation (5.2) directly measures the cyclical component of tax base variability because it shows the percentage change in the tax base that occurs as a result of a 1 percent change in income. A β greater than 1 indicates that the tax base fluctuates more than income over the business cycle, whereas a β less than 1 indicates a tax base that fluctuates less than income over the business cycle. Although unusual, a negative β would indicate that the tax base moves counter to the business cycle, rising during recessions and falling during booms. The specification in equation (5.2) also has the advantage that the variables are stationary, as was shown in the previous section, so it is not subject to the problems associated with the standard levels regression. The greater advantage to using the specification in equation (5.2) rather than in equation (5.1), however, is that equation (5.2) measures the *short-run* relationship between income and the tax base, which is of importance when talking about how a tax fluctuates over the business cycle.

Table 5.2 gives the elasticity estimates from both long-run models of equation (5.1) and short-run models of equation (5.2). The levels OLS estimates in the first column are asymptotically biased, and the next column corrects for any bias by using DOLS with the Newey-West correction. A comparison of those first two columns shows that there are only slight differences between the corrected and uncorrected estimates, indicating that these more sophisticated time series techniques have a relatively small effect on the results with this data. This is an important finding because it implies that the estimates found in previous works are not severely biased and are still of value as measures of long-run growth potential. The third column estimates the change form of the model, as represented in equation (5.2), and the fourth column shows the estimate from this model when an error correction term is added to this change form. There are only small differences in the coefficients when comparing the regular change model to the error correction model. Thus, again the policy implications of the regressions are affected relatively little when using the more sophisticated times series procedure with this data. Again this is important because it suggests that studies estimating short-run income elasticities may use the simpler regular change form of equation (5.2) to obtain rough estimates of the actual income elasticities. The big difference is between the first and second columns, which are the levels regressions typically used to estimate tax base variability, and the third and fourth columns, which report the change specifications of the model.

Table 5.2
Tax Base Elasticity Estimates

| Variable | Estimates of Long-Run Elasticity | | | | Estimates of Short-Run Elasticity | | | |
| | Levels = OLS | | Levels - DOLS with Newey-West correction | | Regular Change Model | | Error Correction Model | |
	β	R_2	β	R_2	β	R_2	β	R_2
Personal taxable income (PINC)	1.235 (0.018)	0.992	1.215 (0.014)	0.997	1.195 (0.171)	0.569	1.164 (0.161)	0.629
Adjusted gross income (AGI)	0.977 (0.009)	0.997	0.945 (0.007)	0.998	1.015 (0.098)	0.740	0.970 (0.100)	0.757
Corporate Taxable income (CINC)	0.691 (0.009)	0.586	0.670 (0.094)	0.635	3.562 (0.655)	0.523	3.369 (0.685)	0.539
Retail Sales (SALES)	0.691 (0.008)	0.995	0.660 (0.008)	0.997	1.084 (0.096)	0.772	1.039 (0.094)	0.796
Nonfood retail sales (NFSALES)	0.732 (0.012)	0.990	0.701 (0.015)	0.994	1.431 (0.114)	0.804	1.377 (0.108)	0.836
Motor fuel usage (FUEL)	1.098 (0.036)	0.960	0.996 (0.044)	0.969	0.731 (0.182)	0.303	0.729 (0.175)	0.373
Liquor store sales (LIQUOR)	0.259 (0.051)	0.399	0.254 (0.043)	0.752	-0.024 (0.216)	0.001	-0.011 (0.219)	0.008

Note: Standard errors of elasticity estimates are given in parentheses.

THE DIFFERENCE BETWEEN SHORT-RUN
AND LONG-RUN ELASTICITY

From Table 5.2, looking at the first two columns, the standard elasticity estimates for corporate taxable income and retail sales are practically identical. Following the line of reasoning begun by Groves and Kahn regarding tax base elasticity, this would imply that these two taxes have both the same long-run growth potential and also the same short-run cyclical variability. The third and fourth columns of Table 5.2 show that this conclusion would be partially incorrect. Although it is true that the similarity of the long-run elasticities would lead to the conclusion that the two taxes have similar long-run growth potentials, it is incorrect to extrapolate this to conclusions about short-run variability. The estimates of the short-run elasticity from Table 5.2 show that corporate taxable income is much more variable over the business cycle than is retail sales. This was the problem with the estimates from equation (5.1) explained earlier with Figures 5.1 and 5.2. To provide a better applied understanding of the different things being measured by the standard elasticity and the elasticity measured in first-difference form, a graph of the log change in GDP, retail sales, and corporate income is given in Figure 5.3.

Figure 5.3

Log Change in GDP, Retail Sales, and Corporate Taxable Income

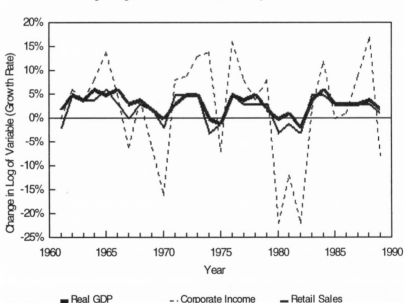

From Figure 5.3 it is easier to see what the different elasticity estimates are measuring in this applied context. Because both corporate taxable income and retail sales have approximately the same long-run growth rate relative to the growth rate

of GDP (as would be shown by a horizontal line in the figure corresponding to each tax's mean growth), they both are estimated to have the same long-run elasticity from the levels regression. But over the business cycle, corporate taxable income varies significantly more than retail sales. This difference in short-run volatility is captured in the estimates from the change specifications in the form of equation (5.2), but is not reflected in the estimates from the levels specifications like equation (5.1). These results show that a tax with a higher elasticity estimated from a levels regression need not fluctuate more over the business cycle. Whereas the long-run elasticity estimate from a levels regression is invariant to the cyclical variability of a tax base, the short-run elasticity is invariant to differences in long-run growth. Not only is this true in principle, the results in Table 5.2 show that in fact there is little relationship between the long-run income elasticity of a tax base and the short-run elasticity.

The long-run elasticity shows how a tax base will tend to grow over time as income grows, whereas the short-run elasticity shows how a tax base will fluctuate over a business cycle as income fluctuates. Based on the error correction model estimates of the short-run elasticities, the most cyclically variable of the tax bases is corporate income, followed by nonfood retail sales, personal taxable income, retail sales, adjusted gross income, motor fuels, and liquor sales. It is worth noting, however, that the estimates for personal income, retail sales, adjusted gross income, and motor fuels are not statistically different from 1. The elasticities of both corporate income and nonfood retail sales are significantly greater than 1, implying that they fluctuate more than income over the business cycle. Although the estimated short-run elasticity of taxable personal income is larger than that of total retail sales, and retail sales is higher than adjusted gross income, the differences are not statistically significant. The difference between the estimated short-run elasticities of the sales tax base with and without food is, however, significant, implying that the food exemption does significantly increase the cyclical variability of a state's retail sales tax. The least cyclic of the tax bases is liquor, which has a negative estimated coefficient (which would imply that it moves countercyclically) but it is not significantly different from zero. The R^2 from this regression is so low that one can conclude that liquor sales are almost unaffected by the business cycle.

The large differences between the estimated short-run and long-run elasticities also have implications for the trade-off between the growth and variability of tax bases. Contrary to the implication of the Groves and Kahn model, these estimates show that it is possible for a state to reduce revenue variability without sacrificing long-run growth. For example, both the personal income tax and motor fuels tax have a higher long-run growth rate and also have a lower cyclical variability than the corporate income tax. Additionally, while the personal income tax has about the same cyclical variability as the retail sales tax, it has a significantly higher long-run growth rate. While several other comparisons could be made with these estimates, it is evident that the tradeoff between growth and variability is not automatic, as has been assumed in the past.

ALTERNATIVE MEASURES OF REVENUE VARIABILITY

Several authors have used a different method to calculate cyclical (or short-run) variability.[22] Their measure is based on the residual variance from a levels regression including only a constant and a time trend. This specification would be correct if tax revenues were trend stationary, but as the results in Part B of Table 5.1 show, they are not. Even if tax revenues were trend stationary, however, this variance measure would still not capture cyclical variability because the deviations from the trend include fluctuations not related to changes in income. Two tax bases that have the same expected downturn during a recession, but one having more year-to-year variance, would be estimated to have different variances. Additionally, a tax that does not respond very much to the business cycle (such as the liquor tax) but has non-cycle-related variation may receive a variance calculation similar to a tax that does respond to the business cycle. The change specification represented in equation (5.2) precisely measures the business-cycle-related variance, as opposed to the simple deviation around the trend. For policy purposes, cycle-related variability is more important because states tend to run into fiscal problems because of recession-related reductions in revenue growth rather than simply because revenues tend to fluctuate around the long-run trend.

Table 5.3 compares these three different ways of measuring the variability of tax bases. Following the procedure of these other authors, the standard deviation of the tax around the trend line in the levels regression was computed for each of the tax bases. The results of this calculation are presented in Table 5.3 along with the corresponding DOLS estimates of the long-run income elasticity and the error correction model estimates of the short-run income elasticity. The associated standard errors of the elasticity estimates are also given in parenthesis.

Table 5.3 shows that the variance measure does a poor job of isolating the revenue variability due to the business cycle. Although it finds that the corporate income tax is the most variable, it also finds that the motor fuels tax and the sin tax have high variability. However, according to the estimates from the error correction model, the motor fuels tax and the sin tax are the least responsive to the business cycle. Clearly, these two taxes have a significant amount of non-cycle-related variance that is being picked up by this variance measure. State policy makers trying to design tax structures that will be less sensitive to business cycle downturns would be severely misguided by these variance estimates.

State policy makers might be interested in both a measure of the cyclical variability a tax and a separate measure of the random variance of the tax. Fortunately, both of these measures can be obtained from a single model. The short-run elasticity estimates serve as the first measure, and the standard errors of the short-run coefficient estimates serve as the second measure. More precisely, the magnitude of the coefficient indicates how much, on average, a tax base will be affected by a change in income, whereas the standard error of the short-run elasticity coefficient estimate shows the predictability of this relationship; that is, how closely the tax follows the business cycle. For example, because the short-run

Table 5.3
Comparison of Measures of Revenue Variability

Variable	Dynamic OLS Estimate of Long-Run Elasticity	Error Correction Model Estimate of Short-Run Elasticity	Standard Deviation of Residuals from Trend Regression
Personal taxable income (PINC)	1.215 (0.014)	1.164 (0.161)	7.024
Adjusted gross income (AGI)	0.945 (0.007)	0.970 (0.100)	4.241
Corporate taxable income (CINC)	0.670 (0.094)	3.369 (0.685)	16.178
Retail sales (SALES)	0.660 (0.008)	1.039 (0.094)	3.514
Nonfood retail sales (NFSALES)	0.701 (0.015)	1.377 (0.108)	4.420
Motor fuel usage (FUEL)	0.996 (0.044)	0.729 (0.175)	10.220
Liquor store sales (LIQUOR)	0.254 (0.043)	-0.011 (0.218)	11.794

elasticity estimates for the personal income tax and the retail sales tax are fairly similar, but the standard error of the elasticity estimate for the personal income tax is higher, these two taxes have similar cyclical variability, but the personal income tax is subject to more non-cycle-related variance than the sales tax. Thus, from a practitioner's standpoint, both the short-run elasticity estimate and its standard error provide useful information. Together they serve as a decomposition of the cycle related and non-cycle-related variability of the tax and are both important to consider in state tax policy decisions.

STABILITY OF THE ELASTICITY ESTIMATES

If these estimates are to be a useful basis for state policy decisions, they must remain fairly stable through time. If, for example, the short-run elasticity of a tax changes frequently, it would make it more difficult to use current estimates to design future tax policy. This section explores the structural stability of both the long-run and short-run elasticities over the past four decades to see whether the elasticity of these taxes changed at some midpoint during the sample period.

If there were some reason to expect that a change occurred in a particular year, a standard F-test could be performed to see if there is a statistically significant difference between the coefficient in the years before and after the break. When the break point is unknown, however, and a search is performed over the entire sample to see which break point yields the highest value of the F-statistic, standard critical values become inappropriate. To correct for this, Andrews calculated the distribution of the highest value of the F-statistic when the test is performed for many alternative points in the sample period.[23] His test, called the sup-Wald test, is performed by finding the highest value of the F-statistic over the sample, and then comparing it to the critical values given in his article. This section uses this test to see if there was a change in income elasticities for these tax bases during the sample.

The F-statistic for a change in the DOLS estimates of the long-run elasticity and the F-statistic for a change in the error correction model estimate of the short-run elasticity were obtained for each year in the sample for each of the tax bases.[24] The largest F-statistic value over these years, along with the estimated change in the elasticity estimate at the implied break-point, are given in Table 5.4. The row labeled F-statistic gives the highest F-statistic over the entire sample period, and the row labeled year gives the year in which the highest value occurred. The final rows give the estimated change in the elasticity estimate. The estimates show a permanent change in the long-run elasticity for every tax base during the sample period. Although these changes are all statistically significant, they are quantitatively insignificant. The largest of the changes in the long-run elasticity occurs for corporate taxable income in 1974, but it is estimated that the elasticity rose by only 0.027 (recall that the original estimate was 3.369). The estimates indicate that the long-run growth potential of every tax base except corporate taxable income fell somewhat during the past few decades, although the decline was very small.

To explore whether there were changes in the short-run elasticities, this procedure was repeated for the error correction model. In this specification, the long-run elasticity was allowed to vary based on the findings just reported, and the results are shown in bottom half of Table 5.4.[25] The estimated changes in the short-run elasticities are of greater magnitude than the changes in the long-run elasticities, but four of the seven are statistically insignificant. For the three major state tax bases—personal taxable income (or adjusted gross income), corporate taxable income, and retail sales—only the retail sales tax base shows a statistically significant change in terms of its short-run variability over the past few decades. This suggests that the variability of taxes stays relatively stable through time, so these estimates can be helpful in the design of tax policy. Even for the two tax bases where there was a change, retail sales and liquor store sales, the changes occurred more than twenty years ago.

Table 5.4
Tests for the Stability of the Estimated Income Elasticities

	Personal Taxalbe Income	Adjusted Gross Income	Corporate Taxable Income	Retail Sales	Nonfood Retail Sales	Motor Fuel Usage	Liquor Store Sales
	Long-Run Elasticity from DOLS Model						
F-statistic	32.71**	63.10**	8.19*	10.94*	29.15**	113.01**	84.46**
Year	1975	1975	1974	1977	1977	1981	1981
Change in Long-run Elasticity	-0.007	-0.004	0.027	-0.002	-0.005	-0.024	-0.022
	Short-Run Elasticity from Error Correction Model						
F-statistic	3.78	5.26	1.79	12.45**	14.80**	7.40	18.50**
Year	1970/1	1967	1970/1	1969	1970/1	1979	1972
Change in short-run elasticity	-0.351	0.342	1.020	0.379	0.453	-0.672	-0.968

Notes: * indicates significance at a 5% level, and ** at a 1% level. Critical values for the F-statistic using the sup-Wald test are 11.48 (1%) and 7.93 (5%)

In an attempt to provide the estimates most relevant for current policy decisions, Table 5.5 shows the estimates of the current short-run elasticities of all of the major state tax bases, taking into account the changes just reported. There are two noticeable changes in the conclusions reached earlier. First, nonfood retail sales is now significantly more variable than either adjusted gross income or personal taxable income. This would suggest that the state personal income tax is more stable over the business cycle than the retail sales tax when food is exempted.[26] The issue is considered further in Chapter 7. There is, however, no significant difference between the variability of the personal income tax and the retail sales tax when food is included. Second, the short-run elasticity for liquor store sales is now significantly negative. This would imply that it moves countercyclically, with liquor purchases rising during recessions, and falling during booms.

Table 5.5
Estimates of the Current Short-Run Elasticities of the Tax Bases

Tax Base	Sample	Short-Run Elasticity
Personal Taxable Income (PINC)	All	1.164 (0.161)
Adjusted Gross Income (AGI)	All	0.970 (0.100)
Corporate Taxable Income (CINC)	All	3.369 (0.685)
Retail Sales	1969 +	1.229 (0.098)
Nonfood Retail Sales (NFSALES)	1970/1 +	1.612 (0.111)
Motor Fuel Usage (FUEL)	All	0.729 (0.175)
Liquor Store Sales (LIQUOR)	1972 +	−0.586 (0.225)

Note: Standard errors of elasticity estimates are given in parentheses.

Taken as a whole, these results suggest that the short-run elasticity of all major state tax bases remains fairly constant through time. Although it appears that the short-run elasticity of the retail sales and sin taxes changed around 1970, there have been no significant changes in any of the tax bases since 1970. This is important with respect to state fiscal policy because it suggests that current estimates can be used as an accurate guide for designing future tax policy aimed at reducing cyclical revenue variability.

CONCLUSIONS ABOUT TAX ELASTICITY ESTIMATION

The income elasticity of tax bases is important in the long run as an indicator of tax revenue growth, and in the short run as a measure of the cyclical variability of tax revenues. Previous studies of the income elasticity of taxes have used several different methodologies to estimate the income elasticities of tax bases, but these methodologies were not always adequate for finding consistent and unbiased estimates. In addition, the important distinction between the long-run income elasticity of a tax base, which indicates how revenues from that base will grow over time as income grows, and the short-run elasticity of a tax base, which indicates how much revenues from that base will fluctuate over the business cycle, has not always been clearly made. For example, corporate taxable income and retail sales have approximately the same long-run income elasticity, but corporate income has a much greater short-run elasticity. Thus, the two tax bases show approximately the same rate of growth as income grows over the long run, even though corporate income taxes will fluctuate much more in response to short-run fluctuations in income. As another example, some studies have concluded that taxes on alcoholic beverages are unstable over the business cycle, but when the model is correctly specified, fluctuations in the alcoholic beverage tax base are, if anything, counter to the business cycle and actually have a stabilizing impact on state revenues.

From a policy perspective, it is important not only to generate consistent and unbiased estimates, but also to have some confidence that those estimates will be stable over time. An examination of the tax base data since the early 1950s suggests that the estimates of income elasticity of the tax bases are relatively stable, and so can be useful guides for designing future tax policy. Because this chapter uses aggregate data for the United States, it is useful for seeing overall state trends. For state policy purposes, a similar type of analysis needs to be done for each individual state. The methodological issues discussed here could be even more significant at the state level, where changes in economic and population trends could have more substantial effects on the time series properties of the data. The following chapters use the techniques developed in this chapter to perform this state-level analysis.

NOTES

1. John L. Mikesell, "Election Periods and State Tax Policy Cycles," *Public Choice* 33, no. 3 (1978): 99–106, finds empirical evidence that state taxes vary systematically over the election cycle, creating a political business cycle at the state level. The present study considers variability of the business cycle as opposed to the election cycle.

2. Steven D. Gold, "Changes in State Government Finances in the 1980s," *National Tax Journal* 44, no. 1 (March 1991): 1–19, notes that state government spending increased faster than revenues in the 1980s, largely due to increases in spending on Medicaid and corrections. A steady increase in revenues allowed these spending increases to continue, and Richard H. Mattoon and William A. Testa, "State and Local Governments' Reaction to

Recession," *Economic Perspectives* 16, no. 2 (March/April 1992): 19–27, (Federal Reserve Bank of Chicago), argue that faced with revenue shortfalls, states will have to begin implementing spending cuts in addition to looking for sources of increased revenues. Charles R. Hulten, "Productivity Changes in State and Local Governments," *Review of Economics and Statistics* 66, no. 2 (May 1984): 256–66, notes that productivity growth of state and local governments from 1959–79 was negative. If this trend has continued, there may be a good argument for reductions in state and local government expenditures. Roy Bahl and David L. Sjoquist, "The State and Local Fiscal Outlook: What Have We Learned and Where are We Headed?" *Natioinal Tax Journal* 43, no. 3 (September 1990): 321–42, note that as a percent of income, state and local government spending did not increase as fast in the 1980s as in prior decades, and debate whether this slowdown will continue into the 1990s.

3.   Fred C. White, "Trade-Off in Growth and Stability in State Taxes," *National Tax Journal* 36, no. 1 (March 1983): 103–14, suggests that states have brought some revenue variability upon themselves by relying more heavily on unstable tax bases. James A. Papke, "The Response of State-Local Government Taxation to Fiscal Crisis," *National Tax Journal* 36, no. 3 (September 1983): 401–05, notes the same phenomenon after the 1982 recession. Large state tax increases were implemented at that time to offset revenue declines caused by the recession. Also see Steven D. Gold, "State Tax Increases of 1983: Prelude to Another Tax Revolt?" *National Tax Journal* 37, no. 1 (March 1984): 9–22, for a discussion of the same phenomenon.

4.   Harold M. Groves and C. Harry Kahn, "The Stability of State and Local Tax Yields," *American Economic Review* 42, no. 2 (March 1952): 87–102.

5.   This is mentioned not only in the papers that estimate the elasticities but also in papers about state fiscal crises. See, for example, Gold, "Changes in State Government Finances in the 1980s" and Mattoon and Testa, "State and Local Governments' Reaction to Recession."

6.   See, for example, Groves and Kahn, "The Stability of State and Local tax Yields," W. T. Wilford, "State Tax Stability Criteria and the Revenue-Income Coefficient Reconsidered," *National Tax Journal* 18, no. 3 (September 1965): 304–12, William Vickrey, "Some Limits to the Income Elasticity of Income Tax Yields," *Review of Economics and Statistics* 31, no. 2 (May 1949): 140–44, John B. Legler and Perry Shapiro, "The Responsiveness of State Tax Revenue to Economic Growth," *National Tax Journal* 21, no. 1 (March 1968): 46–56, Ann F. Friedlaender, Gerald J. Swanson, and John F. Due, "Estimating Sales Tax Revenue Changes in Response to Changes in Personal Income and Sales Tax Rates," *National Tax Journal* 26, no. 1 (March 1973): 103–13, William F. Fox and Charles Campbell, "Stability of the State Sales Tax Income Elasticity," *National Tax Journal* 37, no. 2 (June 1984): 201–12, William V. Williams, Robert M. Anderson, David O. Froehle, and Kaye L. Lamb, "The Stability, Growth, and Stabilizing influence of State Taxes," *National Tax Journal* 26, no. 2 (June 1973): 276–74, and John L. Mikesell, "Income Elasticities of State Sale Tax Base Components," *Quarterly Review of Economics and Business* 17, no. 1 (Spring 1977): 83–94.

7.   For a good overview of the literature on nonstationary time series estimation see Masao Ogaki, "Unit Roots in Macroeconomics: A Survey," *Bank of Japan Monetary and Economic Studies* 11, no. 2 (November 1993): 131–54, James D. Hamilton, *Time Series Analysis* (Princeton, N.J.: Princeton University Press, 1994), or Terence C. Mills, *Time Series Techniques for Economists* (Cambridge: Cambridge University Press, 1990). For more technical details see also C. W. J. Granger and P. Newbold, "Spurious Regressions in Econometrics," *Journal of Econometrics* 2 (1974): 111–20, Peter C. B. Phillips, "Understanding Spurious Regressions in Econometrics," *Journal of Econometrics* 33

(December 1986): 311–40, James H. Stock, "Asymptotic Properties of Least Squares Estimators of Cointegrating Vectors," *Econometrica* 55 (1987): 1035–56, Charles R. Nelson and Charles I. Plosser, "Trends and Random Walks in Macroeconomic Time Series: Some Evidence and Implications," *Journal of Monetary Economics* 10, no. 2 (September 1982): 139–62, Soren Johansen, "Statistical Analysis of Cointegrating Vectors," *Journal of Economic Dynamics and Control* 12, no. 2/3 (June/September 1988): 231–54, and Soren Johansen, "Estimation and Hypothesis Testing of Cointegration Vectors in Gaussian Vector Autoregressive Models," *Econometrica* 59, no. 6 (November 1991): 1551–80.

8.   Williams, Anderson, Froehle, and Lamb, "The Stability, Growth, and Stabilizing Influence of State Taxes," did recognize this problem within the context of elasticity estimation, and attempted to correctly estimated both a short-run and long-run elasticity. Their contribution has largely been ignored in the literature, however, as the more recent studies have used only the long-run measure provided by the levels regression. Fox and Campbell, "Stability of the State Sales Tax Income Elasticity," also attempted to allow for differing elasticities over different phases of the business cycle, but their approach still suffers from not being able to capture the short-run dynamics needed to infer about revenue variability over the business cycle because of the use of levels.

9.   Groves and Kahn, "The Stability of State and Local Tax Yields," find R^2s greater than 0.80 in twenty-one of their twenty-four regressions; Wilford, "State Tax Stability Criteria and the Revenue-Income Coefficient Reconsidered," finds R^2s greater than 0.97 in fifteen of twenty regressions (with nine being larger than 0.99); John B. Legler and Perry Shapiro, "The Responsiveness of State Tax Revenue to Economic Growth," *National Tax Journal* 21, no. 1 (March 1968): 46–56, find R^2s greater than 0.97 in all eight of their regressions (with five being larger than 0.99); Friedlaender, Swanson, and Due, "Estimating Sales Tax Revenue Changes in Response to Changes in Personal Income and Sales Tax Rates," find R^2s above 0.99 in twenty-three of their twenty-four regressions (with the other being 0.97); and Fox and Campbell, "Stability of the State Sales Tax Income Elasticity," find R^2s greater than 0.97 in seven of their ten regressions (the lowest of the ten was 0.82).

10.   Tax revenues can be used in place of the tax base as the dependent variable if another independent variable is included to measure changes in the tax rate. Also per capita income and population are sometimes substituted for aggregate income in this equation. For ease of exposition, aggregate income is used here, but the results also apply to the alternative specification.

11.   If one did not have explicit data on tax bases and had to use revenues as the dependent variable instead, Joon Y. Park, "Canonical Cointegrating Regressions," *Econometrica* 60, no. 1 (January 1992): 119–43, has shown that asymptotically, the estimate of β will be correct if an independent variable denoting the change in the tax rate is included in the regression (and it is stationary) and the variables B_t and Y_t are transformed in a manner consistent with canonical cointegrating regressions (CCR).

12.   Of the forty-six states that currently have a general sales tax, twenty-six exempt food purchases.

13.   See David A. Dickey and Wayne A. Fuller, "Distribution of the Estimators for Autoregressive Time Series with a Unit Root," *Journal of the American Statistical Association* 74, no. 366 (June 1979): 427–31, Said E. Said and David A. Dickey, "Testing for Unit Roots in Autoregressive-Moving Average Models of Unknown Order," *Biometrica* 71 (1984): 599–607, and Wayne A. Fuller, *Introduction to Statistical Time Series* (New York: John Wiley & Sons, 1976).

14.   The ADF critical values used for this paper are calculated using the tables and sample size adjustment formula from James G. MacKinnon, "Critical Values for

Cointegration Tests," in *Long-Run Economics Relationships: Readings in Cointegration*, R. F. Engle and C. W. J. Granger, eds., (Oxford: Oxford University Press, 1990), 267–77.

15.   For examples of this methodology see Fred C. White, "Trade-Off in Growth and Stability in State Taxes," *National Tax Journal* 36, no. 1 (March 1983): 103–14 and Richard F. Dye and Therese J. McGuire, "Growth and Variability of State Individual Income and Sales Taxes," *National Tax Journal* 44, no. 1 (March 1991): 55–66. Their measure is discussed in more detail later in the chapter.

16.   James H. Stock and Mark W. Watson, "A Simple Estimator of Cointegrating Vectors in Higher Order Integrated Systems," *Econometrica* 61, no. 4 (July 1993): 783–820.

17.   See also Pentti Saikkonen, "Asymptotically Efficient Estimation of Cointegrating Regressions," *Econometric Theory* 7, no. 1 (March 1991): 1–21, and Peter C. B. Phillips and Mico Loretan, "Estimating Long-Run Economic Equilibria," *Reveiw of Economic Studies* 58, no. 3 (May 1991): 407–36.

18.   Whitney K. Newey and Kenneth D. West, "A Simple, Positive Semi-Definite, Heteroskedasticity and Autocorrelation Consistent Covariance Matrix," *Econometrica* 55, no. 3 (May 1987): 703–08.

19.   See Hamilton, *Time Series Analysis*, for a good discussion of these techniques.

20.   Robert F. Engle and Clive W. J. Granger, "Co-Integration and Error Correction: Representation, Estimation, and Testing," *Econometrica* 55, no. 2 (March 1987): 251–76.

21.   This is only a partial correction because there is not a similar term for Δy_t. Soren Johansen, "Cointegration in Partial Systems and the Efficiency of Single-Equation Analysis," *Journal of Econometrics* 52, no. 3 (June 1992): 389–402, notes that this is sufficient if Y_t is weakly exogenous, and a test based upon J. Geweke, R. Meese, and W. Dent, "Comparing Alternative Tests of Causality in Temporal Systems," *Journal of Econometrics* 21 (1982): 161–94, shows that the partial error correction model is adequate. The *F*-statistics for the test (and significance levels) were PINC 1.325 (0.31), CINC 1.844 (0.26), SALES 2.071 (0.13), NFSALES 1.875 (0.16), FUEL 1.266 (0.33), and LIQUOR 1.901 (0.16).

22.   See, for examples, White, "Trade-Off in Growth and Stability in State Taxes," and Dye and McGuire, "Growth and Variability of State Individual Income and General Sales Taxes."

23.   See Donald W. K. Andrews, "Tests for Parameter Instability and Structural Change with Unknown Change Point," *Econometrica* 61, no. 4 (July 1993): 821–56.

24.   This test can only be performed for midpoints in the sample because it is impossible to get accurate estimates of the elasticities using less than ten observations.

25.   Because of the small magnitude of the changes in the long-run elasticities, however, almost identical results are found when the error correction model is searched without allowing the long-run elasticity to change.

26.   This implication will hold if the sales tax taxes the entire retail sales tax base, but nothing more. Raymond J. Ring, Jr., "The Proportion of Consumers' and Producers' Goods in the General Sales Tax," *National Tax Journal* 42, no. 2 (June 1989): 167–79, notes that in the average state only 59 percent of the retail sales tax base is retail sales because nonretail transactions are a part of the sales tax base.

Chapter 6

The Cyclical Variability of State Government Revenues

The previous chapter identified a methodology for measuring cyclical variability of state government revenues, concentrating on that component of variability that is specifically associated with business cycles in the economy. This chapter uses that methodology to estimate how cyclical each state's revenues are relative to the national business cycle and relative to the state's own business cycle. Any elasticity estimate done using revenues, rather than tax bases, is subject to some problems, however. Revenues are influenced by state policy changes, and if these policy changes are correlated with the state's income cycle, the estimates will be influenced by the use of revenue instead of the tax base.

If a state tends to increase tax rates during recessions and lower them during economic booms, their revenue stream will appear more stable than it would if the estimates were performed using only the tax base. If state policy changes are completely uncorrelated with the business cycle, tending to be done in a random manner, the elasticity estimates will not be influenced, but the fit of the regression and the constant term will. It might be possible to correct a specific tax revenue stream for state policy changes by including a variable in the regression to reflect the tax rate. For a general sales tax this would be easy, but for a personal income tax with many rates and brackets, this would be more difficult. Including the tax rate, however, would only partially remove the policy factor, because changes in state tax bases and exemptions will also influence revenue.

The estimates done in this chapter use the state's total revenues, and because there is no single tax rate for all state revenues, there is no way to even partially correct the estimates. Because it is logical that state tax policies are influenced by the business cycle, it is possible to think of the estimates in this chapter as reduced-form estimates. Imagine a separate equation that specified state tax policy as the dependent variable, being determined by the economy. The tax policy variable in the revenue elasticity regression could be substituted out using the first equation, producing a final equation that depended only on the economy. This is what is being estimated in this chapter. The elasticity coefficients on the economic variable will measure both the direct impact that the economy has on the revenues and the impact that it has directly through causing a change in state tax policy.

Recognizing that what is estimated in this chapter does not represent the effects of tax base changes alone, there are still several reasons why it makes sense to look at changes in tax revenues over the business cycle rather than focusing on tax bases. First, the variability of revenues is what really matters to state government finance. Instability in revenues, rather than bases per se, aggravates fiscal crises. Second, the tax rates on some tax bases may be easier to change than on others, so some tax rates may be more responsive in times of fiscal stress. By looking at revenues, the changes in both bases and rates are taken into account. Third, tax rates influence tax bases, so a measure of tax bases independent of rates would be difficult to obtain. If income tax rates are raised, for example, taxable income will go down as a result. Even a good measure of taxable income (the tax base) will be a function of the rate at which the base is taxed, so tax rates and tax bases are inevitably linked. Later chapters do examine tax bases in addition to tax revenues, but this chapter focuses on revenue variability over the business cycle.

VARIABILITY OF TOTAL REVENUES OVER THE NATIONAL BUSINESS CYCLE

One measure of variability would be a measure of how cyclical a state's total revenues are when compared to national income, or GDP. Using the models discussed in the previous chapter, estimates of both the long- and short-run elasticities of each state's total general revenues were obtained using data from 1972–1993. The reason for beginning the sample in 1972 is the important changes in state revenue trends around the early 1970s that were found in previous chapters. Both GDP and the state revenue data were converted to per capita amounts to remove the impact that population trends have on revenue growth. The results of all four specifications for each state are given in Table 6.1.

The first column in Table 6.1 gives the OLS estimate of the long-run elasticity of state general revenues with respect to GDP. This is the (asymptotically biased) estimate from the levels regression in natural log form. The second column shows the (inconsistently estimated) standard error of this coefficient estimate, and the third column shows the rank of the long-run elasticity estimates across states. A rank of 1 corresponds to the highest estimated long-run revenue elasticity. The following three columns show the long-run elasticities obtained from Stock and Watson's dynamic OLS (DOLS) procedure along with the standard error of this estimate obtained by employing the Newey-West correction, and the ranking of the elasticity estimates from highest to lowest. For the DOLS estimation, two leads and lags of the change in the independent variable were used.[1]

Later in this chapter, a more detailed analysis of the differences between the estimates is done. Generally, the use of the DOLS procedure to remove the asymptotic bias produces a smaller long-run elasticity estimate than regular OLS. The differences are not quantitatively large, and the relative rankings do not change much. Using the DOLS estimates of the long-run elasticity it is possible to reach some conclusions about the long-run growth potential of state government general revenues. The states with the highest rankings are Connecticut and New Jersey, both having per capita real revenue growth more than three times the growth in per capita real GDP over the long run. Including Massachusetts, Ohio, New York, Indiana, Maine, Missouri, Wyoming, Delaware, and Iowa completes the list of states that have long-run revenue growth at more than twice the growth rate of GDP.

The states with the lowest long-run revenue growth potential are Nevada, Colorado, Mississippi, Oregon, and New Mexico. All of these states have long-run per capita real revenue growth that is less than the growth rate of real per capita GDP. Over the long run, Nevada's general revenues have been growing by only about one quarter of the growth in the national economy. The states whose long-run revenue growth is closest to that of the national economy are Texas and West Virginia. Both of these states will have long-run revenue growth corresponding to the growth in the national economy at nearly a one-to-one ratio.

Turning to the estimates of the short-run elasticities, the first sets of estimates are from the regular change model. This is the model estimated in first difference form without an error correction term. The final set of columns shows the short-run elasticity estimates from the error correction model, along with the *t*-statistic and significance level of the error correction term. Generally, the error correction model estimates are slightly higher than the estimates from the regular change model. Again, more specifics on the differences between the models are discussed later in this chapter.

From the error correction model estimates, the states with the highest cyclical variability in revenues are Michigan, Maine, Connecticut, New York, and New Hampshire. Michigan's revenues fluctuate at a rate more than 1.5 times the fluctuation in the national economy. From the estimates, there are seventeen states that can expect their total revenues to fall by more than 1 percent in response to a 1 percent decline in GDP. The states with the most stable revenues over the business cycle are North Dakota, New Mexico, Oklahoma, Louisiana, and Wyoming. All of these states can expect their revenues to fall by less than 0.4 times the fall in GDP during a recession. Interestingly, all of these states rely on natural resources for a substantial portion of their state income, and thus rely more heavily on severance taxes for revenue. Alaska has an estimate that is negative, suggesting that its revenues run countercyclically, rising during national economic slowdowns. Clearly, Alaska is an extreme outlier. The states whose revenue cycles most closely approximate the national business cycle are Arizona, North Carolina, and Georgia. Each of these states can expect about a 1 percent change in their state revenues in response to a 1 percent change in the national economy during an economic recession.

Table 6.1
Long-Run and Short-Run Elasticities of State Total General Revenue with Respect to GDP, 1972 to 1993

| | Estimates of Long-Run Elasticity | | | | | | Estimates of Short-Run Elasticity | | | | | | |
| | OLS | | | DOLS (with N/W, 2L & L) | | | Regular Change Model | | | Error Correction Model (using DOLS LR) | | | |
State	LR Elasticity	Std. Error	Rank	LR Elasticity	Std. Error	Rank	SR Elasticity	Std. Error	Rank	SR Elasticity	Std. Error	Rank	T-EC (**=1%, *=5%)
Alabama	1.554	0.149	24	1.496	0.140	24	1.110	0.337	9	1.171	0.318	12	-1.895
Alaska	2.028	1.315	10	1.851	1.488	14	-3.177	1.179	50	-2.902	1.192	50	-1.162
Arizona	1.349	0.162	38	1.183	0.248	39	0.990	0.293	15	0.996	0.287	18	-1.350
Arkansas	1.663	0.181	20	1.319	0.148	33	0.885	0.298	20	0.885	0.307	24	-0.035
California	1.394	0.099	33	1.218	0.131	37	0.761	0.291	27	0.890	0.253	23	-2.814*
Colorado	0.988	0.171	49	0.751	0.168	49	0.757	0.290	30	0.750	0.293	33	-0.775
Connecticut	3.061	0.278	2	3.563	0.259	1	1.281	0.347	2	1.407	0.391	3	-0.729
Delaware	1.944	0.146	15	2.086	0.128	10	0.710	0.241	35	0.814	0.304	30	-0.575
Florida	1.569	0.248	23	1.831	0.236	15	1.190	0.336	4	1.146	0.326	15	-1.514
Georgia	1.339	0.113	40	1.502	0.114	23	0.953	0.229	17	1.026	0.215	17	-2.032
Hawaii	1.409	0.238	32	1.437	0.331	27	0.730	0.306	33	0.734	0.304	34	-1.139
Idaho	1.374	0.233	36	1.306	0.278	35	0.615	0.312	38	0.620	0.318	39	-0.516
Illinois	1.084	0.123	47	1.181	0.127	40	0.593	0.250	39	0.656	0.228	37	-2.293*
Indiana	2.414	0.193	5	2.464	0.181	6	0.822	0.320	26	0.979	0.374	20	-0.832
Iowa	1.957	0.170	14	2.040	0.178	11	0.300	0.220	44	0.463	0.228	43	-1.776
Kansas	1.572	0.145	22	1.429	0.143	28	0.842	0.256	24	0.870	0.264	27	-0.624
Kentucky	1.652	0.175	21	1.481	0.293	25	0.758	0.289	28	0.796	0.283	31	-1.389
Louisiana	1.231	0.154	41	1.127	0.143	42	0.262	0.308	45	0.338	0.309	46	-1.276
Maine	2.135	0.165	7	2.344	0.100	7	1.048	0.384	12	1.419	0.414	2	-1.838
Maryland	1.468	0.084	28	1.392	0.070	30	1.103	0.155	10	1.149	0.108	14	-4.580**
Massachusetts	2.543	0.181	4	2.815	0.239	3	0.977	0.307	16	1.209	0.337	9	-1.478
Michigan	1.521	0.089	26	1.531	0.088	22	1.438	0.244	1	1.563	0.217	1	-2.681*
Minnesota	1.463	0.128	29	1.386	0.081	31	0.741	0.232	32	0.952	0.249	22	-1.803
Mississippi	1.031	0.155	48	0.789	0.189	48	0.837	0.230	25	0.882	0.241	26	0.728
Missouri	2.010	0.173	11	2.148	0.159	8	0.851	0.248	23	0.954	0.282	21	-0.799
Montana	1.536	0.167	25	1.373	0.166	32	0.533	0.310	40	0.607	0.319	41	-0.990
Nebraska	2.042	0.177	9	1.991	0.218	12	0.717	0.242	34	0.768	0.273	32	-0.443
Nevada	0.513	0.159	50	0.249	0.143	50	0.758	0.398	29	0.731	0.365	35	-2.125*
New Hampshire	2.004	0.286	12	1.573	0.136	21	1.265	0.561	3	1.337	0.588	5	-0.528
New Jersey	3.270	0.323	1	3.548	0.273	2	0.855	0.384	22	0.882	0.459	25	-0.114

New Mexico	1.142	0.267	46	0.934	0.204	46	0.086	0.339	48	0.158	0.339	48	-1.229
New York	2.127	0.190	8	2.482	0.108	5	1.157	0.376	7	1.373	0.460	4	-0.831
North Carolina	1.688	0.143	18	1.591	0.128	20	0.925	0.275	19	0.992	0.285	19	-0.931
North Dakota	1.366	0.268	37	1.155	0.205	41	-0.229	0.388	49	0.020	0.392	49	-1.797
Ohio	2.618	0.221	3	2.776	0.213	4	0.880	0.219	21	0.866	0.262	28	0.104
Oklahoma	1.171	0.162	44	1.216	0.176	38	0.186	0.298	47	0.318	0.287	47	-1.939
Oregon	1.376	0.173	34	0.910	0.150	47	0.680	0.248	36	0.635	0.234	38	-1.890
Pennsylvania	1.483	0.189	27	1.254	0.050	36	1.045	0.431	13	1.159	0.426	13	-1.440
Rhode Island	1.989	0.193	13	1.965	0.194	13	0.669	0.214	37	0.729	0.243	36	-0.563
South Carolina	1.765	0.125	17	1.743	0.156	17	1.115	0.204	8	1.172	0.192	11	-1.966
South Dakota	1.374	0.122	35	1.422	0.153	29	0.458	0.252	42	0.607	0.229	40	-2.542*
Tennessee	1.871	0.153	16	1.824	0.133	16	1.158	0.260	6	1.218	0.259	8	-1.352
Texas	1.225	0.174	43	0.992	0.166	45	0.414	0.348	43	0.410	0.341	44	-1.341
Utah	1.154	0.114	45	1.102	0.133	43	0.935	0.325	18	1.185	0.283	10	-3.068**
Vermont	1.348	0.167	39	1.663	0.130	19	0.749	0.199	31	0.831	0.215	29	-1.012
Virginia	1.666	0.078	19	1.696	0.085	18	1.014	0.152	14	1.118	0.123	16	-3.564**
Washington	1.446	0.111	31	1.449	0.184	26	1.068	0.304	11	1.286	0.281	7	-2.540*
West Virginia	1.229	0.176	42	1.000	0.226	44	0.516	0.299	41	0.524	0.308	42	-0.324
Wisconsin	1.449	0.092	30	1.312	0.089	34	1.161	0.209	5	1.323	0.168	6	-3.699**
Wyoming	2.230	0.510	6	2.131	0.446	9	0.229	0.587	46	0.367	0.637	45	-0.619

There are important differences between the elasticities estimated by the technique used in this book when compared to older methods. Most important is the distinction between short- and long-run elasticities. To help in understanding the difference, Figures 6.1 and 6.2 show the revenues of two states, Rhode Island and Utah. Figure 6.1 shows the long-run growth in real per capita general revenue, and Figure 6.2 shows the short-run fluctuations over the business cycle. Returning to the estimates in Table 6.1, Rhode Island and Utah have very different long-run elasticities. Rhode Island's long-run revenue elasticity is 1.965, much greater than Utah's 1.102 long-run elasticity. In Figure 6.1 this difference in long-run growth is evident. Utah's long-run revenue growth is almost identical to the long-run growth of GDP, as would be suggested by the long-run elasticity close to 1.0. Rhode Island's long-run revenue growth is greater than GDP, implying a long-run revenue elasticity greater than 1, and also greater than Utah's long-run revenue elasticity.

If one were to assume the widely accepted Groves and Kahn reasoning and methodology, the estimates in Table 6.1 would imply that Rhode Island's revenues would fluctuate much more over the business cycle than those of Utah. Figure 6.2 shows that this is not the case. In fact, Utah's revenues tended to fluctuate more than Rhode Island's over the past business cycles. During all three of the recessions in the figure, Utah's revenues fell by more than those of Rhode Island. Additionally, during the business cycle upswings, Utah's revenues peaked at rates of growth higher than those of Rhode Island. Looking at the short-run elasticity estimates from Table 6.1, Rhode Island has an estimate of 0.729, whereas Utah has 1.185. These estimates imply that Utah has greater revenue variability over the business cycle than Rhode Island, which is clearly correct given the data presented in Figure 6.2. As the short-run elasticity estimates suggest, Utah's revenues fluctuate over the business cycle at a greater magnitude than GDP (because the state's estimate is greater than 1.0), whereas Rhode Island's revenues tend to fluctuate less over the business cycle than GDP. These two figures make clear the distinction between long-run and short-run income elasticities. Whereas Rhode Island has a higher long-run elasticity, it has a lower short-run elasticity. Thus, over the longer run, Rhode Island can expect more revenue growth with the economy, but will suffer less from cyclical fluctuations than Utah.

In Figure 6.2 it is slightly noticeable that Rhode Island's revenues track the business cycle more closely than do those of Utah. The standard errors of the short-run elasticity estimates provide a measure of how closely the state's revenues track the national business cycle. The larger the standard error, the less predictable is the relationship between state revenues and GDP given by the elasticity estimate. The standard error of the coefficient estimate of Rhode Island's short-run elasticity, from Table 6.1, is 0.243, whereas Utah's is 0.283 Thus, the smaller standard error implies that Rhode Island's revenues track the national business cycle slightly more closely than those of Utah.

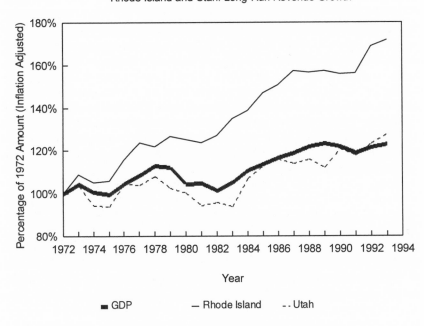

Figure 6.1
Rhode Island and Utah: Long-Run Revenue Growth

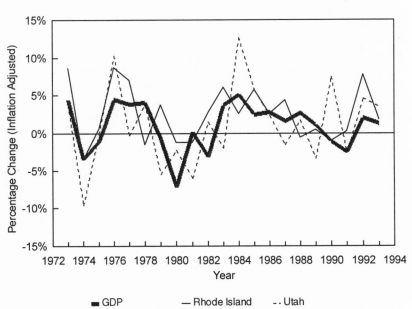

Figure 6.2
Rhode Island and Utah: Short-Run Revenue Variability

VARIABILITY OF TOTAL REVENUES OVER THE STATE BUSINESS CYCLE

An alternative way to measure variability is relative to the state's own business cycle, rather than the national business cycle. The estimates in Table 6.1 reflect both the sensitivity of the state tax structure to the economy and how the state's economy fluctuates with the national business cycle. It is possible that a state may have a very stable tax structure but have a very unstable state economy. This state may receive a higher short-run elasticity relative to GDP than a state with an unstable state tax structure but a stable state economy. The estimates done with respect to GDP provide a better picture of the relative susceptibility of each state to a fiscal crises during national recessions. Because each state's revenues are being compared to the same income base, it is easier to draw direct comparisons across states with the GDP based estimates of elasticity.

This section estimates the same elasticities with respect to the state's economy as measured by total state personal income.[2] This method will allow an estimate that is more specific to state tax structure, because it removes any effect of state business cycles differing from the national business cycle. These estimates are, however, less comparable across states when discussing susceptibility to recessionary fiscal crises. The estimates from these regressions are give in Table 6.2.

Many of the same states appear at the top and bottom of the rankings when the estimates are performed using state personal income rather than national income. The states with the highest long-run growth relative to state income are Iowa, Alaska, Ohio, and Indiana. All of these states have total revenue growth more than twice the rate of growth in state income. The states with the lowest long-run elasticities are Colorado, Louisiana, New Hampshire, and Maryland. All of these states have long-run rates of revenue growth of 0.75 percent or less in response to a 1 percent long-run growth rate in the state economy.

The states with the most short-run cyclical variability when compared to state income are Wisconsin, Washington, Utah, and New Jersey. These states can all expect at least a 1.7 percent change in total general revenues in response to a 1 percent change in the state economy. The states with the least short-run cyclical variability are Iowa, North Dakota, Louisiana, Wyoming, and Arizona. All of these states can expect a 0.30 or lower percent change in state revenues in response to a 1 percent change in the state economy. The states whose revenues most closely track the state business cycle, as measured by the standard error of the short-run elasticity estimate, are North Dakota, South Dakota, and Michigan.

There are some noticeable changes when comparing the estimates from Tables 6.1 and 6.2. Although most states received a higher short-run elasticity when compared to their state economy, they mostly received lower long-run elasticity. The largest changes in the short-run elasticities occurred for Alaska, Wisconsin, Kentucky, and Washington. All of these states received a higher short-run elasticity when compared to the state economy than when compared to the national economy. New Hampshire and Arizona were the two largest changes in the opposite direction, having lower estimated short-run elasticities when compared to state income. The largest changes in the long-run elasticities occurred for Connecticut, New Jersey,

Massachusetts, Maine, and New York. All of these states received lower estimates of long-run growth when compared to the state economy than when compared to the national economy. Iowa and Alaska had the two largest changes in the opposite direction, receiving a higher long-run elasticity when compared to state income.

VARIABILITY OF TAX REVENUES OVER THE BUSINESS CYCLE

Tables 6.1 and 6.2 show how state total general revenues change with the national and state economies. This perhaps paints a clearer picture of how much a state's total resources suffer during economic slowdowns. An alternative is to measure the variability of total tax revenue, rather than total general revenue. Tax revenue excludes federal grants, lottery proceeds, and other nontax forms of revenue. Estimates based on tax revenues alone further isolate the tax structure characteristics responsible for revenue growth and stability. The estimates in Tables 6.1 and 6.2 were repeated, substituting total tax revenue for total general revenue in the regressions. The results of these new models are given in Tables 6.3 and 6.4.

Table 6.3 summarizes the results of the elasticity estimates for per capita real state total tax revenue with respect to the national economy, per capita real GDP. The states with the highest long-run elasticity are New Jersey, Connecticut, Massachusetts, Maine, and Ohio. These same states were also in the fastest growing when their total general revenues were compared to GDP in Table 6.1. The states with the lowest long-run elasticities are Wyoming, Oregon, Colorado, Mississippi, and Pennsylvania. The very low DOLS estimate of the long-run elasticity for Wyoming is troubling, however. In Tables 6.1 and 6.2 Wyoming was estimated to have a rather high long-run elasticity. Additionally, the regular OLS estimate of the long-run elasticity in Table 6.3 is substantially different from the DOLS estimate. This points to one drawback of using the more sophisticated DOLS technique to estimate the long-run elasticities. Althouth it removes the asymptotic bias in the coefficient estimate, the technique is much more sensitive to data abnormalities. In addition, the DOLS technique includes both leads and lags, requiring that the sample be reduced. The elimination of the first and last few observations can have a major impact on the estimate if these observations are substantially different from the rest of the sample. The estimate for Wyoming is probably a case where the drawbacks of this technique outweighed the benefits, and thus the regular OLS estimate is more reliable. This ability to double check the results of the more sophisticated techniques is one reason why both the OLS and DOLS results are presented throughout this book in addition to both the regular change and error correction model results. The results from the DOLS model and

Table 6.2
Long-Run and Short-Run Elasticities of State Total General Revenue with Respect to State Personal Income, 1972 to 1993

| | Estimates of Long-Run Elasticity | | | | | | Estimates of Short-Run Elasticity | | | | | | |
| | OLS | | | DOLS (with N/W, 2L & L) | | | Regular Change Model | | | Error Correction Model (using DOLS LR) | | | |
State	LR Elasticity	Std. Error	Rank	LR Elasticity	Std. Error	Rank	SR Elasticity	Std. Error	Rank	SR Elasticity	Std. Error	Rank	T-EC (**=1%, *=5%)
Alabama	1.082	0.050	32	1.041	0.042	30	1.256	0.516	16	1.251	0.381	17	-4.101**
Alaska	2.125	0.342	4	2.975	0.522	2	0.528	0.501	40	0.683	0.546	39	-0.759
Arizona	1.035	0.056	37	0.864	0.055	44	0.337	0.353	44	0.307	0.366	46	-0.457
Arkansas	1.190	0.083	22	1.137	0.067	25	0.701	0.372	37	0.871	0.389	30	-1.287
California	1.116	0.045	27	0.952	0.033	36	1.349	0.527	10	1.181	0.559	20	-0.926
Colorado	0.805	0.081	49	0.497	0.124	50	0.323	0.457	45	0.352	0.493	44	0.185
Connecticut	1.456	0.066	11	1.393	0.069	13	1.513	0.486	5	1.452	0.470	9	-0.562
Delaware	1.459	0.080	10	1.242	0.113	16	0.787	0.367	33	1.056	0.420	23	-1.255
Florida	1.018	0.066	40	0.933	0.032	38	1.332	0.502	11	1.488	0.601	7	0.495
Georgia	0.898	0.030	45	0.903	0.029	40	0.986	0.271	23	0.822	0.269	35	-1.895
Hawaii	1.166	0.060	23	1.224	0.117	17	1.783	0.480	2	1.405	0.605	11	-1.024
Idaho	1.285	0.075	16	1.355	0.055	14	0.737	0.246	36	0.922	0.341	28	-0.789
Illinois	1.109	0.097	28	1.205	0.097	19	0.985	0.441	24	1.183	0.383	18	-2.826*
Indiana	2.201	0.118	3	2.199	0.097	4	0.848	0.391	29	1.271	0.537	16	-1.139
Iowa	2.300	0.324	2	3.312	0.266	1	0.188	0.212	48	-0.043	0.345	50	0.854
Kansas	1.279	0.109	17	1.022	0.126	32	0.834	0.503	31	0.833	0.515	34	-0.342
Kentucky	1.314	0.078	15	1.459	0.119	10	1.319	0.388	14	1.669	0.396	51	-2.075
Louisiana	0.877	0.108	46	0.713	0.161	49	0.279	0.359	46	0.270	0.371	48	-0.193
Maine	1.129	0.057	24	0.985	0.021	35	1.047	0.499	21	1.024	0.455	26	-2.209*
Maryland	0.907	0.047	44	0.750	0.059	47	1.137	0.304	18	1.030	0.256	25	-3.078**
Massachusetts	1.234	0.077	18	1.131	0.151	26	1.000	0.374	22	0.836	0.363	32	-1.851
Michigan	1.439	0.089	12	1.481	0.100	9	1.323	0.179	13	1.428	0.181	10	-1.705
Minnesota	1.078	0.053	34	0.993	0.038	34	0.449	0.351	42	0.833	0.334	33	-2.749*
Mississippi	0.876	0.080	47	0.883	0.102	41	0.919	0.309	27	0.993	0.321	27	-0.906
Missouri	1.460	0.085	9	1.442	0.065	11	1.303	0.327	15	1.320	0.316	13	-1.560
Montana	1.766	0.158	7	1.873	0.158	5	-0.047	0.340	50	0.601	0.478	42	-1.830
Nebraska	1.768	0.098	6	1.591	0.129	7	0.383	0.290	43	0.651	0.295	41	-2.114*
Nevada	0.923	0.030	42	0.922	0.032	39	0.672	0.417	39	0.769	0.387	37	-2.107*

State													
New Hampshire	0.921	0.082	43	0.732	0.045	48	0.502	0.567	41	0.469	0.593	43	-0.291
New Jersey	1.697	0.078	8	1.438	0.105	12	1.092	0.554	19	1.710	0.574	4	-2.235*
New Mexico	1.198	0.056	21	1.012	0.136	33	0.936	0.517	25	0.857	0.501	31	-1.546
New York	1.350	0.081	13	1.144	0.087	24	1.593	0.506	3	1.521	0.407	6	-3.397**
North Carolina	1.032	0.043	38	0.945	0.044	37	0.675	0.398	38	0.665	0.375	40	-1.855
North Dakota	0.663	0.342	50	1.539	0.208	8	-0.028	0.130	49	0.086	0.132	49	-2.051
Ohio	2.578	0.143	1	2.587	0.118	3	1.357	0.323	9	1.381	0.391	12	-0.115
Oklahoma	1.124	0.079	25	1.173	0.082	21	0.819	0.284	32	0.901	0.275	29	-1.724
Oregon	1.342	0.037	14	1.199	0.037	20	1.168	0.302	17	1.041	0.263	24	-2.784*
Pennsylvania	1.124	0.128	26	0.772	0.072	46	1.057	0.637	20	1.131	0.616	22	-1.561
Rhode Island	1.229	0.076	19	1.035	0.047	31	0.838	0.296	30	1.182	0.300	19	-2.429*
South Carolina	1.108	0.037	29	1.048	0.037	29	1.326	0.357	12	1.152	0.346	21	-1.930
South Dakota	1.078	0.121	35	1.063	0.102	27	0.221	0.153	47	0.329	0.172	45	-1.284
Tennessee	1.100	0.059	30	1.058	0.057	28	1.410	0.388	8	1.473	0.365	8	-1.900
Texas	1.019	0.071	39	0.866	0.153	43	0.774	0.423	34	0.774	0.436	36	0.001
Utah	1.087	0.041	31	1.212	0.066	18	1.591	0.516	4	1.821	0.412	3	-3.543**
Vermont	0.849	0.055	48	0.878	0.066	42	0.760	0.267	35	0.709	0.264	38	-1.335
Virginia	0.963	0.034	41	0.860	0.021	45	1.468	0.310	7	1.304	0.369	14	-0.836
Washington	1.066	0.044	36	1.152	0.023	23	1.484	0.672	6	2.154	0.586	2	-3.246**
West Virginia	1.079	0.158	33	1.745	0.188	6	0.932	0.336	26	1.275	0.378	15	-1.701
Wisconsin	1.214	0.061	20	1.161	0.064	22	1.956	0.425	1	2.382	0.231	1	-7.154**
Wyoming	1.787	0.190	5	1.254	0.174	15	0.894	0.359	28	0.303	0.389	47	-2.588*

Table 6.3
Long-Run and Short-Run Elasticities of State Total Tax Revenue with Respect to GDP, 1972 to 1993

| | Estimates of Long-Run Elasticity | | | | | | Estimates of Short-Run Elasticity | | | | | | |
| | OLS | | | DOLS (with N/W, 2L & L) | | | Regular Change Model | | | Error Correction Model (using DOLS LR) | | | |
State	LR Elasticity	Std. Error	Rank	LR Elasticity	Std. Error	Rank	SR Elasticity	Std. Error	Rank	SR Elasticity	Std. Error	Rank	T-EC (**=1%, *=5%)
Alabama	1.298	0.052	29	1.262	0.052	28	1.216	0.141	14	1.334	0.131	16	-2.620*
Alaska	1.014	1.797	42	-1.898	1.572	50	-2.395	2.237	50	-2.295	2.054	50	-2.132*
Arizona	1.268	0.138	31	1.011	0.171	34	1.166	0.336	16	1.195	0.307	21	-2.182*
Arkansas	1.565	0.121	15	1.388	0.093	25	0.795	0.267	33	0.897	0.271	32	-1.388
California	1.450	0.146	24	1.183	0.143	30	0.660	0.339	39	0.666	0.291	36	-2.791*
Colorado	0.898	0.163	45	0.577	0.178	46	0.867	0.406	27	0.749	0.378	35	-2.084
Connecticut	2.913	0.289	2	3.531	0.228	2	1.632	0.467	2	1.939	0.510	2	-1.352
Delaware	1.304	0.102	28	1.320	0.109	27	0.828	0.310	29	1.151	0.253	24	-3.766**
Florida	1.247	0.206	32	1.585	0.151	21	1.527	0.271	3	1.485	0.260	10	-1.707
Georgia	1.527	0.110	18	1.858	0.108	11	1.035	0.230	23	1.112	0.189	26	-3.231**
Hawaii	1.646	0.210	11	1.920	0.266	10	0.640	0.319	40	0.662	0.277	37	-2.694*
Idaho	1.537	0.232	17	1.563	0.295	23	0.708	0.355	37	0.752	0.360	34	-0.939
Illinois	0.846	0.119	47	0.823	0.149	41	0.665	0.238	38	0.577	0.222	39	-2.140*
Indiana	1.890	0.176	6	1.827	0.203	12	0.800	0.477	32	1.189	0.423	23	-2.957**
Iowa	1.480	0.131	21	1.611	0.140	19	0.340	0.245	44	0.527	0.221	42	-2.812*
Kansas	1.577	0.119	14	1.584	0.120	22	0.817	0.302	30	1.042	0.259	28	-3.164**
Kentucky	1.591	0.157	13	1.438	0.317	24	0.816	0.343	31	0.830	0.301	33	-2.582*
Louisiana	0.104	0.123	50	-0.036	0.139	49	0.272	0.435	45	0.041	0.323	48	-4.176**
Maine	2.158	0.221	5	2.763	0.203	4	1.248	0.624	12	1.964	0.679	1	-2.015
Maryland	1.454	0.083	23	1.621	0.097	18	1.279	0.190	10	1.376	0.192	12	-1.625
Massachusetts	2.409	0.187	3	2.940	0.209	3	1.082	0.332	21	1.191	0.405	22	-0.491
Michigan	1.107	0.174	35	1.115	0.073	31	2.105	0.387	1	1.883	0.353	3	-2.519*
Minnesota	1.376	0.146	25	1.231	0.089	29	1.088	0.369	20	1.370	0.294	13	-3.753**
Mississippi	0.728	0.116	49	0.649	0.138	45	1.098	0.260	19	0.999	0.263	30	-1.418
Missouri	1.835	0.157	8	2.327	0.110	6	1.431	0.248	5	1.544	0.243	5	-1.812
Montana	1.317	0.216	27	0.907	0.215	38	0.462	0.554	42	0.439	0.523	44	-1.821
Nebraska	1.873	0.192	7	1.641	0.287	17	0.964	0.412	25	1.027	0.382	29	-2.060
Nevada	1.029	0.216	41	1.000	0.201	35	0.780	0.628	34	1.228	0.549	20	-2.977**
New Hampshire	1.181	0.327	34	0.919	0.213	37	1.425	0.641	6	1.496	0.631	9	-1.328

108

New Jersey	3.276	0.352	1	3.627	0.337	1	1.020	0.435	24	1.140	0.489	25	-0.580
New Mexico	1.099	0.179	36	0.863	0.116	39	0.725	0.490	36	0.553	0.442	40	-2.429*
New York	1.475	0.168	22	2.005	0.109	7	0.891	0.287	26	0.994	0.332	31	-0.654
North Carolina	1.760	0.134	10	1.976	0.102	8	1.147	0.238	18	1.291	0.232	17	-2.007
North Dakota	0.953	0.308	43	0.798	0.210	43	-0.368	0.588	49	0.142	0.636	46	-1.702
Ohio	2.263	0.197	4	2.618	0.133	5	1.412	0.267	7	1.391	0.319	11	0.128
Oklahoma	1.369	0.309	26	1.380	0.278	26	-0.198	0.472	48	-0.034	0.463	49	-1.659
Oregon	1.039	0.180	40	0.494	0.251	47	0.862	0.474	28	0.512	0.451	43	-2.353*
Pennsylvania	0.862	0.151	46	0.701	0.068	44	1.167	0.336	15	1.104	0.318	27	-1.858
Rhode Island	1.480	0.116	20	1.754	0.091	15	0.774	0.313	35	1.229	0.303	19	-3.010**
South Carolina	1.496	0.090	19	1.724	0.064	16	1.307	0.223	9	1.339	0.206	15	-2.087
South Dakota	0.807	0.108	48	1.055	0.113	32	0.513	0.329	41	0.604	0.271	38	-3.194**
Tennessee	1.539	0.160	16	1.588	0.129	20	1.454	0.316	4	1.499	0.292	8	-2.096
Texas	0.935	0.130	44	0.849	0.133	40	0.360	0.374	43	0.536	0.309	41	-3.267**
Utah	1.051	0.143	38	0.963	0.249	36	1.062	0.502	22	1.232	0.361	18	-4.379**
Vermont	1.288	0.254	30	1.822	0.193	13	1.345	0.333	8	1.536	0.310	6	-2.351*
Virginia	1.609	0.094	12	1.933	0.112	9	1.279	0.193	11	1.357	0.208	14	-1.024
Washington	1.760	0.134	9	1.805	0.163	14	1.164	0.373	17	1.856	0.421	4	-2.606*
West Virginia	1.187	0.192	33	0.804	0.261	42	-0.075	0.481	46	0.220	0.463	45	-2.120*
Wisconsin	1.046	0.093	39	1.029	0.072	33	1.218	0.254	13	1.504	0.208	7	-3.825**
Wyoming	1.062	0.729	37	0.113	0.605	48	-0.188	0.893	47	0.055	0.862	47	-1.714

the error correction model are, however, the ones used to make inferences except in the very few cases like this for Wyoming.

Returning to the estimates in Table 6.3, both Alaska and Louisiana received negative long-run elasticity estimates, but neither is significantly different from 0 at the 5% level of confidence. Overall, the long-run elasticity estimates in Table 6.3 tend to be smaller than the estimates in Table 6.1, which also used GDP as the income base. The short-run elasticities for total tax revenues with respect to GDP tended to be larger than the corresponding total general revenue elasticities. Maine, Connecticut, Michigan, Washington, and Missouri topped the ranking as the states who can expect the largest tax revenue fluctuations over the national business cycle. Alaska and Oklahoma received negative short-run elasticity estimates, suggesting that their tax revenues run counter to the national business cycle, however, again neither is significantly different from 0, implying no significant correlation with the national business cycle. The states with the lowest (positive but closest to 0) estimates are Wyoming, North Dakota, West Virginia, Montana, and Oregon. It is again interesting that the majority of the states ranking very low are states that rely heavily on severance taxes. This suggests that severance taxes tend to be more stable over the national business cycle than other taxes. A separate case study for West Virginia, a state that relies heavily on severance revenues found that severance tax revenues were generally found to be very stable compared to GDP, but very unstable when compared to state income.[3] During national economic recessions, the demand for natural resource products tends to be very stable, producing a stable stream of severance revenues during the national recession. However, because the state economy is heavily reliant on natural resources, when something negative does happen to the industry (such as a strike or environmental regulation), severance revenues fall dramatically and the state economy falls into a recession that is unrelated to national economic forces. Thus, it is possible for states that rely heavily on natural resource industries and severance tax revenues to receive lower short-run elasticities when estimated relative to GDP than when estimated relative to state income. As mentioned earlier, this is a result of the fact that some states have business cycles that are dissimilar to the national business cycles.

Table 6.4 contains the tax revenue elasticity estimates with respect to state personal income. The states estimated to have the highest long-run elasticities are Iowa, Ohio, North Dakota, Indiana, and West Virginia. The states with the lowest estimated long-run elasticities are Louisiana, Pennsylvania, Colorado, New Hampshire, and Maryland. On average, the long-run elasticity estimates tended to be smaller when estimated against state personal income than against GDP. Additionally, the long-run estimates for tax revenues against the state economy tended to be smaller than the estimates for total revenues against the state economy. The states receiving the highest estimated short-run elasticities are Wisconsin, Washington, Tennessee, New Jersey, and Maine. Along with Virginia, Oklahoma, and Ohio, all of these states have estimates short-run elasticities greater than 2.0. This would suggest that these states can expect their total tax revenues to fluctuate twice as much as their state economy. Interestingly, Oklahoma here receives a high short-run elasticity when tax revenues are estimated with respect to state income, but it received very low estimates when estimated relative to GDP. Oklahoma is another case of a state that relies heavily on severance taxes. The states receiving the lowest estimated short-run elasticities are Colorado, North Dakota, Louisiana, Iowa, and Nebraska. While no state was estimated to have a negative elasticity, all of these states have very low ones. The first three of these states can expect their tax revenues to fluctuate by less than half of the fluctuation in the state economy. Alabama and South Dakota have the smallest standard errors on their short-run elasticities, suggesting that these states tax revenues more closely track their state business cycles than the other states.

SOME OVERALL TRENDS

When the results of Tables 6.1 through 6.4 are taken together, there are several states that consistently appear at the top and bottom of the lists. In terms of long-run growth, Indiana, Iowa, and Ohio consistently rank among the highest, whereas Louisiana and Colorado consistently rank among the lowest. To gain a better understanding of the differences, Figure 6.3 shows the per capita total general revenue growth of Ohio, one of the highest growth states, and Colorado, one of the

Figure 6.3
States with Fast and Slow Long-Run Growth

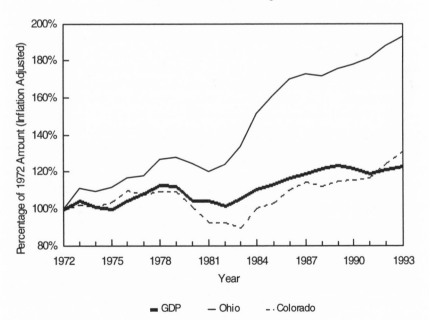

Table 6.4
Long-Run and Short-Run Elasticities of State Total Tax Revenue with Respect to State Personal Income, 1972 to 1993

| | Estimates of Long-Run Elasticity | | | | | | Estimates of Short-Run Elasticity | | | | | | |
| | OLS | | | DOLS (with N/W, 2L & L) | | | Regular Change Model | | | Error Correction Model (using DOLS LR) | | | |
State	LR Elasticity	Std. Error	Rank	LR Elasticity	Std. Error	Rank	SR Elasticity	Std. Error	Rank	SR Elasticity	Std. Error	Rank	T-EC (**=1%, *=5%)
Alabama	0.900	0.031	8	0.927	0.036	34	1.410	0.257	21	1.470	0.191	20	-4.039**
Alaska	2.364	0.429	1	1.156	0.626	20	2.066	0.729	4	1.791	0.731	13	-1.484
Arizona	1.011	0.047	29	0.878	0.061	40	0.592	0.419	44	0.574	0.407	45	-1.462
Arkansas	1.118	0.061	22	1.259	0.044	17	0.800	0.310	39	1.257	0.323	28	-2.612*
California	1.150	0.046	19	0.957	0.031	29	1.520	0.566	19	1.380	0.533	24	-1.960
Colorado	0.763	0.076	45	0.474	0.135	48	0.538	0.625	45	0.178	0.675	50	-1.286
Connecticut	1.385	0.084	10	1.350	0.061	15	1.824	0.668	8	1.818	0.592	11	-2.493*
Delaware	1.100	0.056	23	0.851	0.100	41	1.070	0.448	33	1.233	0.418	32	-2.135*
Florida	0.919	0.055	37	0.923	0.040	35	1.686	0.454	11	1.570	0.478	18	-0.836
Georgia	0.954	0.027	34	1.012	0.026	28	1.287	0.228	27	1.050	0.232	35	-2.265*
Hawaii	1.248	0.056	16	1.353	0.124	14	1.659	0.528	14	1.404	0.564	23	-1.196
Idaho	1.346	0.083	11	1.435	0.094	11	0.739	0.313	42	1.216	0.440	33	-1.497
Illinois	0.852	0.103	42	0.929	0.106	33	1.222	0.394	29	1.094	0.370	34	-2.041
Indiana	1.701	0.144	5	1.690	0.144	4	1.031	0.564	35	1.439	0.533	21	-2.388*
Iowa	1.722	0.227	4	2.540	0.240	1	0.455	0.217	46	0.542	0.336	47	-0.346
Kansas	1.277	0.096	13	1.133	0.129	21	0.883	0.559	38	0.740	0.526	42	-1.967
Kentucky	1.249	0.078	15	1.457	0.122	9	1.446	0.449	20	1.738	0.433	15	-2.151*
Louisiana	0.417	0.061	50	0.099	0.069	50	1.050	0.443	34	0.478	0.530	48	-1.768
Maine	1.132	0.078	21	1.122	0.042	23	1.659	0.758	13	2.162	0.588	5	-3.891**
Maryland	0.888	0.047	40	0.755	0.045	46	1.660	0.289	12	1.558	0.286	19	-1.577
Massachusetts	1.206	0.052	17	1.124	0.101	22	1.403	0.359	22	1.586	0.291	17	-3.460**
Michigan	1.077	0.144	24	1.160	0.132	19	1.876	0.310	6	1.815	0.261	12	-2.985**
Minnesota	1.005	0.074	30	0.930	0.065	32	1.123	0.506	32	1.343	0.396	25	-3.694**
Mississippi	0.661	0.064	47	0.782	0.070	45	1.139	0.368	31	1.262	0.322	27	-2.707*
Missouri	1.280	0.111	12	1.498	0.102	7	1.986	0.347	5	1.879	0.346	10	-1.445
Montana	1.651	0.174	7	1.452	0.177	10	0.021	0.579	50	0.860	0.562	40	-2.984**
Nebraska	1.587	0.147	8	1.368	0.232	12	0.326	0.478	48	0.545	0.430	46	-2.532*
Nevada	1.039	0.049	28	1.099	0.051	24	0.765	0.683	41	0.801	0.617	41	-2.305*
New Hampshire	0.658	0.089	48	0.515	0.058	47	1.030	0.622	36	0.990	0.679	37	-0.174
New Jersey	1.695	0.102	6	1.471	0.133	8	1.342	0.622	24	2.165	0.623	4	-2.666*

State													
New Mexico	1.059	0.057	25	0.816	0.053	43	0.705	0.787	43	0.587	0.754	44	-1.702
New York	0.973	0.074	32	0.892	0.082	39	1.382	0.360	23	1.248	0.341	29	-2.008
North Carolina	1.049	0.040	26	1.063	0.035	26	1.300	0.311	26	1.233	0.273	31	-2.605*
North Dakota	0.765	0.309	44	1.957	0.286	3	0.104	0.197	49	0.343	0.219	49	-1.971
Ohio	2.169	0.173	2	2.353	0.156	2	1.848	0.466	7	2.039	0.539	8	-0.728
Oklahoma	1.471	0.063	9	1.596	0.074	6	1.554	0.414	17	2.089	0.312	7	-4.572**
Oregon	1.147	0.063	20	1.028	0.118	27	1.319	0.608	25	0.992	0.452	36	-4.162**
Pennsylvania	0.610	0.122	49	0.406	0.089	49	1.283	0.514	28	1.239	0.485	30	-1.834
Rhode Island	0.953	0.050	35	0.906	0.083	37	1.144	0.359	30	0.977	0.293	38	-3.353**
South Carolina	0.977	0.046	31	1.071	0.032	25	1.749	0.381	10	1.760	0.367	14	-1.568
South Dakota	0.716	0.075	46	0.794	0.076	44	0.408	0.176	47	0.659	0.157	43	-3.509**
Tennessee	0.897	0.076	39	0.938	0.060	31	2.198	0.334	2	2.182	0.298	3	-1.925
Texas	0.962	0.043	33	0.847	0.081	42	0.995	0.440	37	0.907	0.414	39	-3.553**
Utah	1.048	0.051	27	1.221	0.069	18	1.808	0.810	9	1.952	0.640	9	-1.957
Vermont	0.796	0.089	43	0.917	0.118	36	1.528	0.424	18	1.419	0.400	22	-0.857
Virginia	0.921	0.044	36	0.900	0.033	38	2.226	0.276	1	2.143	0.294	6	-3.410**
Washington	1.172	0.053	18	1.260	0.037	16	1.599	0.813	16	2.551	0.708	2	-2.812*
West Virginia	1.265	0.150	14	1.599	0.216	5	0.771	0.570	40	1.618	0.574	16	-4.673**
Wisconsin	0.875	0.087	41	0.946	0.067	30	2.105	0.480	3	2.592	0.347	1	-0.897
Wyoming	1.865	0.199	3	1.358	0.313	13	1.658	0.475	15	1.273	0.642	26	

lowest, along with per capita real GDP. In the figure, the differences in the long-run growth are evident. Between 1972 and 1994, Ohio's per capita real general revenues almost doubled, whereas that of Colorado increased by only around 20 percent. Ohio's per capita revenue growth was much faster than the growth of GDP, especially in the boom years of the mid and late 1980s, whereas Colorado's growth lagged behind that of GDP for almost the entire period. Recall, however, that these growth figures are for state revenues (not the tax base) so they include any changes in tax rates and laws. Thus, a state may have a high growth in revenues because they have continuously increased their tax rates over this sample period.

In terms of short-run variability, several states also have common trends as being at the top and bottom of the lists. Louisiana and North Dakota consistently have very low estimated short-run elasticities and Michigan and Washington consistently have very high short-run elasticities. Figure 6.4 shows the annual change in per capita real general revenue for Louisiana, which has very low cyclical variability, and Michigan, which has very high cyclical variability. In the figure, the difference between the states is apparent when looking at their experiences during the 1974–1975, 1980–1982, and 1990–1991 recessions. During all of these recessions,

Figure 6.4
States with High and Low Cyclical Variability

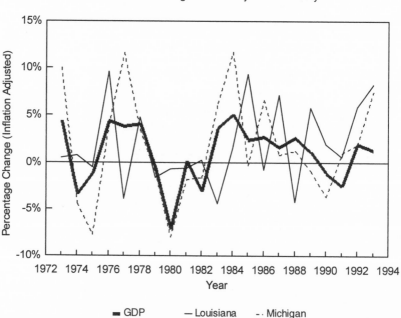

Michigan's revenues declined by more than the decline in GDP, whereas Louisiana's revenues declined by less than GDP. During both of the first two recessions, Michigan's per capita real general revenues fell by more than 7 percent. Louisiana fared the 1990–1991 recession fairly well, with revenue growth slowing, but never becoming negative.

Clearly the differences in these states' short-run variability is at least partially due to the characteristics of the state economies, rather than just which types of taxes are used. Michigan has a heavy reliance on the auto industry, which fluctuates highly with the national economy, whereas Louisiana relies on many different industries, including oil, which tend to be more stable during national recessions.

Again it is important to stress that a state's revenues may be highly variable even if the state has a stable tax structure, if the state has an economy that is highly variable. Of course, a highly unstable tax structure and a stable state economy may also produce the same result. When trying to identify which states are most likely to experience fiscal problems during national recessions, it is important to combine these two factors by looking at the estimates with respect to GDP. However, for policy purposes, it may be more important to know which taxes produce the most stable revenue stream given the variability of the state economy. For this purpose, the estimates with respect to the state economy are most important. In the next chapter, the two major state taxes, the individual income tax and retail sales tax, will be explored with respect to state income to see whether there are significant differences between these taxes that may be exploited by states to reduce revenue variability.

A STATISTICAL COMPARISON OF THE ELASTICITY ESTIMATES

With Tables 6.1 through 6.4 containing so many estimates, it is sometimes hard to see the differences among them. Although particular states sometimes stick out, the overall trends do not. Table 6.5 contains descriptive statistics for all of the elasticity estimates presented in the above tables.

The first column gives the average elasticity estimate across all states. The second column gives the standard deviation of the elasticity estimates across the states. This is not the average of the estimated standard errors, but rather how much the elasticity estimate differed among the fifty states. This is an indicator of how much uniformity there is across states in revenue growth and variability. The final column gives the average R^2 from the actual regressions across states. The R^2 was not reported in the earlier tables. This is given as an indicator of which measures most closely fit the revenues of the states.

One of the interesting features of Table 6.5 is the differences in the standard deviations. States tend to differ more in their short-run elasticities than in their long-run elasticities. In terms of the elasticity estimates themselves, short-run elasticities tend to be smaller on average than long-run elasticities. In addition, the elasticities with respect to GDP tend to be larger for the long-run estimates, but smaller for the short-run estimates. The average regression R^2 for the long-run

Table 6.5
Descriptive Statistics of Elasticity Estimates

	Average	Standard Deviation Across States	Average Regression R^2
General revenue elasticities			
With respect to GDP			
Long-run (OLS)	1.430	0.467	0.9898
Long-run (DOLS)	1.351	0.511	0.9903
Short-run (regular change model)	0.701	0.654	0.4206
Short-run (error correction model)	0.801	0.632	0.4864
With respect to state personal income			
Long-run (OLS)	1.258	0.399	0.9904
Long-run (DOLS)	1.249	0.540	0.9954
Short-run (regular change model)	0.942	0.463	0.4846
Short-run (error correction model)	1.022	0.500	0.5654
Tax revenue elasticities			
With respect to GDP			
Long-run (OLS)	1.276	0.514	0.9998
Long-run (DOLS)	1.222	0.561	0.9999
Short-run (regular change model)	0.802	0.732	0.3562
Short-run (error correction model)	0.913	0.656	0.5060
With respect to state personal income			
Long-run (OLS)	1.141	0.386	0.9999
Long-run (DOLS)	1.132	0.437	0.9999
Short-run (regular change model)	1.266	0.541	0.4389
Short-run (error correction model)	1.355	0.578	0.5709

elasticity regressions tends to be very close to 1. This upward bias in the R^2 was pointed out in the previous chapter, and appears again here. The average R^2 from the short-run regressions was smaller, typically between 0.4 and 0.6 across short-run specifications. Most interesting is whether the models using GDP produced a better or worse fit than the ones using state income. It appears that for both general revenue elasticities and tax revenue the model using state personal income fit more closely. The averages do not differ by very much, however.

Table 6.6
Correlation of Estimates across Estimation Techniques

	Correlation
General revenue elasticities	
With respect to GDP	
Long-run OLS and DOLS	0.97
Short-run regular change and ECM	0.99
With respect to state personal income	
Long-run OLS and DOLS	0.86
Short-run regular change and ECM	0.87
Tax revenue elasticities	
With respect to GDP	
Long-run OLS and DOLS	0.84
Short-run regular change and ECM	0.95
With respect to state personal income	
Long-run OLS and DOLS	0.71
Short-run regular change and ECM	0.82

To further explore the similarities across the estimates, Table 6.6 shows the simple correlations between the estimates from the different econometric techniques. It is convenient to remember that the correlation coefficient squared is the R^2 that would be found by regressing one of the estimates on the other. There is very high correlation between the estimates, with the short-run elasticities depending more on the inclusion of the error correction term than the long-run elasticities do on the inclusion of the dynamic terms. Nonetheless, the correlations are not 1, which means that there are estimation improvements arising from the

DOLS correction for the asymptotic bias in the long-run elasticity, and the error correction model improvement in the estimation of the short-run elasticity.

Table 6.7
Correlation between GDP and Personal Income Elasticities

	Correlation
General revenue elasticities	
Long-run (OLS)	0.61
Long-run (DOLS)	0.36
Short-run (regular change model)	0.40
Short-run (error correction model)	0.38
Tax revenue elasticities	
Long-run (OLS)	0.48
Long-run (DOLS)	0.31
Short-run (regular change model)	0.23
Short-run (error correction model)	0.31

Although the estimation techniques had very high correlations among their estimates, the correlations between the estimates received from the use of different income bases is much lower. Table 6.7 shows how closely correlated the estimates obtained from using GDP as the income base are to the estimates obtained from using state personal income as the base. The highest correlation is 0.61, but most are less than 0.4. Recall that a correlation coefficient of 0.61 translates into an R^2 between the estimates of only 0.37. It appears that the long-run OLS estimates are more closely correlated across the income bases, however, the bias removed DOLS estimates have correlations that are lower and similar to those for the short-run elasticities.

Table 6.8 shows how closely correlated the estimates for state total tax revenue were with the ones for state total general revenue. The correlations between the estimates are fairly high, suggesting that the main determinant of total revenue variability is the variability of tax revenue.

Table 6.9 is perhaps the most important of all of the correlation tables. It shows the correlations between the short-run and long-run elasticities. If the Groves and Kahn reasoning that the estimates from the levels regression can be used to infer about short-run variability were true, these should be very close to 1. Even if they are not equivalent, the prevailing thought that there is a trade-off between long-run

Table 6.8
Correlation between Tax and General Revenue Elasticities

	Correlation
With respect to GDP	
Long-run (OLS)	0.79
Long-run (DOLS)	0.81
Short-run (regular change model)	0.92
Short-run (error correction model)	0.92
With respect to state personal income	
Long-run (OLS)	0.87
Long-run (DOLS)	0.79
Short-run (regular change model)	0.80
Short-run (error correction model)	0.79

Table 6.9
Correlation between Short-Run and Long-Run Elasticities

	Correlation
General revenue elasticities	
With respect to GDP	
Long-run (OLS) and short-run (regular change model)	0.05
Long-run (DOLS) and short-run (error correction model)	0.15
With respect to state personal income	
Long-run (OLS) and short-run (regular change model)	-0.02
Long-run (DOLS) and short-run (error correction model)	-0.06
Tax revenue elasticities	
With respect to GDP	
Long-run (OLS) and short-run (regular change model)	0.32
Long-run (DOLS) and short-run (error correction model)	0.71
With respect to state personal income	
Long-run (OLS) and short-run (regular change model)	0.09
Long-run (DOLS) and short-run (error correction model)	0.18

growth and short-run variability would imply a high positive correlation between the estimates. This table clearly shows that this is not the case. In fact, some of the correlations are negative, implying that states with higher long-run growth potential have, on average, less cyclical variability, and vice versa. The highest positive correlation is between the short- and long-run elasticity estimates on tax revenue using the two best models. This correlation is 0.71 which translates into an R^2 of about 0.50, which still remains small enough to cast doubt on the prevailing idea of a tradeoff. A more detailed analysis of this issue is given later in the book. The main conclusion to be reached from Table 6.9 is that there is an important difference between short-run revenue variability and long-run growth potential.

CONCLUSION

One problem that has plagued state governments in the early 1990s has been cyclical variability in their revenue streams. After the recession in 1982, the remainder of the decade was prosperous, allowing state governments to grow along with overall economic activity. The recession in the early 1990s caused a downturn in state revenue growth and prompted a fiscal crisis in many states. This chapter has reported several measures of cyclical variability using modern time series techniques to gain a better understanding of the degree of revenue variability among the states. These measures show that some states exhibit much more cyclical variability than others. Additionally, there are large differences between the long-run and short-run income elasticities of state government revenues and taxes. This highlights the need for the empirical techniques used in this book, which measure these characteristics independently.

NOTES

1.   Dynamic OLS is usually performed using five leads and five lags of the change in the independent variable in the levels regression. The sample here contained only twenty-one observations and this would have resulted in a loss of almost half of the sample, causing a loss in efficiency that outweighted the loss in asymptotic bias. The use of five was actually tried, but resulted in very unstable coefficient estimates. Thus, for the final empirical estimates, two leads and lags were used to produce the DOLS estimates.

2.   State total personal income was calculated as the quarterly average over the state fiscal year from U.S. Department of Commerce, Bureau of Economic Analysis, *Regional Economic Information System* (May 1995) CD ROM data. All but four of the states have fiscal years running from July 1 to June 31, and all of the state data was calculated corresponding to the fiscal year of the particular state.

3.   See Russell S. Sobel, "West Virginia's Tax Structure and Rainy Day Fund," *West Virginia Public Affairs Reporter* 13, no. 1 (Winter 1996).

Chapter 7

The Variability of State Income and Sales Taxes

The cyclical variability of state revenues has been the main factor leading to state fiscal crises and, as the previous chapter has shown, there is a considerable amount of variation in cyclical variability of revenues among the states. This chapter takes a closer look at that issue by examining in more detail the two major sources of state tax revenue—individual (or personal) income taxes and general sales taxes.[1] If one revenue source is more variable than the other, it may be that states could modify their reliance on these taxes to reduce their cyclical variability.

In 1992 general sales and gross receipts taxes accounted for 32.8 percent of state tax revenues, and personal income tax revenues accounted for 31.8 percent, so these two types of taxes account for over 60 percent of all state tax revenues.[2] Although states do rely on other tax revenues, income and sales taxes so dominate state taxation that policy changes intended to have any significant effect on state revenue variability would have to deal with these taxes. This chapter presents measures of cyclical variability in these revenue sources and compares the cyclical variability of the two taxes.

A comparison of the cyclical variability of these two taxes might be of interest for several reasons. Although most states have both types of taxes, several do not. In states with only one of the taxes, the argument is sometimes made that the cyclical variability in tax revenues could be reduced if both tax bases were used.[3] For states that use both taxes, substitution at the margin might be possible by reducing sales taxes and increasing income tax rates, or reducing income tax rates in exchange for higher rates, or a broader base, for sales taxes. Even if tax proposals were not made specifically for the purpose of affecting the cyclical variability of revenues, the implications for cyclical variability could be a consideration. The cyclical variability of these tax bases is very relevant to state tax policy issues.

Aggregate comparisons of the growth and variability of these tax sources was performed in Chapter 5 using data that were aggregated across all states to the national level. Although in the aggregate the state income tax base is about as cyclically variable as general sales, and the food exemption increases the variability of the sales tax base, there may be some significant differences among the states. This chapter performs state-by-state comparisons and examines factors that cause cyclical variability within the two tax bases.

TAX BASES, TAX REVENUES, AND THE INCOME BASE

There are always issues regarding measurement in an empirical study, and one important measurement issue with regard to the cyclical variability of specific taxes is whether the tax base or tax revenues should be used to estimate variability. Some studies have used measures of actual revenues to evaluate the variability of a tax, whereas others have used measures of the tax base.[4] With regard to the issue of variability, tax revenues have something to recommend them, because ultimately it is variability in revenues, not in the tax base, that contributes to state fiscal problems. Using tax revenues, however, includes any impacts that legislated changes in tax rates and the tax base have on revenue variability. For this reason, many researchers find it preferable to look at the tax base directly, rather than at tax revenues. But if stabilizing changes can be made to one tax more readily than to another, there appears to be a strong argument in favor of having a measure that would account for that.[5] Given that both measures provide useful information, this chapter performs the analysis for both the tax base and tax revenues. By doing the analysis in both ways, it is also possible to see how much difference is made by using one measure rather than the other.

For this chapter, state personal income is used as the measure of the business cycle. Recalling the discussion from the previous chapter, this is important if the estimate is to reflect only the characteristics of the tax itself. If GDP, rather than state income, was used as the income base, the estimated elasticities would also reflect the variability of the state's economy. By focusing on how the tax fluctuates with respect to the state's economy, it becomes possible to draw conclusions about which of these two taxes is more stable given a particular change in the state economy. A state with a stable economy, however, will still have less fluctuations in its tax revenues, however, than a state with an unstable economy, even if the states have the same elasticity estimates. Only if every states economy was impacted identically by a national recession could these estimates tell which states are more likely to experience revenue problems during recessions. The estimates in this chapter focus on whether one of these two major taxes is more stable than the other, allowing some insight into whether states may lower their revenue variability by adjusting their reliance on these taxes. This issue is, however, more important for a state with an unstable economy.

CYCLICAL VARIABILITY OF STATE INDIVIDUAL INCOME TAXES

The tax base data used here is, for the personal income tax, federal adjusted gross income in the state. This data encompassing the period from 1972–1993 was collected from the Internal Revenue Service's *Statistics of Income* series. Although it is the total adjusted gross income in the state reported on federal income tax forms, most states base their personal income taxes on a measure of adjusted gross income very similar to the federal amount. One benefit from using the federal adjusted gross income amount is that it eliminates some of the differences in state tax base laws. For example, some states tax only dividend and interest income, whereas others levy no personal income tax at all. The use of federal level data allows an estimate of the growth and variability of the income tax base even in states that do not levy a personal income tax, or that levy only a limited one.

Using the methodology discussed in the previous chapters, the long- and short-run income elasticities for the state personal income tax were estimated using both the tax base as described above and actual state personal income tax revenues. These estimates are performed with respect to the state business cycle, as measured by state personal income. The results of the estimates for the personal income tax base are given in Table 7.1.

The last two lines of the table show the average estimate across all states and the standard deviation of the estimates. This standard deviation shows how different the estimates are across the states. Interestingly, almost all of the long-run elasticity estimates are less than 1, with the average being 0.893. Even for the few states whose estimates are greater than 1, they are not much greater, with the largest being 1.049. This suggests that the individual income tax base grows in the long run at a rate slower than the growth rate of the state economy. The estimated long-run elasticities are quite similar across the states with the standard deviation being only 0.159. The states whose personal income tax base grows the fastest with respect to the state economy are Delaware, Michigan, Georgia, Nevada, and Florida. Along with South Dakota and North Carolina these states all received estimates just higher than 1. The states whose personal income tax base grows the slowest are North Dakota, West Virginia, Montana, Nebraska, and Kansas. All of these states can expect their tax base to grow at a rate less than three quarters of the growth rate of their state economy.

The estimated short-run elasticities show more variation across the states than the estimated long-run elasticities as can be seen by the higher standard deviation. The average estimated elasticity is 1.192, which suggests that the average state can expect its personal income tax base to fall approximately 1.2 percent during a recession for every 1 percent decline in the state economy. The states with the most cyclic personal income tax bases are California, Oregon, Hawaii, Wisconsin, and Virginia, and the states with the most stable personal income tax bases are North Dakota, Nebraska, Colorado, Kansas, and Montana.

Table 7.2 contains the income elasticity estimates for the personal income tax when actual tax revenue, rather than the tax base, is used. The sample period for

Table 7.1
Long-Run and Short-Run Elasticities of State Individual Income Tax Base, 1972 to 1993

| | Estimates of Long-Run Elasticity | | | | | | Estimates of Short-Run Elasticity | | | | | |
| | OLS | | | DOLS (with N/W, 2L & L) | | | Regular Change Model | | | Error Correction Model (using DOLS LR) | | |
State	LR Elasticity	Std. Error	Rank	LR Elasticity	Std. Error	Rank	SR Elasticity	Std. Error	Rank	SR Elasticity	Std. Error	Rank
Alabama	0.890	0.037	20	0.989	0.039	11	1.436	0.276	14	1.471	0.259	14
Alaska	0.931	0.057	12	0.857	0.061	41	0.652	0.169	43	0.868	0.170	40
Arizona	0.899	0.022	18	0.909	0.024	28	1.176	0.211	27	1.227	0.178	27
Arkansas	0.830	0.049	33	0.980	0.061	14	1.071	0.291	28	1.281	0.279	26
California	0.930	0.042	13	0.935	0.060	23	1.894	0.425	1	1.797	0.452	1
Colorado	0.825	0.032	34	0.895	0.022	34	0.488	0.249	48	0.679	0.329	48
Connecticut	0.976	0.045	6	0.963	0.035	17	1.590	0.385	6	1.518	0.353	12
Delaware	1.014	0.049	1	1.049	0.055	1	1.471	0.408	11	1.382	0.390	20
Florida	0.949	0.031	9	1.030	0.034	5	1.210	0.351	24	1.568	0.322	9
Georgia	0.969	0.053	7	1.039	0.053	3	1.375	0.950	17	0.729	0.700	44
Hawaii	0.977	0.052	5	0.871	0.103	40	0.953	0.551	30	1.637	0.613	3
Idaho	0.855	0.074	28	0.889	0.064	35	0.685	0.298	38	0.903	0.349	37
Illinois	0.805	0.109	36	0.967	0.089	16	1.581	0.515	7	1.587	0.487	6
Indiana	0.774	0.084	38	0.897	0.075	33	1.293	0.230	18	1.352	0.209	21
Iowa	0.492	0.195	48	0.883	0.224	36	0.635	0.263	44	0.770	0.277	42
Kansas	0.739	0.063	43	0.709	0.072	46	0.679	0.323	40	0.681	0.311	47
Kentucky	0.769	0.068	40	0.997	0.072	10	0.573	0.426	47	1.127	0.470	30
Louisiana	0.670	0.054	45	0.842	0.089	43	0.790	0.233	33	1.341	0.409	22
Maine	0.881	0.042	21	0.906	0.022	30	1.282	0.313	19	1.338	0.298	23
Maryland	0.864	0.036	25	0.852	0.019	42	1.256	0.307	20	1.141	0.296	29
Massachusetts	0.940	0.041	10	0.949	0.018	20	1.499	0.224	10	1.452	0.206	15
Michigan	0.859	0.094	26	1.043	0.059	2	1.436	0.142	15	1.419	0.129	18
Minnesota	0.917	0.052	14	0.945	0.052	21	0.715	0.265	36	0.742	0.253	43
Mississippi	0.837	0.044	32	0.956	0.058	19	0.681	0.293	39	0.882	0.285	39
Missouri	0.763	0.048	41	0.793	0.034	45	1.252	0.318	21	1.063	0.313	32
Montana	0.572	0.117	47	0.448	0.116	48	0.653	0.262	42	0.718	0.270	46

State												
Nebraska	0.597	0.101	46	0.659	0.100	47	0.314	0.257	50	0.368	0.257	49
Nevada	0.985	0.032	2	1.030	0.024	4	1.176	0.344	26	1.421	0.345	17
New Hampshire	0.914	0.031	16	0.874	0.026	38	1.439	0.235	13	1.386	0.225	19
New Jersey	0.984	0.046	3	0.982	0.035	13	1.608	0.368	4	1.566	0.348	10
New Mexico	0.866	0.029	24	0.905	0.039	31	0.894	0.488	31	1.308	0.421	25
New York	0.911	0.065	17	0.872	0.062	39	1.227	0.362	23	1.054	0.380	33
North Carolina	0.932	0.034	11	1.023	0.017	7	1.386	0.264	16	1.313	0.252	24
North Dakota	0.440	0.117	49	0.190	0.168	50	0.325	0.087	49	0.246	0.077	50
Ohio	0.713	0.090	44	0.838	0.076	44	1.617	0.342	3	1.585	0.326	7
Oklahoma	0.758	0.048	42	0.926	0.049	25	0.611	0.235	45	0.932	0.523	36
Oregon	0.813	0.072	35	0.975	0.063	15	1.249	0.325	22	1.737	0.327	2
Pennsylvania	0.772	0.080	39	0.903	0.068	32	0.575	0.403	46	0.728	0.376	45
Rhode Island	0.917	0.060	15	0.916	0.026	27	1.591	0.350	5	1.451	0.364	16
South Carolina	0.877	0.035	22	0.956	0.028	18	1.466	0.394	12	1.580	0.359	8
South Dakota	0.981	0.112	4	1.027	0.124	6	0.765	0.197	35	0.818	0.188	41
Tennessee	0.846	0.037	30	0.923	0.031	26	1.529	0.280	9	1.518	0.259	11
Texas	0.859	0.023	27	0.909	0.036	29	0.773	0.235	34	1.085	0.284	31
Utah	0.845	0.035	31	0.930	0.035	24	0.835	0.334	32	1.029	0.362	34
Vermont	0.959	0.053	8	0.999	0.034	8	1.185	0.445	25	1.211	0.401	28
Virginia	0.869	0.033	23	0.883	0.027	37	1.734	0.373	2	1.598	0.380	5
Washington	0.895	0.049	19	0.989	0.037	12	1.034	0.461	29	1.510	0.534	13
West Virginia	0.374	0.074	50	0.433	0.111	49	0.714	0.249	37	0.882	0.238	38
Wisconsin	0.849	0.083	29	0.998	0.069	9	1.563	0.437	8	1.626	0.407	4
Wyoming	0.790	0.071	37	0.938	0.054	22	0.673	0.208	41	0.974	0.395	35
Average	0.833	0.060		0.893	0.059		1.092	0.327		1.192	0.333	
Standard Deviation	0.138	0.032		0.159	0.039		0.406	0.130		0.364	0.115	

Table 7.2
Long-Run and Short-Run Elasticities of State Individual Income Tax Revenue, 1972 to 1993

State	Estimates of Long-Run Elasticity						Estimates of Short-Run Elasticity					
	OLS			DOLS (with N/W, 2L & L)			Regular Change Model			Error Correction Model (using DOLS LR)		
	LR Elasticity	Std. Error	Rank	LR Elasticity	Std. Error	Rank	SR Elasticity	Std. Error	Rank	SR Elasticity	Std. Error	Rank
Alabama	2.120	0.058	12	2.192	0.066	14	1.853	0.755	7	1.555	0.662	18
Alaska												
Arizona	1.505	0.046	29	1.452	0.081	28	0.384	0.427	32	0.268	0.371	36
Arkansas	2328	0.073	10	2.467	0.103	12	0.893	0.631	23	1.325	0.517	20
California	1.733	0.083	21	1.673	0.086	23	2.392	1.615	5	4.509	1.372	2
Colorado	1.412	0.124	31	1.048	0.216	36	0.107	0.834	35	-0.262	0.867	37
Connecticut												
Delaware	0.902	0.129	39	0.582	0.154	39	-0.465	0.886	37	0.434	0.913	34
Florida												
Georgia	1.840	0.065	19	1.782	0.063	20	1.014	0.355	21	1.109	0.368	23
Hawaii	1.378	0.075	32	1.131	0.192	34	2.854	1.247	3	3.630	1.040	3
Idaho	1.851	0.074	17	1.656	0.062	25	0.648	0.487	27	0.870	0.480	30
Illinois	1.696	0.125	22	1.772	0.196	21	0.472	1.413	31	1.205	1.038	22
Indiana	3.332	0.291	2	3.732	0.267	2	-1.140	1.475	39	1.817	2.148	13
Iowa	2.772	0.191	5	3.132	0.232	3	0.831	0.297	25	1.102	0.361	26
Kansas	2.525	0.128	8	2.488	0.129	11	1.121	0.904	19	0.850	0.740	31
Kentucky	2.411	0.101	9	2.736	0.220	6	0.550	0.847	30	1.700	1.188	15
Louisiana	1.844	0.402	18	2.123	0.390	15	-0.635	1.509	38	-0.434	1.455	38
Maine	3.094	0.174	3	3.074	0.275	4	1.677	0.883	8	1.869	0.930	12
Maryland	1.188	0.039	35	1.218	0.035	32	1.171	0.411	17	1.106	0.370	24
Massachusetts	1.513	0.064	28	1.489	0.142	27	0.769	0.572	26	1.081	0.463	27
Michigan	1.873	0.269	16	2.097	0.280	16	2.999	0.919	2	3.127	0.799	5
Minnesota	1.200	0.114	34	1.168	0.105	33	0.567	0.866	29	0.933	0.741	29
Mississippi	1.948	0.166	14	2.460	0.199	13	1.220	1.563	15	3.216	1.580	4
Missouri	2.230	0.102	11	2.511	0.087	9	1.583	0.878	10	1.603	0.763	17
Montana	0.929	0.231	38	0.822	0.237	38	0.188	0.546	34	0.376	0.625	35

State												
Nebraska	3.036	0.268	4	2.619	0.299	8	0.631	1.268	28	1.225	1.073	21
Nevada												
New Hampshire												
New Jersey	2.009	0.098	13	1.979	0.059	17	0.204	1.133	33	1.104	1.172	25
New Mexico	1.624	0.775	24	2.666	2.048	7	-9.387	7.782	40	-5.799	7.833	40
New York	1.553	0.122	27	1.447	0.135	29	1.125	0.754	18	3.048	0.699	6
North Carolina	1.696	0.051	23	1.679	0.038	22	1.003	0.504	22	1.024	0.453	28
North Dakota	0.393	0.710	40	-2.281	0.982	40	0.074	0.653	36	-0.828	0.815	39
Ohio	6.013	0.575	1	5.888	0.397	1	4.355	3.517	1	4.974	2.493	1
Oklahoma	2.600	0.156	7	2.497	0.289	10	1.535	0.603	12	1.629	0.596	16
Oregon	1.606	0.083	25	1.407	0.121	30	1.095	0.929	20	0.800	0.680	32
Pennsylvania	1.237	0.155	33	1.097	0.121	35	2.581	1.328	4	2.061	1.168	11
Rhode Island	1.941	0.118	15	1.848	0.204	18	0.855	0.843	24	2.236	1.061	10
South Carolina	1.764	0.079	20	1.821	0.081	19	1.624	0.875	9	1.752	0.848	14
South Dakota												
Tennessee												
Texas	1.593	0.087	26	1.673	0.132	24	1.500	2.145	13	2.545	1.362	8
Utah	1.122	0.077	36	1.344	0.113	31	1.232	0.808	14	0.468	0.719	33
Vermont	1.495	0.034	30	1.494	0.037	26	2.054	0.585	6	2.456	0.520	9
Virginia												
Washington												
West Virginia	2.646	0.265	6	3.028	0.317	5	1.186	0.942	16	1.454	0.864	19
Wisconsin	0.990	0.085	37	0.876	0.098	37	1.566	1.032	11	2.546	0.650	7
Wyoming												
Average	1.924	0.172		1.897	0.232		0.857	1.151		1.392	1.070	
Standard Deviation	0.909	0.168		1.152	0.331		1.924	1.202		1.665	1.173	

the estimation is again 1972–1993, except for New Jersey which enacted its personal income tax in 1976. The states excluded from the analysis are those that have no income tax (Alaska, Florida, Nevada, South Dakota, Texas, Washington, and Wyoming), those that have a limited income tax (New Hampshire and Tennessee who only tax interest and dividends), and Connecticut which enacted its income tax in 1991 and only had a limited income tax prior to that date. Looking at Table 7.2 it is clear that using revenues changes the estimates substantially. The average long-run growth estimate more than doubles from 0.893 to 1.897. Of the forty states common to both Tables 7.1 and 7.2, thirty-seven states had higher long-run elasticity estimates when estimated on tax revenues rather than the tax base. This increase can be seen as a measure of how dramatically tax law and tax rate changes have increased the long-run growth of personal income tax revenues. Ohio, Indiana, Iowa, Maine, and West Virginia all receive very large long-run elasticity estimates. It is interesting to find Ohio in this group because it was one of the states in the last chapter that had very high general revenue growth. This growth has evidently been driven by the growth of income tax revenues, and because the long-run estimate for the income tax base itself for Ohio was fairly low, it can be concluded that much of the reason why Ohio has had rapid growth has been discretionary changes in the tax code. A check of Ohio's top marginal income tax rate shows that it has doubled from 3.5 percent in 1972 to 7.5 percent in 1993.

The average estimated short-run elasticity for personal income tax revenues is larger than the average estimate using the tax base, but not by as much as the average long-run elasticity. The average using the tax base was 1.192, whereas the average using revenues is 1.392. Of the forty states common to both tables, twenty-five receive higher estimated short-run elasticities for tax revenue than for the tax base. This suggests that tax law changes exert more of influence on the long-run growth of the personal income tax than on its short-run variability. Although states can greatly increase the long-run growth of the tax by changing tax rates and laws, they appear to not to be able to reduce the cyclical variability of the tax in the same manner. The deviation of the estimates across states is, however, much larger than it was for the respective estimates done using the tax base. Although the average short-run elasticity estimate does not change much from Table 7.1, for some individual states, the changes are dramatic. There are quite a few states who receive abnormally high and low estimates. For example, New Mexico receives a negative estimate (although it is not significantly different from 0). Even with all of the additional problems with using tax revenues, many of the states retain their respective rankings, however. For example, California and Hawaii remain in the top three. It is clear that using tax rates, instead of the tax base, influences the estimated elasticities. However, for both the short- and long-run elasticities there is a positive correlation between the estimates from the tax base and tax revenues once the few outlier states are excluded.

CYCLICAL VARIABILITY OF STATE RETAIL SALES TAXES

To measure the cyclical variability and long-run growth potential of the state retail sales tax, two different measures of the tax base are used: total retail sales in the state and total retail sales excluding food sales (nonfood retail sales). This allows a better exploration of the impact of the food exemption. Both of these series of data encompassing the period 1972–1994 were collected from *Sales and Marketing Management* (various issues) published by Bill Communications. Again, one benefit of using base, rather than revenue, data is that the income elasticity estimates can be obtained even for states who do not have a retail sales tax.[6]

The long- and short-run income elasticities for the state retail sales tax were estimated using both the tax base as described above and actual state retail sales tax revenues. Just as with the personal income tax estimates, these are performed with respect to the state business cycle, as measured by state personal income. The results of the estimates for the retail sales tax base (including food) are given in Table 7.3.

As was found with the personal income tax base, almost all of the long-run elasticity estimates are less than 1, with the average being 0.546. This average is lower than the average long-run elasticity of the personal income tax base, which was 0.893. Comparing all fifty individual states, forty-five had higher estimated long-run elasticities for the personal income tax base than for the retail sales tax including food. This suggests that the retail sales tax base (with food included) has lower long-run growth potential than the personal income tax base. The estimated long-run elasticities are again similar across the states with the standard deviation being 0.256, just higher than it was for the deviation of the personal income tax base. The states whose retail sales tax base grew the fastest with respect to the state economy are Hawaii, Delaware, and Alaska. All three of these states received estimates higher than 1. The states with the next fastest growing retail sales tax bases are Vermont, Maine, Oregon, and New Hampshire. The states whose retail sales tax base grew the slowest are West Virginia, Nebraska, Ohio, Kansas, New York, Mississippi, and Illinois. All of these states retail sales tax base grew at a rate less than 25 percent of the growth in the state economy. West Virginia's estimate is negative using DOLS, and again the regular OLS serves as a check on this estimate. In the regular OLS model, West Virginia's estimate is still very low, but not negative, and again this is a case were the costs of the more sophisticated technique outweighed the benefit.

Just as with the estimates for the personal income tax base, the estimated short-run elasticities show more variation across the states than the estimated long-run elasticities. The average estimated short-run elasticity is 0.968, which is lower than the average estimate for the personal income tax base, which was 1.192. This suggests that the average state can expect its personal income tax base to fluctuate more than its retail sales tax if food is included. The states with the most cyclic retail sales tax bases are Wisconsin, Hawaii, Ohio, Delaware, Tennessee, and South Carolina. Along with Massachusetts, California, Indiana, and Maine, all of these states can expect their retail sales to fluctuate at a rate more than 1.5 times the

Table 7.3
Long-Run and Short-Run Elasticities of State Retail Sales Tax Base Including Food, 1972 to 1994

| | Estimates of Long-Run Elasticity | | | | | | Estimates of Short-Run Elasticity | | | | | |
| | OLS | | | DOLS (with N/W, 2L & L) | | | Regular Change Model | | | Error Correction Model (using DOLS LR) | | |
State	LR Elasticity	Std. Error	Rank	LR Elasticity	Std. Error	Rank	SR Elasticity	Std. Error	Rank	SR Elasticity	Std. Error	Rank
Alabama	0.499	0.064	39	0.405	0.078	36	1.301	0.546	14	1.241	0.548	18
Alaska	1.032	0.055	3	1.024	0.106	3	0.695	0.197	37	0.511	0.139	40
Arizona	0.737	0.049	10	0.608	0.060	20	0.669	0.439	38	0.629	0.444	39
Arkansas	0.526	0.054	36	0.342	0.066	40	0.776	0.374	32	0.368	0.383	42
California	0.626	0.028	27	0.669	0.034	15	0.583	0.458	40	1.556	0.470	8
Colorado	0.677	0.044	18	0.541	0.066	28	1.254	0.444	16	1.124	0.475	19
Connecticut	0.651	0.072	22	0.731	0.118	9	0.784	0.630	31	1.034	0.596	23
Delaware	1.274	0.071	1	1.090	0.095	2	1.526	0.735	10	1.940	0.445	4
Florida	0.437	0.053	45	0.347	0.060	39	1.558	0.604	7	1.083	0.722	21
Georgia	0.638	0.031	24	0.616	0.016	19	1.720	0.350	3	1.490	0.388	11
Hawaii	1.116	0.037	2	1.092	0.057	1	2.037	0.673	1	1.970	0.525	2
Idaho	0.629	0.098	25	0.376	0.097	38	0.703	0.548	35	0.697	0.576	36
Illinois	0.346	0.097	49	0.247	0.124	44	1.231	0.568	18	1.384	0.543	15
Indiana	0.431	0.078	46	0.285	0.074	43	1.144	0.358	21	1.543	0.310	9
Iowa	0.519	0.178	37	0.538	0.253	30	-0.100	0.354	49	0.184	0.351	44
Kansas	0.443	0.077	44	0.229	0.072	47	0.202	0.461	46	0.259	0.477	43
Kentucky	0.655	0.055	20	0.556	0.060	26	1.332	0.558	12	0.649	0.542	38
Louisiana	0.651	0.055	21	0.590	0.063	23	0.231	0.346	45	0.111	0.308	45
Maine	0.810	0.039	7	0.872	0.045	5	0.724	0.583	34	1.511	0.453	10
Maryland	0.552	0.034	34	0.470	0.044	32	0.728	0.395	33	1.363	0.400	16
Massachusetts	0.591	0.076	30	0.553	0.069	27	1.271	0.415	15	1.580	0.385	7
Michigan	0.627	0.079	26	0.445	0.074	34	1.156	0.258	20	1.042	0.287	22
Minnesota	0.713	0.039	15	0.656	0.050	16	0.701	0.332	36	0.980	0.298	25
Mississippi	0.341	0.071	50	0.245	0.085	45	1.537	0.438	9	1.272	0.418	17
Missouri	0.503	0.061	38	0.398	0.047	37	1.233	0.456	17	1.430	0.453	13
Montana	0.702	0.133	16	0.607	0.127	21	1.173	0.464	19	1.100	0.439	20

Nebraska	0.396	0.097	47	0.171	0.093	49	-0.257	0.350	50	-0.278	50
Nevada	0.737	0.039	11	0.712	0.038	12	1.134	0.521	23	0.769	33
New Hampshire	0.867	0.036	5	0.862	0.049	7	1.143	0.477	22	0.793	30
New Jersey	0.559	0.040	33	0.533	0.039	31	0.855	0.422	29	0.873	28
New Mexico	0.687	0.049	17	0.593	0.067	22	1.579	0.612	6	1.451	12
New York	0.371	0.061	48	0.245	0.052	46	0.844	0.366	30	0.771	32
North Carolina	0.721	0.028	12	0.713	0.025	11	1.109	0.382	24	1.407	14
North Dakota	0.559	0.225	32	0.725	0.255	10	-0.043	0.135	47	0.018	48
Ohio	0.495	0.102	40	0.206	0.083	48	1.864	0.416	2	1.964	3
Oklahoma	0.540	0.084	35	0.321	0.171	41	0.487	0.465	42	0.072	46
Oregon	0.847	0.069	6	0.863	0.058	6	1.328	0.514	13	0.937	26
Pennsylvania	0.454	0.075	43	0.319	0.088	42	0.630	0.501	39	0.724	34
Rhode Island	0.474	0.150	41	0.628	0.143	17	1.455	1.926	11	-0.057	49
South Carolina	0.759	0.030	8	0.754	0.023	8	1.718	0.523	4	1.602	6
South Dakota	0.666	0.142	19	0.581	0.204	24	-0.068	0.256	48	0.063	47
Tennessee	0.572	0.056	31	0.467	0.035	33	1.555	0.522	8	1.903	5
Texas	0.649	0.031	23	0.622	0.053	18	0.856	0.322	28	0.886	27
Utah	0.610	0.042	29	0.540	0.031	29	0.443	0.597	43	1.008	24
Vermont	0.715	0.071	14	0.883	0.082	4	0.397	0.674	44	0.701	35
Virginia	0.755	0.034	9	0.686	0.037	13	1.064	0.724	25	0.779	31
Washington	0.720	0.028	13	0.677	0.028	14	0.565	0.433	41	0.803	29
West Virginia	0.469	0.166	42	-0.337	0.100	50	0.951	0.545	26	0.388	41
Wisconsin	0.611	0.109	28	0.572	0.099	25	1.621	0.725	5	2.099	1
Wyoming	0.878	0.154	4	0.414	0.337	35	0.950	0.429	27	0.660	37
Average	0.637	0.073		0.546	0.085		0.967	0.496		0.968	
Standard Deviation	0.184	0.044		0.256	0.063		0.529	0.243		0.582	

fluctuations in the state economy. The states with the most stable retail sales tax bases are Nebraska, Rhode Island, North Dakota, South Dakota, Oklahoma, Louisiana, Iowa, and Kansas. Nebraska and Rhode Island receive negative estimates; however, they are not different from 0. Another interesting comparison between the personal income tax base and the retail sales tax base is to see which is subject to more random variance. This unpredictability is measured by how closely the tax follows the state business cycle, which is the estimated standard error of the short-run elasticity estimate. From Table 7.1 the average standard error of the short-run elasticity estimates was 0.333, whereas for the retail sales tax base it is 0.469. In fact, forty-two of the fifty states have higher standard errors for the retail sales tax than for the personal income tax. This suggests that the retail sales tax follows the state business cycle less closely than the personal income tax.

Table 7.4 contains the income elasticity estimates for the retail sales tax base when food is excluded. Several differences are apparent when comparing these estimates to the ones in Table 7.3, where food is included. The average long-run elasticity estimate is somewhat higher, rising from 0.546 to 0.607. Of the fifty states, forty have higher long-run elasticity estimates for the tax base when food is exempt. This strongly suggests that reliance on a retail sales tax with food exempt produces more long-run growth than relying on a retail sales tax that includes food. The states with the highest and lowest long-run elasticities are very similar to those in Table 7.3 with food included. Of the top six in both tables, all six are the same, Delaware, Hawaii, Oregon, Alaska, Vermont, and Maine, and of the bottom six, three are the same, West Virginia, Nebraska, and Kansas. With respect to the short-run elasticities, the average estimate increases from 0.968 with food included to 1.104 with food exempt. Of the fifty states, forty receive higher short-run elasticity estimates when food is not included. This is strong evidence that exempting food increases the cyclical variability of a state's retail sales tax. The states with the highest and lowest short-run elasticities are also very similar across Tables 7.3 and 7.4. Of the top 6 in both tables, again all six are the same, Wisconsin, Ohio, Tennessee, Delaware, Hawaii, and South Carolina. Of the bottom six in both tables, five are the same, Rhode Island, Nebraska, Oklahoma, North Dakota, and South Dakota.[7]

The states for which the food exemption appears to matter the most are Kentucky, Ohio, Maryland, Tennessee, Georgia, Alabama, Maine, Washington, Indiana, Texas, and Michigan. All of these states have much higher short-run variability when food is exempted relative to when it is included. Of these states, only Tennessee, Georgia, and Alabama currently include food in the sales tax. This suggests that the other eight states listed above could stabilize their retail sales tax revenues by removing the food exemption. This would also bring in additional revenue, unless the overall sales tax rate was lowered.

Table 7.5 contains the income elasticity estimates for the retail sales tax when actual tax revenue, rather than the tax base, is used. The sample period for the estimation is 1972–1993. The states excluded from the analysis are those that have no retail sales tax (Alaska, Delaware, Montana, New Hampshire, and Oregon). Again it is clear that using revenues rather than bases changes the estimates substantially. The average long-run growth estimate is higher than it was for either version of the tax base, the average across all states being 1.189. The states that exempt food had an average estimate of 1.36, and the respective estimate for the tax base excluding food was 0.607. The states that include food in their retail sales tax had an average estimate of 0.976 compared to the estimate for the tax base including food, which was 0.546. Again it is evident that using revenues results in a much higher estimated long-run elasticity, suggesting that state tax policy significantly increases the long-run growth of revenues from the retail sales tax. At the top of the long-run elasticity list are Iowa, Ohio, Minnesota, Massachusetts, and Idaho, all receiving estimates greater than 2.0. Again, it is interesting to find Ohio in this group because it was one of the states in the last chapter that had very high general revenue growth. Earlier this chapter reported that Ohio's long-run estimate for personal income tax revenues was also very high. The lowest ranking states are West Virginia, Colorado, North Dakota, Alabama, and New York. West Virginia was also at the bottom of the list when its long-run elasticity was estimated for its retail sales tax base.

The average short-run elasticity estimate for retail sales tax revenues is higher than it was for either version of the tax base, the average across all states being 1.295. The states that exempt food had an average estimate of 1.169, while the respective estimate for the tax base excluding food was 1.104. The states that include food in their retail sales tax had an average estimate of 1.451 compared to the estimate for the tax base including food, which was 0.968. Again it is evident that state tax changes affect long-run growth much more than cyclical variability. If state tax changes reduced revenue variability, then the estimates from the revenues should have been lower, not higher, than the ones for the tax bases.

Comparing the averages for states with food included and food exempt, however, appears to contradict earlier findings that the food exemption increases the cyclical variability of the sales tax. The average short-run estimate for states exempting food is lower than for states including food in the tax. The wide variation of the estimates, and the complications introduced by using revenues could be used to discount this result; however, this finding may suggest an even more important problem with cross-sectional studies of revenue variability. Even if it is true that states who exempt food have less revenue variability than states that include food, it still can be true that if a given state was to exempt food, it would increase the variability of that state's revenues. This result could happen if, for example, states with highly variable retail sales tax bases are more likely to include food, whereas states with stable retail sales tax bases are more likely to exempt food. In fact, if taxing food does decrease cyclical variability, it seems logical that the states with the most variable retail sales tax bases would find it more attractive to tax food, producing the situation described above. This finding draws into question the adequacy of cross-sectional comparisons and seems to suggest that more accurate conclusions can be drawn from within-state comparisons, such as showing that for forty-five of the fifty states, retail sales excluding food vary more over the business cycle than retail sales including food.

Table 7.4
Long-Run and Short-Run Elasticities of State Retail Sales Tax Base Excluding Food, 1972 to 1994

| | Estimates of Long-Run Elasticity | | | | | | Estimates of Short-Run Elasticity | | | | | |
| | OLS | | | DOLS (with N/W, 2L & L) | | | Regular Change Model | | | Error Correction Model (using DOLS LR) | | |
State	LR Elasticity	Std. Error	Rank	LR Elasticity	Std. Error	Rank	SR Elasticity	Std. Error	Rank	SR Elasticity	Std. Error	Rank
Alabama	0.572	0.078	36	0.517	0.096	33	1.606	0.624	11	1.594	0.622	14
Alaska	1.019	0.069	3	1.038	0.138	4	0.744	0.240	37	0.518	0.189	41
Arizona	0.718	0.062	18	0.567	0.080	30	0.734	0.529	39	0.690	0.538	38
Arkansas	0.596	0.060	35	0.425	0.075	40	0.750	0.413	36	0.597	0.420	39
California	0.687	0.036	24	0.736	0.051	14	0.727	0.561	40	1.380	0.551	18
Colorado	0.638	0.056	31	0.465	0.071	38	1.104	0.576	24	0.959	0.609	32
Connecticut	0.716	0.081	19	0.801	0.136	9	0.904	0.678	30	1.129	0.645	23
Delaware	1.348	0.071	1	1.123	0.093	1	1.720	0.773	8	2.271	0.502	4
Florida	0.515	0.061	44	0.439	0.074	39	1.616	0.677	10	1.197	0.764	21
Georgia	0.697	0.046	20	0.659	0.021	22	1.923	0.479	4	1.854	0.533	8
Hawaii	1.174	0.037	2	1.108	0.069	2	2.149	0.691	2	2.188	0.533	5
Idaho	0.601	0.105	34	0.335	0.095	46	0.738	0.600	38	0.754	0.624	37
Illinois	0.488	0.118	45	0.368	0.149	44	1.471	0.655	15	1.754	0.635	12
Indiana	0.602	0.095	33	0.470	0.087	37	1.306	0.404	21	1.805	0.377	10
Iowa	0.472	0.210	46	0.538	0.293	32	-0.176	0.393	49	0.176	0.397	43
Kansas	0.417	0.092	49	0.165	0.082	48	0.092	0.491	46	0.105	0.508	45
Kentucky	0.762	0.062	13	0.763	0.102	12	1.318	0.635	20	1.297	0.562	19
Louisiana	0.697	0.072	21	0.610	0.097	28	0.256	0.456	45	0.174	0.427	44
Maine	0.853	0.043	7	0.927	0.039	6	0.945	0.587	29	1.861	0.487	7
Maryland	0.634	0.042	32	0.540	0.053	31	0.993	0.586	28	1.840	0.516	9
Massachusetts	0.647	0.087	27	0.639	0.083	24	1.479	0.490	14	1.778	0.454	11
Michigan	0.919	0.077	5	0.774	0.073	11	1.378	0.265	16	1.249	0.285	20
Minnesota	0.747	0.044	14	0.687	0.048	17	0.762	0.379	35	1.082	0.343	25
Mississippi	0.425	0.097	48	0.499	0.154	34	1.572	0.653	12	1.614	0.599	13
Missouri	0.571	0.071	37	0.477	0.045	36	1.367	0.490	17	1.507	0.492	15
Montana	0.696	0.161	22	0.660	0.133	20	1.256	0.565	22	1.191	0.526	22

Nebraska	0.382	0.107	50	0.148	0.109	49	-0.263	0.378	50	-0.288	0.393	49
Nevada	0.727	0.042	17	0.683	0.040	18	1.327	0.543	19	0.951	0.601	33
New Hampshire	0.911	0.043	6	0.905	0.056	7	1.341	0.497	18	1.019	0.448	28
New Jersey	0.655	0.053	30	0.614	0.050	27	1.061	0.528	26	1.020	0.489	27
New Mexico	0.681	0.050	26	0.590	0.069	9	1.562	0.664	13	1.505	0.636	16
New York	0.539	0.071	43	0.384	0.059	42	1.016	0.476	27	0.912	0.464	34
North Carolina	0.786	0.033	11	0.788	0.027	10	1.197	0.405	23	1.436	0.358	17
North Dakota	0.559	0.229	40	0.666	0.276	19	-0.034	0.149	47	0.028	0.152	47
Ohio	0.672	0.127	28	0.389	0.100	41	2.220	0.505	1	2.441	0.498	2
Oklahoma	0.566	0.089	38	0.326	0.169	47	0.303	0.548	44	-0.184	0.493	48
Oregon	0.985	0.086	4	1.057	0.061	3	1.644	0.705	9	1.016	0.691	29
Pennsylvania	0.549	0.092	41	0.368	0.102	43	0.652	0.616	41	0.800	0.607	36
Rhode Island	0.472	0.206	47	0.660	0.179	21	1.726	2.664	7	-0.733	1.867	50
South Carolina	0.835	0.034	9	0.842	0.024	8	1.812	0.557	6	1.875	0.456	6
South Dakota	0.687	0.154	23	0.620	0.215	25	-0.080	0.284	48	0.097	0.303	46
Tennessee	0.681	0.063	25	0.618	0.050	26	1.966	0.520	3	2.328	0.481	3
Texas	0.668	0.033	29	0.655	0.060	23	0.885	0.352	32	1.114	0.287	24
Utah	0.560	0.046	39	0.487	0.035	35	0.502	0.669	43	1.006	0.712	30
Vermont	0.743	0.076	15	0.932	0.085	5	0.588	0.639	42	0.833	0.686	35
Virginia	0.810	0.035	10	0.753	0.034	13	1.090	0.730	25	0.990	0.675	31
Washington	0.778	0.032	12	0.735	0.035	15	0.864	0.500	34	1.066	0.520	26
West Virginia	0.541	0.157	42	-0.277	0.094	50	0.870	0.559	33	0.268	0.677	42
Wisconsin	0.737	0.127	16	0.723	0.110	16	1.917	0.787	5	2.541	0.794	1
Wyoming	0.836	0.157	8	0.354	0.353	45	0.888	0.453	31	0.573	0.549	40
Average	0.692	0.084		0.607	0.097		1.076	0.572		1.104	0.540	
Standard Deviation	0.182	0.048		0.255	0.068		0.600	0.328		0.730	0.233	

Table 7.5
Long-Run and Short-Run Elasticities of State Retail Sales Tax Revenues, 1972 to 1993

| State | Food Exempt | Estimates of Long-Run Elasticity | | | | | | Estimates of Short-Run Elasticity | | | | | |
| | | OLS | | | DOLS (with N/W, 2L & L) | | | Regular Change Model | | | Error Correction Model (using DOLS LR) | | |
		LR Elasticity	Std. Error	Rank	LR Elasticity	Std. Error	Rank	SR Elasticity	Std. Error	Rank	SR Elasticity	Std. Error	Rank
Alabama	No	0.529	0.044	43	0.498	0.047	42	1.299	0.359	19	1.319	0.318	23
Alaska													
Arizona	Yes	1.090	0.058	27	0.834	0.073	33	1.113	0.558	29	1.041	0.512	29
Arkansas	No	1.468	0.085	11	1.761	0.118	8	1.362	0.489	17	2.140	0.516	5
California	Yes	1.097	0.068	26	0.801	0.037	35	0.452	0.683	40	0.711	0.607	35
Colorado	Yes	0.526	0.083	44	0.398	0.138	44	1.503	0.711	16	1.394	0.634	21
Connecticut	Yes	1.341	0.078	16	1.721	0.068	11	2.101	0.860	5	2.074	0.873	8
Delaware													
Florida	Yes	1.337	0.056	17	1.437	0.074	16	1.649	0.561	11	1.808	0.500	11
Georgia	No	0.937	0.055	34	0.972	0.085	28	0.823	0.621	34	0.424	0.582	39
Hawaii	No	1.161	0.039	21	1.140	0.098	22	1.597	0.357	13	1.480	0.346	20
Idaho	No	1.730	0.136	6	2.038	0.172	5	0.842	0.614	33	1.386	0.700	22
Illinois	No	0.637	0.129	41	0.539	0.132	40	2.614	0.605	1	2.515	0.571	4
Indiana	Yes	1.285	0.259	18	1.169	0.111	21	1.228	1.303	23	0.527	1.145	38
Iowa	Yes	1.780	0.300	5	2.589	0.400	1	0.535	0.619	39	1.221	0.681	24
Kansas	No	1.118	0.144	25	0.774	0.179	36	0.610	0.721	36	0.583	0.740	37
Kentucky	Yes	0.730	0.105	38	0.978	0.103	27	0.750	0.642	35	2.135	0.587	6
Louisiana	No	0.990	0.104	30	0.923	0.169	29	1.084	0.635	30	0.669	0.611	36
Maine	Yes	0.963	0.060	32	0.883	0.028	30	1.572	0.446	14	1.628	0.434	18
Maryland	Yes	0.970	0.069	31	0.812	0.157	34	1.210	0.713	25	1.662	0.654	16
Massachusetts	Yes	2.245	0.214	1	2.123	0.422	4	1.898	0.853	7	3.407	1.035	1
Michigan	Yes	0.693	0.151	39	0.837	0.110	32	1.226	0.502	24	1.213	0.426	25
Minnesota	Yes	1.943	0.256	3	2.280	0.216	3	-1.856	1.636	45	-0.638	1.806	45
Mississippi	No	0.665	0.065	40	0.596	0.073	39	1.163	0.530	26	0.826	0.503	33
Missouri	No	1.449	0.121	13	1.635	0.096	12	1.288	1.003	20	1.763	0.953	14
Montana													

State	Food Exempt												
Nebraska	Yes	1.669	0.173	7	1.222	0.170	19	-0.382	0.611	43	-0.114	0.612	44
Nevada	Yes	1.437	0.075	14	1.569	0.073	14	0.541	1.100	38	0.091	0.982	42
New Hampshire													
New Jersey	Yes	1.518	0.088	8	1.761	0.152	9	1.119	0.906	28	0.843	0.877	32
New Mexico	No	1.178	0.070	20	1.047	0.113	25	1.260	1.163	21	1.698	1.052	15
New York	Yes	0.777	0.077	37	0.529	0.103	41	1.151	0.472	27	1.091	0.460	28
North Carolina	No	1.134	0.071	24	1.123	0.043	24	2.138	0.659	4	2.081	0.607	7
North Dakota	Yes	0.565	0.223	42	0.484	0.419	43	0.092	0.230	42	0.079	0.196	43
Ohio	Yes	1.979	0.200	2	2.379	0.208	2	1.606	0.805	12	1.927	0.901	10
Oklahoma	No	1.835	0.201	4	1.726	0.253	10	0.989	0.684	31	0.906	0.674	31
Oregon													
Pennsylvania	Yes	1.135	0.086	23	1.126	0.068	23	1.301	0.455	18	1.594	0.443	19
Rhode Island	Yes	1.155	0.080	22	1.380	0.132	17	2.150	0.702	3	1.776	0.668	13
South Carolina	No	1.062	0.066	28	1.205	0.064	20	1.736	0.636	10	1.962	0.622	9
South Dakota	No	0.852	0.148	36	0.649	0.163	38	0.135	0.290	41	0.130	0.256	41
Tennessee	No	1.404	0.072	15	1.444	0.056	15	2.451	0.663	2	2.661	0.605	2
Texas	Yes	1.475	0.109	10	1.570	0.165	13	0.544	0.621	37	0.755	0.673	34
Utah	No	1.020	0.044	29	1.046	0.080	26	1.863	0.852	8	2.536	0.621	3
Vermont	Yes	1.483	0.112	9	1.900	0.136	6	1.539	0.947	15	1.635	0.893	17
Virginia	No	0.888	0.043	35	0.860	0.055	31	1.252	0.559	22	0.991	0.598	30
Washington	Yes	1.276	0.062	19	1.361	0.034	18	-0.522	0.862	44	0.214	1.087	40
West Virginia	No	0.331	0.383	45	-1.217	0.525	45	2.020	1.237	6	1.142	1.315	27
Wisconsin	Yes	1.466	0.107	12	1.868	0.067	7	0.912	0.765	32	1.165	0.854	26
Wyoming	No	0.962	0.186	33	0.757	0.225	37	1.818	0.208	9	1.803	0.209	12
Average (All States)		1.184	0.119		1.189	0.142		1.151	0.699		1.295	0.687	
Standard Deviation (All States)		0.422	0.076		0.654	0.109		0.806	0.278		0.808	0.298	
Average (Food Exempt)		1.277	0.126		1.360	0.147		0.937	0.743		1.169	0.742	
Average (Food Not Exempt)		1.067	0.110		0.976	0.137		1.417	0.644		1.451	0.620	

Looking at the states ranking highest in the variability of sales tax revenues, the top are Massachusetts, Tennessee, Vermont, Illinois, Arkansas, and Kentucky. Of these, Tennessee was also at the top of the cyclical variability list when looking at the state retail sales tax base. The states with the most stable retail sales tax revenues are Minnesota, Nebraska, North Dakota, Nevada, and South Dakota, and Washington. Of these, Nebraska, North Dakota, and South Dakota were also estimated to have low variability when looking at the state retail sales tax base.

COMPARING THE GROWTH AND VARIABILITY OF INCOME AND SALES TAXES

One primary objective of this chapter is to compare the growth and stability of income and sales taxes over the business cycle. In terms of long-run growth, the average elasticity estimate for the personal income tax base was 0.893, whereas the estimate for the retail sales tax base was 0.546 with food included and 0.607 with food exempt. Of the fifty states, forty-five had long-run elasticity estimates that were greater for the personal income tax base than for total retail sales, whereas forty-two had estimates greater for the personal income tax than for nonfood retail sales. Additionally, for the tax revenues, the respective long-run elasticity estimates were 1.897 for the personal income tax and 1.189 for the retail sales tax. Of the thirty-seven states that have both income and sales taxes, twenty-nine had higher long-run elasticity estimates for personal income tax revenues than for retail sales tax revenues. All of the results in this chapter suggest that personal income taxes are a better source of long-run revenue growth than retail sales taxes.

For short-run cyclical variability, the average elasticity estimate for the personal income tax base was 1.192, whereas the estimate for the retail sales tax base was 0.968 with food included and 1.104 with food exempt. Of the fifty states, thirty-two had short-run elasticity estimates that were greater for the personal income tax base than for total retail sales, whereas twenty-seven had estimates greater for the personal income tax than for nonfood retail sales. For tax revenues, the respective short-run elasticity estimates were 1.392 for the personal income tax and 1.295 for the retail sales tax. Of the thirty-seven states that have both income and sales taxes, twenty-one had higher short-run elasticity estimates for personal income tax revenues than for retail sales tax revenues. These results, although not as strong as for long-run growth, suggest that retail sales taxes, especially when they include food, are more stable over the business cycle than personal income taxes for most (but not all) states. This finding is consistent with a conclusion reached using aggregate U.S. data in Chapter 5 that retail sales taxes including food were more stable than personal income taxes. Comparing retail sales taxes that exempt food with personal income taxes, the results are not strong enough to suggest a consistently significant difference in the variability of these two taxes in either direction.

Although overall, the difference between the short-run variability of the personal income and retail sales taxes does not appear strong; for several individual states, it appears that the difference may be substantial. The states whose personal income tax base has much higher variability than their retail sales tax base are Louisiana, Oklahoma, Arkansas, South Dakota, Nebraska, New Jersey, Iowa, Arizona, and North Dakota. The above results seem to suggest that these states might be able to substantially increase the stability of their state tax revenues with heavier reliance on the retail sales tax base and less reliance on the personal income tax base. Interestingly, of these states, South Dakota currently does not have a personal income tax. On the other end, Mississippi appears to have a much more stable personal income tax base than retail sales tax base. For Mississippi, the implication would work in the other direction, with a heavier reliance on the personal income tax potentially creating more stability in the state's revenues.

As mentioned earlier, there are several states that do not have either income or sales taxes. Within these states, proposals to adopt these taxes are frequent and the debates are often vigorous. For this reason, it is worth looking specifically at the results in this chapter for these states to see whether they could either increase the long-run growth or reduce the cyclical variability of their tax revenues by enacting the missing tax. Table 7.6 shows both the long- and short-run elasticities for the personal income tax base and retail sales tax base for these states.

The first set of states are those that currently have an individual income tax but do not have a retail sales tax. In terms of long-run growth, Delaware's untapped retail sales tax base appears to be just barely higher than their current personal income tax base. There is not enough difference to conclude that they could increase the long-run growth potential of their tax revenues by adding a retail sales tax. Delaware's untapped retail sales tax base, however, appears to be much more cyclically variable than their current personal income tax base. This suggests that if Delaware were to add a retail sales tax that it might result in a decrease in the stability of their tax revenues over the business cycle. Montana's untapped retail sales tax base does appear to have a higher long-run growth potential than their current income tax base. Adding this tax might, however, result in a decrease in the stability of their tax revenues over the business cycle, just as for Delaware. For Oregon, the long-run growth potential of their untapped retail sales tax base would appear to be mildly higher than their current personal income tax base if they were to exempt food, but lower if they were to include food in the tax. Unlike for the other two states, however, Oregon's revenues might be stabilized over the business cycle if they were to adopt a retail sales tax. This is mostly because Oregon's personal income tax base received the second highest short-run elasticity out of the fifty states.

The second set of states are those that currently have a retail sales tax but no individual income tax. Tennessee actually has an income tax, but it is limited in terms of taxing only interest and dividend income. In terms of long-run growth, the untapped personal income tax bases for all of the states listed appear to be higher than the long-run growth of their current retail sales tax bases. For five of the seven states (Florida, Nevada, South Dakota, Washington, and Wyoming), however, the short-run variability of their untapped personal income tax bases appears to be more cyclically variable than their current retail sales tax bases. This suggests that if these states were to add a personal income tax, it might result in a decrease in the

Table 7.6
States with No Individual Income or Retail Sales Tax

	Long-Run Elasticities (DOLS)			Short-Run Elasticities (ECM)		
	Individual Income Tax Base	Retail Sales Tax Base		Individual Income Tax Base	Retail Sales Tax Base	
		Including Food	Food Exempt		Including Food	Food Exempt
Individual income tax but no retail sales tax						
Delaware	1.049	1.090	1.123	1.382	1.940	2.271
Montana	0.448	0.607	0.660	0.718	1.100	1.191
Oregon	0.975	0.863	1.057	1.737	0.937	1.016
Retail sales tax but no individual income tax						
Florida	1.030		0.439	1.568		1.197
Nevada	1.030		0.683	1.421		0.951
South Dakota	1.027	0.581		0.818	0.063	
Tennessee*	0.923	0.467		1.518	1.903	
Texas	0.909		0.655	1.085		1.114
Washington	0.989		0.735	1.510		1.066
Wyoming	0.938	0.414		0.974	0.660	
No individual income tax and no retail sales tax						
Alaska	0.857	1.024	1.038	0.868	0.511	0.518
New Hampshire*	0.874	0.862	0.905	1.386	0.793	1.019

Note: * Indicates states with only a limited income tax on interest and dividends.

stability of their tax revenues over the business cycle. If Tennessee were to change their limited income tax into a full-blown personal income tax base, these results suggest that unlike the above five states, their revenues might actually become more stable. This result is found because the short-run elasticity of Tennessee's current retail sales tax is very high, ranking fifth highest in the nation. Texas's untapped personal income tax base is just slightly more stable than their current retail sales tax base, suggesting little, if any, improvement in revenue stability by adding this tax. Thus, for the vast majority of the states that currently have a retail sales tax, but no personal income tax, it appears that state revenues would become less stable over the business cycle if the states adopt a personal income tax. An additional consideration is that five of the states that do not have a personal income tax (Nevada, South Dakota, Texas, Washington, and Wyoming) also do not have a corporation income tax. Many states that adopt personal income taxes also simultaneously adopt corporate income taxes, so for these five states the total impact of adopting an income tax might need to include the additional variability created by the corporation income tax. Recall in from Chapter 5 that the corporation income tax was shown to be the most cyclically variable of all taxes. Thus, the adoption of an income tax in these states might lead to a large increase in the cyclical variability of tax revenues if a corporation income tax were also adopted.

The third set of states have neither tax. If Alaska were to adopt one of the taxes, the retail sales tax might provide both more long-run growth and more stability than the personal income tax. New Hampshire actually has a limited income tax, but if they were to expand this to a full-blown income tax it might provide just about the same long-run revenue growth as if they were to adopt a retail sales tax. The retail sales tax might, however, be much more stable over the business cycle.

Thus, interestingly, for seven of the ten states with only one type of tax, either income or sales, it appears that adding the other tax might lead to an increase in long-run revenue growth but a decrease in the stability of state revenues over the business cycle. Therefore, these states are currently taking advantage of the tax base that is most stable.

CONCLUSION

This chapter has undertaken a comprehensive analysis of the differences between the state personal income tax and the state retail sales tax in terms of both long-run growth potential and cyclical stability. Although there are some significant differences among the individual states in the conclusions reached, there are a few overall trends. First, estimates of the income elasticities using revenues instead of the tax base generally produce higher estimated long-run elasticities, showing the positive impact that discretionary changes in state tax codes have on the long-run growth of revenues. In short, tax rates have gone up. Second, looking at overall averages, cyclical variability estimates are not reduced when looking at revenues rather than tax bases, implying that state tax code changes cannot significantly reduce revenue variability. Third, exempting food from the retail sales tax increases the long-run growth potential of the tax, but it also increases the cyclical variability of the tax. Fourth, personal income taxes appear to have more long-run growth potential than retail sales taxes. Although the evidence is less clear, it appears likely that personal income taxes are more cyclically variable than retail sales taxes that include food. The evidence is mixed on whether the personal income tax is more or less stable than retail sales taxes that exempt food. Finally, of the states that currently only have one of these two taxes, the vast majority would suffer increased revenue variability by adding the other tax. They may, however, be able to improve the long-run growth of state revenues by adding the other tax. The conclusions listed here raise an interesting issue as to whether there is a trade-off between the long-run growth and cyclical variability of taxes. That is, do taxes with the highest long-run growth have the lowest cyclical variability? That is the subject of the next chapter.

NOTES

1.   A less technically developed analysis of the relative variability of income and sales tax revenues can be found in Randall G. Holcombe and Russell S. Sobel, "The Relative Variability of State Income and Sales Taxes Over the Revenue Cycle," *Atlantic Economic Journal* 23, no. 2 (June 1995): 97–112.

2.   The figure for sales taxes does not include excise taxes on motor fuels and alcoholic beverages. These figures are from the Tax Foundation's *Facts and Figures on Government Finance*, 1994 edition.

3.   William F. Fox and Charles Campbell, "Stability of the State Sales Tax Income Elasticity," *National Tax Journal* 37, no. 2 (June 1984): 201–12, document the procyclical nature of the state sales tax. However, Fred C. White, "Trade-Off in Growth and Stability in State Taxes," *National Tax Journal* 36, no. 1 (March 1983): 103–14, finds that sales taxes are more stable sources of revenue than income taxes.

4.   Fox and Campbell, "Stability of the State Sales Tax Income Elasticity," and Richard F. Dye and Therese J. McGuire, "Growth and Variability of State Individual Income and General Sales Taxes," *National Tax Journal* 44, no. 1 (March 1991): 55–66, look at the tax base, while William V. Williams, Robert M. Anderson, David O. Froehle, and Kaye L. Lamb, "The Stability, Growth, and Stabilizing Influence of State Taxes," *National Tax Journal* 26, no. 2 (June 1973): 267–74, and White, "Trade-Off in Growth and Stabilization in State Taxes," use tax revenues. W. T. Wilford, "A Comment on 'The Stability, Growth, and Stabilizing Influence of State Taxes,' " *National Tax Journal* 28, no. 4 (December 1975): 452–58, critiques the approach taken by Williams et al. "The Stability; Growth, and Stabilizing Influence of State Taxes," for using revenues instead of bases.

5.   See Paul R. Blackley and Larry DeBoer, "Explaining State Government Discretionary Revenue Increases in Fiscal Years 1991 and 1992," *National Tax Journal* 46, no. 1 (March 1993): 1–12, for example, who explain that state tax rates are changed in response to cyclical downturns. This implies that to fully capture cyclical variability, a measure should capture both changes in the base and changes in the rate, which argues in favor of an examination of the variability of revenues.

6.   It is worth mentioning that total retail sales are a poor measure of the actual state tax base. Besides the food exemption, most states also have excmptions for items such as prescription drugs, clothing, services, and various other categories of sales. Additionally, state sales tax laws are complex enough that many items are double-taxed, whereas many

others escape taxation altogether. Raymond J. Ring, "The Proportion of Consumers' and Producers' Goods in the General Sales Tax," *National Tax Journal* 42, no. 2 (June 1989): 167–79, estimates that consumer goods as a proportion of the state sales tax base ranges from 35 to 82 percent, with the average being 59 percent.

7.   Another consideration is that food purchases made with food stamps or drafts issued by state supplemental food programs for women, infants, and children (WIC) are required by federal law to be exempt from state retail sales taxes. Thus, in states that tax food, some food purchases are still exempt, and in the states that exempt food, the extension of the tax to include food would not tax all food purchases. One common argument for exempting food is the relatively heavier burden it places on lower-income families. The federally mandated food exemption on food stamp and WIC purchases reduces this regressivity of the sales tax on food. The amount of food purchases exempt will differ across states. In West Virginia, for example, approximately one of every eight dollars spent on food groceries is exempt from the state sales tax (which taxes food purchases) because of this federally mandated exemption. See *West Virginia Tax Expenditure Study: Expenditures for Consumer Sales Tax and Use Tax* (West Virginia Department of Tax and Revenue, January 1995), 121.

Chapter 8

Is There a Trade-Off between Variability and Growth in State Government Tax Bases?

The previous chapter showed that for most of the states currently without either a personal income tax or a retail sales tax, the addition of the other tax might increase the long-run growth potential of tax revenues but might decrease the cyclical stability of revenues. Additionally, it was found that retail sales taxes that exempt food are generally more variable over the business cycle, but that they have higher long-run growth. These facts might suggest that there is a trade-off between growth and variability in state taxes. That is, if a state wishes to lower the cyclical variability of its tax revenues, it must also suffer reduced long-run growth potential. Beginning with Groves and Kahn,[1] the single estimate of income elasticity (the OLS long-run elasticity) presented in Chapter 5 was used as both a measure of long-run growth potential and cyclical variability. Following this logic, there is an assumed trade-off between growth and stability in tax bases, with more income-elastic bases necessarily growing faster and being less stable over the business cycle. Although some authors have questioned whether this trade-off automatically exists, it is often accepted in the literature without much question.[2] The technical analysis done in Chapter 5 showed that, in fact, the Groves and Kahn type of estimate provides information about only the long-run growth potential of a tax, and does not measure cyclical variability. Additionally, the standard estimate is subject to biases (that can be corrected using DOLS), which might make the standard estimate a poor measure of even long-run growth. Because cyclical variability and long-run growth can be measured separately using the techniques presented in this book, the existence of this trade-off demands further exploration. If the long- and short-run elasticities were perfectly correlated, then there would be no reason to question the trade-off (and no reason to provide separate estimates). The results in the earlier chapters showed, however, that these estimates are not perfectly correlated. This chapter brings together the results from previous chapters and provides new evidence on whether there is at least a strong positive correlation between the short- and long-run elasticity estimates. If a strong positive correlation is found, this suggests that states may have to sacrifice long-run growth to obtain more stable revenues. If there is a zero correlation, it suggests that states may gain cyclical stability without changing long-run growth, and finally, if there is a negative correlation, it suggests that states may simultaneously increase cyclical stability and long-run growth.

It is important to distinguish between a trade-off between taxes and a trade-off between states. For example, it may be the case that states that have higher long-run growth also have higher cyclical variability, but this does not necessarily mean that for any given state there is a trade-off between specific taxes. It could still remain the case that a given state could reduce revenue variability without sacrificing long-run growth. This means that results obtained from a cross section of states do not necessarily hold for a particular state. Also, it is important to distinguish between tax base trade-offs and tax revenue trade-offs. It may be the case that evidence from tax bases and evidence from tax revenues provide different results. As was shown in the previous chapter, estimates for tax revenues include the impact of state tax policy, which was shown to have a significant effect on the elasticity estimates, especially for long-run growth.

CROSS-SECTIONAL TRADE-OFFS AMONG THE STATES

Chapter 6 provided several estimates of the long- and short-run elasticities of state revenues. For both state general revenue and state tax revenue, elasticity estimates were obtained with respect to both GDP and state personal income. This section uses these results to explore whether a trade-off between growth and variability exists when looking across the fifty states in a cross-sectional manner. The question to be addressed is whether states with higher long-run growth potentials have higher short-run cyclical variability. Figure 8.1 shows a scatter plot of the states using the DOLS estimates of long-run elasticity and the error correction model estimates of short-run elasticity for state general revenue with respect to the national economy, GDP.

A quick glance at Figure 8.1 seems to suggest a positive correlation between long-run and short-run elasticities across the states. States such as Maine, New York, Massachusetts, New Jersey, and Connecticut have more long-run growth, but also higher cyclical variability in their revenues than do states such as New Mexico, Texas, Louisiana, West Virginia, and Oklahoma. This apparent trade-off does not hold rigidly, as some states such as Wyoming and Iowa have more long-run growth but *lower* cyclical variability than states such as Utah, Pennsylvania, and Arizona. Indeed, regressing the long-run elasticity against the short-run elasticity using the same data plotted in Figure 8.1 yields a *t*-statistic of 1.06, suggesting that the apparent positive correlation suggested in Figure 8.1 is not statistically significant.

Figure 8.2 shows the same scatter plot for states using the general revenue elasticity estimates done using state personal income. The positive correlation does

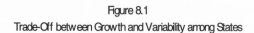

Figure 8.1
Trade-Off between Growth and Variability among States

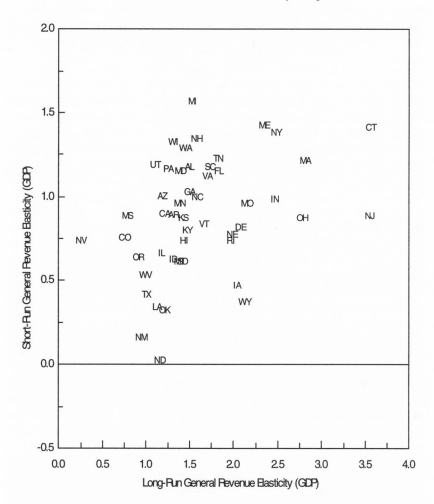

not appear as strong when using state income as it did when national income was used. Regressing the variables in this figure yields a *t*-value of 0.43, so there is no statistically significant relationship. Nonetheless, some individual examples of the cross-state trade-off can be found, as states such as Connecticut, New Jersey, and Kentucky have higher long-run growth and also higher cyclical variability than states such as Louisiana, Arizona, Colorado, and South Dakota. In the opposite direction, some states, such as Montana, Nebraska, and North Dakota, have higher long-run growth but less cyclical variability than states such as Florida, Virginia, and Pennsylvania.

Figures 8.1 and 8.2 show the elasticity estimates for state general revenues. Figures 8.3 and 8.4 show the corresponding plots of the estimates for state tax

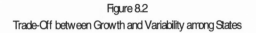

Figure 8.2
Trade-Off between Growth and Variability among States

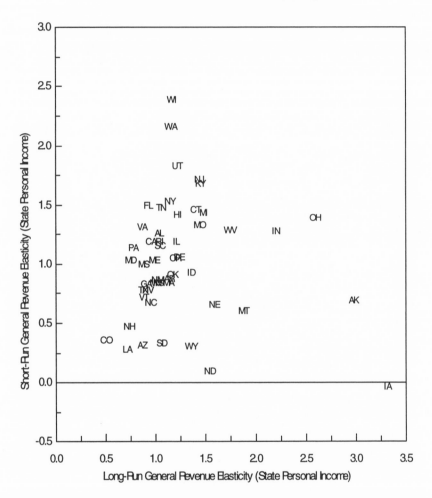

revenues done using both GDP and state personal income. These two figures tell much the same story as the first two figures. There again appears to be some positive correlation between short- and long-run estimates across the states, with the correlation being stronger for the GDP estimates than for the state personal income estimates. Again there are examples where state comparisons show trade-offs and other examples where there is not a trade-off. Regressing the variables in Figure 8.3 yields a *t*-statistic of 7.03, which indicates that there is a strong statistical relationship between the short-run and long-run tax revenue elasticities with respect to GDP. Regressing the data in Figure 8.4 produces a *t*-statistic of 1.26, which is not statistically significant at normally accepted levels.

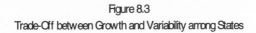

Figure 8.3
Trade-Off between Growth and Variability among States

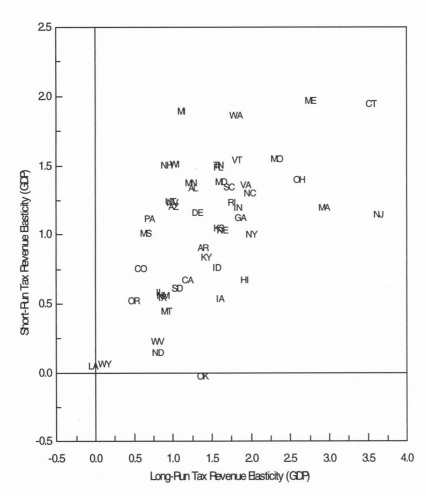

Taken as a whole, Figures 8.1 through 8.4 suggest that if states that exhibit higher long-run tax base or tax revenue growth also exhibit greater short-run variability in their tax revenues, the relationship is weak at best. For purposes of designing individual state policy, however, a cross-sectional analysis of states does not provide sufficient information. The issue of importance is not how states compare with each other, but whether a specific state must reduce its long-run growth potential to achieve more cyclical stability. The cross-state comparisons do not directly shed light on this issue. For example, returning to Figure 8.4, Ohio has both more long-run growth and more cyclical variability in its tax revenues than does Texas. Suppose that in an effort to reduce its cyclical variability Ohio changed its tax structure to exactly mirror the tax structure of Texas. Would this change

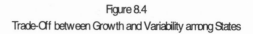

Figure 8.4
Trade-Off between Growth and Variability among States

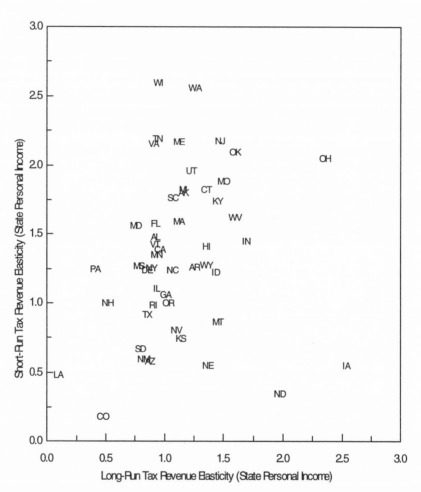

necessarily result in a decrease in Ohio's cyclical variability and its long-run growth? Working in the other direction, suppose Texas changed its tax structure to mirror the tax structure of Ohio. Would this change necessarily result in Texas having more long-run growth and more cyclical variability? The answers to these questions are not clear. The answer lies in what factors make Ohio have more growth and more variability than Texas. If it was solely the difference in tax structures, the answer to the above questions would be yes, but if the reason the states have differing growth and variability in their taxes lies in other non-tax-related reasons, the answer may be no. Perhaps the structure of the Texas economy makes them have the revenue pattern they do. If so, then if Texas were to change its tax structure to mirror that of Ohio, Texas might gain long-run growth but also lower its cyclical variability. Similarly, if Ohio were to change its tax structure to mirror that of Texas, Ohio might lower its long-run growth but also gain cyclical variability.

Figure 8.5 shows the hypothetical possibility that tax structure changes might move states diagonally in the figure from upper left to lower right, implying that there is no trade-off for a particular state. Rather, because of their state economies, some states naturally tend to have more stability and higher tax base growth than others. Using the example illustrated in Figure 8.5, if Texas and Ohio were to adopt similar tax structures, moving them along the dashed lines from TX to [TX] and OH to [OH], the apparent trade-off that appears in the cross-sectional data does not in fact exist for a particular state. Alternatively, it might be the case that a state has

Figure 8.5

Trade-Off between Growth and Variability among States

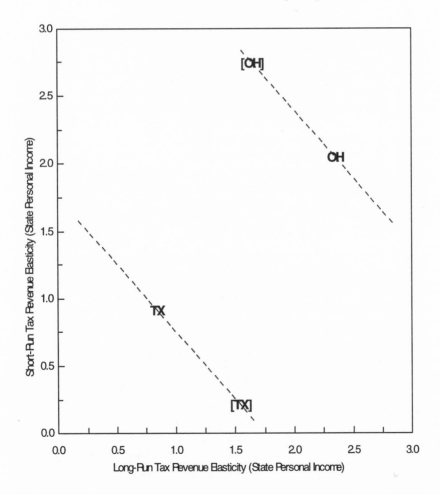

no control over its short-run variability and that tax structure changes affect only long-run growth. If this were the case, the diagonal lines would be horizontal and again the apparent cross-sectional trade-off would not apply to particular states. The trade-off between growth and variability is an important issue in state tax policy only if it applies to each individual state.

TRADE-OFFS IN TAX BASES VERSUS TAX REVENUES

Because cross-state comparisons cannot be used to generate any firm conclusions about the existence of a trade-off between growth and variability, this section attempts to address the issue more directly by looking at the growth and variability of particular tax sources when they are aggregated to the national level. This provides information that abstracts from any peculiarities of particular states. Figure 8.6 shows a plot of the long-run growth potential estimates and the short-run

Figure 8.6
Trade-Off between Growth and Variability in Tax Bases

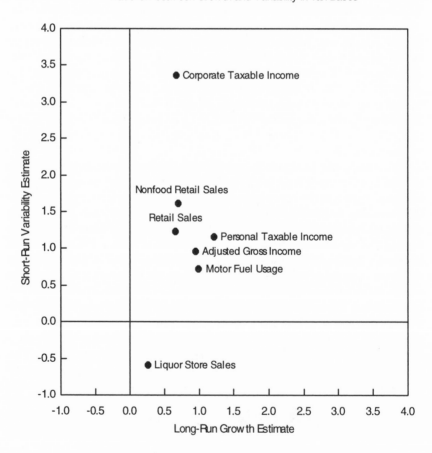

cyclical variability estimates for all major tax bases using the final results from Chapter 5. Figure 8.7 shows a similar plot for the same estimates done using actual tax revenues, instead of tax bases, aggregated across all states.

The plot in Figure 8.6 suggests that the trade-off between growth and cyclical variability is not very strong among state tax bases. A regression run on the two variables in Figure 8.6 produces a *t*-statistic of 0.54, showing that there is not a statistically significant relationship among all of the tax bases shown in the figure. Although there is a trade-off between some taxes, there is no trade-off between others. For example, nonfood retail sales have higher long-run growth but also more cyclical variability than all retail sales, suggesting a trade-off. On the other hand, personal income taxes are both faster growing and more stable than corporate income taxes, suggesting no trade-off. Additionally, personal income taxes (by either tax base measure) are both more stable and faster growing than retail sales taxes that exempt food.

The data in Figure 8.6 suggest that it might be possible for a state to reduce revenue variability without sacrificing long-run growth. Less reliance on corporation income taxes relative to personal income taxes and the removal of the food exemption on retail sales for those states that currently do not tax food are the most obvious ways that states can simultaneously reduce revenue variability and gain long-run growth. Most of the taxes in Figure 8.6 are close together with regard to both variability and growth, with the two longest outliers being liquor store sales and corporate taxable income. Both have slightly slower than average growth, but liquor store sales are slightly countercyclical, implying that liquor taxes can actually be stabilizing, whereas corporate taxable income is much more cyclically variable than other tax bases, suggesting that relying on corporate taxable income as a tax base will produce no more growth than other bases, but much more variability over the business cycle.

The data plotted in Figure 8.7 are the same estimates done at an aggregated national level for actual tax revenues, rather than tax bases. Interestingly, the trade-offs appear stronger in tax revenues than in tax bases. Motor fuels taxes are both faster growing and more variable than alcohol and tobacco taxes, the corporate income tax is both faster growing and more variable than the motor fuels tax, and the personal income tax is both faster growing and less stable than the corporate income tax (and retail sales tax). The only place where a trade-off does not appear is for the retail sales tax, which dominates both the motor fuels and corporate income taxes, because it grows faster and has less cyclical variability.

The data in Figure 8.7 seem to suggest that there are trade-offs in state revenues, whereas the data in Figure 8.6 seem to suggest that the trade-offs do not exist among the actual state tax bases. The *t*-statistic for a regression using the data in Figure 8.7 is 1.89, which is significant at better than the 10 percent level. This implies that state tax policy (which is included in the revenue data) acts to increase the appearance of a trade-off between growth and variability. A reason for this phenomenon may be that states are likely to increase the tax rate on a cyclically variable tax base during a recession. For a cyclically variable tax base, revenues fall off by more during a recession, perhaps inducing the state to increase the tax

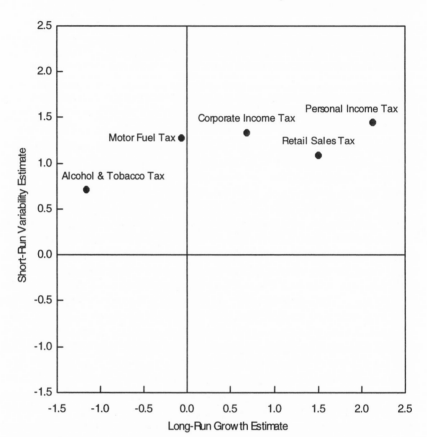

Figure 8.7

Trade-Off between Growth and Variability in Tax Revenues

rate on this base. After coming out of the recession the revenues from this tax are higher than before the recession because it is now taxed at a higher rate. This ratcheting up in tax rates on cyclically variable tax bases could produce a situation where the trade-off appears stronger in tax revenue data than in tax base data. Unfortunately, it implies that over time states end up relying more heavily on the most cyclically variable tax bases, making each recession even more damaging to the state revenue stream than the last recession.

When looking at the data on cyclical variability of actual tax revenues, as plotted in Figure 8.7, one must be struck by the fact that revenue growth varies quite a bit among different tax bases, but the cyclical variabilities among tax sources are not very different. This contrasts with the findings on tax bases pictured in Figure 8.6, which showed more variation in the cyclical variability of the tax relative to the long-run growth of the tax base. The main reason for differences in the variation in revenue growth (as opposed to base growth) has been changes in tax rates. In particular, note that the two taxes with the slowest long-run growth in revenues shown in Figure 8.7 are on motor fuels and alcohol and tobacco. These taxes tend to be formulated as a fixed amount per unit (per gallon, per pack, etc.), and so do not automatically adjust for inflation, whereas income and sales tax revenues do automatically rise when income and sales rise due to inflation. Thus, differences in revenue-generating potential—as opposed to actual revenues raised—are overstated in Figure 8.7.

WITHIN-STATE TRADE-OFFS BETWEEN SALES AND INCOME TAXES

The previous section has found that when tax base data are aggregated to the national level, the existence of a trade-off across all tax bases is questionable at best. It does appear to exist, however, for a few specific taxes. The personal income tax base, for example, was both more stable and faster growing than retail sales taxes that exempt food. This section explores whether this conclusion holds for all states equally. This analysis can be done using the estimates from Chapter 7 of the state-level growth and variability estimates for income and sales taxes. The estimates in Chapter 7 were performed for both state tax revenues and state tax bases. Given the bias found in the previous section that was introduced by looking at revenues rather than tax bases, this section looks at the estimates done for the state tax bases. The important issue to be addressed is whether this trade-off exists at the individual state level between sales and income taxes.

Figure 8.8 shows a plot of the difference between the long- and short-run elasticity estimates when comparing state income and sales taxes that include food in the sales tax base. This subtraction of the estimates of sales tax elasticities from income tax elasticities helps illustrate the possible existence of a trade-off because it allows the upper right and lower left quadrants of the graph to represent cases where a trade-off does exist, whereas the lower right and upper left quadrants represent cases where a trade-off does not exist. If a state does have a trade-off because its personal income tax base has both a higher long-run growth rate and a higher cyclical variability than its retail sales tax base (including food), the state's observation will lie in the upper right quadrant of the graph. The alternative trade-off exists when the retail sales tax base has both a higher long-run growth rate and a higher cyclical variability than its personal income tax base, and results in an observation in the lower left quadrant of the graph. Thus, the upper right and lower left quadrants denote a trade-off between growth and variability between the sales and income taxes in the state. If one of the tax bases has higher long-run growth but lower short-run variability, suggesting no trade-off, the observation will lie in either the upper left or lower right quadrants.

In Figure 8.8 a total of thirty-three states lie in the two trade-off quadrants. Of these, thirty lie in the upper right quadrant suggesting that the state's income tax base has both more growth and more variability than its retail sales tax base including food. Only three states have the opposite tradeoff where the sales tax

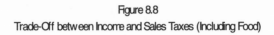

Figure 8.8
Trade-Off between Income and Sales Taxes (Including Food)

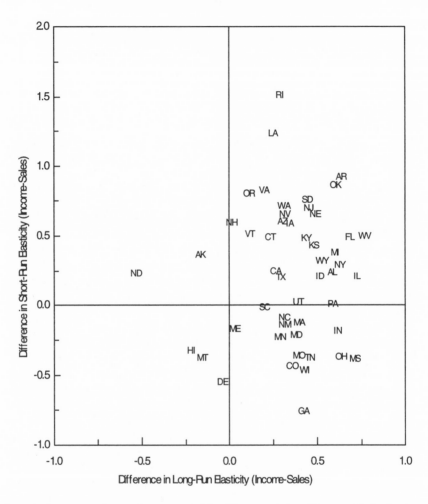

base is faster growing and more variable. The remaining 17 states lie in the two quadrants denoting no trade-off because the tax that is the fastest growing also has the least cyclical variability. For fifteen of these seventeen states, it is the income tax that has the higher growth and less variability. Figure 8.9 shows a similar comparison done between the personal income tax base and the retail sales tax base, but this time using the estimates for the retail sales tax base when the state exempts food from the retail sales tax.

The number of states with a trade-off is now twenty-seven, less than in the previous figure. For twenty-three of the twenty-seven trade-off states, it is the income tax that exhibits more growth but also more variability. For the remaining twenty-three states in which no trade-off exists, the majority (nineteen) have income

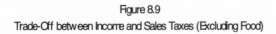

Figure 8.9
Trade-Off between Income and Sales Taxes (Excluding Food)

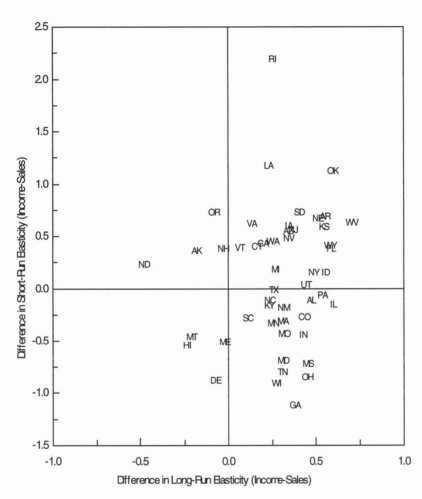

tax bases that grow faster and exhibit less variability than the sales tax bases exempting food. Figures 8.8 and 8.9 firmly show that although a trade-off between these two tax sources does exist for some states, it does not exist for all states. In other words, shifting reliance from the sales to the income tax would result in higher growth for the vast majority of states, but some states would experience declines in cyclical variability, whereas others would experience increases in cyclical variability. The presence of a trade-off between growth and variability cannot be accepted as a rule applicable to all states and all tax bases, nor as a uniform guide to state tax policy across all fifty states. This trade-off is present in some states and between some tax bases, but not across all states and not across all tax bases.

Figure 8.10 shows a similar plot of the trade-off between state retail sales tax bases when it includes food and when it exempts food. For forty of the fifty states, there does appear to be a trade-off in the case of the food exemption in the retail sales tax base. For thirty-five of these forty trade-off states, the retail sales tax base exempting food is both more cyclically variable and faster growing than the retail sales tax base when it includes food. For most of the ten states where there is no trade-off, the observations are borderline, with the two bases having almost a zero difference in at least one of the elasticity estimates. This trade-off that exists between retail sales tax bases that include food with those that exclude food is

Figure 8.10
Trade-Off between Sales Tax Including and Excluding Food

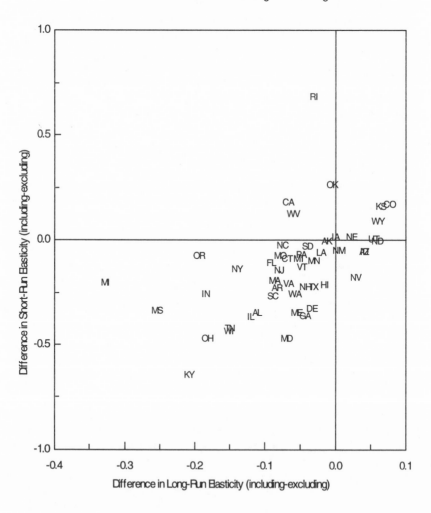

perhaps the only trade-off strong enough to be relied on by all states as a guide to tax policy.

CONCLUSION

The conventional wisdom is that there is a trade-off between variability and growth in state government tax bases. The conventional wisdom has its origin in the idea that greater income elasticity of a revenue source will make it more variable and will make it grow faster over time. The evidence presented here casts doubt on this conventional wisdom. The presence of consistent tradeoffs appears to exist when looking at tax revenues, but disappears when looking at tax bases and when looking at individual states. The fact that the trade-off appears to exist more strongly when looking at revenues, rather than bases, suggests that state tax policy acts to increase the appearance of a tradeoff that indeed does not inherently exist among the tax bases. The evidence in this chapter suggests that the presumed tradeoff between growth and variability cannot be used as a blanket guide to state tax policy across all tax bases and across all states. Only in one particular case, the food exemption from the retail sales tax base, does this tradeoff appear to be strong enough to be used as a guide to policy.

NOTES

1.   Harold M. Groves and C. Harry Kahn, "The Stability of State and Local Tax Yields," *American Economic Reveiw* 42, no. 1 (March 1952): 87–102.

2.   This is mentioned not only in the papers that estimate the elasticities, but also in papers about state fiscal crises. See, for example, Steven D. Gold, "Changes in State Government Finances in the 1980s," *National Tax Journal* 44, no. 1 (March 1991): 1–19, and Richard H. Mattoon and William A. Testa, "State and Local Governments' Reaction to Recession," *Economic Perspectives* 16, no. 2 (March/April 1992): 19–27. (Federal Reserve Bank of Chicago)

Chapter 9

The Role of Rainy Day Funds in Easing State Fiscal Crises

The primary cause of state fiscal crises is the cyclical variability of state government revenues. State revenues tend to be procyclic, whereas the demand for state expenditures tends to be countercyclic, so during recessions, states find themselves experiencing fiscal crises because revenues are insufficient to meet expenditure demands. Faced with fiscal crises, in the short run, states are pressured to reduce expenditures and increase taxes.[1] In addition, states may use temporary measures such as accelerating tax collections and deferring expenditures, as well as bending accounting practices.[2] Over the longer run, states might try to reduce their susceptibility to fiscal crises by relying on less cyclically variable tax bases, but the analysis of the previous chapters has shown that this is not a very promising route. As an alternative, states can smooth expenditures over the business cycle by creating and saving budget surpluses in boom years to finance expenditures during lean years. After the fiscal crises that states experienced during the 1980–1982 recession, many states responded by creating rainy day, or budget stabilization, funds specifically for this purpose. Currently, over three quarters of the states have some type of rainy day fund. This chapter examines the degree to which these rainy day funds eased the fiscal stress experienced by states during the 1990–1991 recession, and so provides an indication of the potential for rainy day funds to mitigate state fiscal crises.

Because most state governments face balanced budget constraints, budget stabilization funds and general fund surpluses are useful tools for smoothing state expenditures due to temporary fluctuations in tax revenues. The chapter examines states' actual reliance on tax increases, general fund surpluses, and rainy day funds to maintain expenditures during the declines in revenues suffered by states during the past three recessions. A measure of state fiscal stress during the 1990–1991 recession is developed, and a regression analysis is performed to see whether the presence of an explicit state rainy day fund had a significant impact in lessening state fiscal stress, and whether the impact differed depending on the specific provisions of the state rainy day fund.

STATE FISCAL POLICY AND THE ROLE OF BUDGET STABILIZATION FUNDS

In the analysis that follows, a state fiscal policy of neutrality over the business cycle is used as a benchmark for evaluating the use of budget stabilization funds.[3] Under a policy of neutrality, states do not change their tax structures over the business cycle, so revenues move procyclically, and state expenditures grow at a constant rate through the business cycle. If states are constrained against deficit finance (as most are), a policy of neutrality would require building up surplus funds during the good years and using those funds during recessions.[4] The reason states desire rainy day funds is to mitigate against the impacts of recessions that require states to reduce their expenditure growth or raise taxes, so the benchmark of neutrality makes sense as a measure of the effectiveness of rainy day funds. The use of fiscal neutrality as a benchmark does not constitute a policy recommendation, however. States may want to slow expenditure growth or increase taxes to some degree during a recession. Although no stand is taken on the desirability of fiscal neutrality as a policy goal, it is a good benchmark to measure the performance of a rainy day fund, because the purpose of a rainy day fund is to reduce the need for tax increases and expenditure cuts.

Unlike the federal government, states are faced with constraints that limit their ability to finance temporary revenue fluctuations with budget deficits and surpluses. Only one state, Vermont, is completely free of balanced budget requirements.[5] There are also ten states that allowed to carry over a deficit, but of these ten, two are allowed to carry this deficit over for only one year, and a third can carry over only unanticipated deficits. Fortunately, the majority of these state balanced budget requirements are stock, rather than flow, in nature.[6] This means that most states are allowed to spend more than they collect in tax revenues in a given year as long as they have surplus balances accumulated in prior years to cover the deficit. Because of these constraints, states have adopted the policy of building up budget surpluses during the boom years to help mitigate the fiscal problems associated with recessions.

From a practical standpoint, for most states it does not matter whether these surplus balances are kept in rainy day funds, or just maintained as excess general fund balances. For the few states whose balanced budget requirements are flow in nature, such as Michigan, the setting up of a rainy day fund is the only way to circumvent the balanced budget constraint.[7] As of fiscal year 1994, forty-four states had some type of rainy day fund, with almost three quarters of these being established after the state fiscal crises experienced during the 1980–1982 recession.[8] Table 9.1 shows the number of states with rainy day funds between fiscal years 1982 and 1994.

Table 9.1
Number of States with Rainy Day Funds, Fiscal Years 1982–1994

Fiscal Year	Number of States with Rainy Day Funds
1982	12
1983	19
1984	23
1985	25
1986	28
1987	35
1988	35
1989	38
1990	38
1991	39
1992	43
1993	44
1994	44

Although many states could just rely on their surplus general fund balances, there are several reasons why establishing a rainy day fund may be preferable.[9] Unlike general fund balances, rainy day funds often have specific provisions for saving and withdrawing funds, which prevents legislators from giving in to special interest demands to spend all of their revenues during boom years. Additionally, some tax and expenditure caps enacted during the tax revolt of the late 1970s and early 1980s contain provisions requiring state legislatures to at least partially refund tax revenues in excess of expenditures. As Gold points out, California's large surplus was an important factor in generating support for Proposition 13 reforms.[10] A properly structured rainy day fund can provide a vehicle for saving during boom years to help cover revenue shortfalls during recessions.

The cyclical nature of revenues, however, is not the only reason why a state may wish to establish a rainy day fund. Some rainy day funds are structured so that they allow states to use them in cases of unanticipated revenue shortfalls, such as could happen with a bad revenue forecast, or in case of federal tax changes that may adversely affect state revenues.[11] The use of these funds in case of adverse effects from federal tax law changes is specifically mentioned in the rules governing Virginia's rainy day fund. A substantial literature discusses the impact of the federal Tax Reform Act of 1986 on state tax revenues.[12] Although the 1986 reform created a windfall gain for most states, the possibility of a change that adversely affects state revenue is always present.

The majority of state rainy day funds require only regular legislative approval for the funds to be used, which allows states to cover unanticipated revenue shortfalls, but has the drawback of not providing very stringent controls to ensure that funds are left untouched until they are really needed. Some states have created rainy day funds without requiring that money be deposited in them, so the funds may have little or no money in them when a revenue downturn arrives. The current provisions and purposes of state rainy day funds differ substantially across states, so specific provisions may influence how effective rainy day funds are at mitigating the effects of revenue downturns. The effectiveness of rainy day funds is examined after first looking at the fiscal stress that rainy day funds are intended to reduce.

THE IMPACT OF RECESSIONS ON STATE FINANCES

Rainy day funds are set aside to lessen the degree to which states will have to reduce expenditure growth or raise taxes to cope with a recession. This section of the chapter looks at data from the last three recessions to see how recessions have affected the taxes and expenditures of states. The contractionary stages of these three recessions, from peak to trough, are November 1973 to March 1975, January 1980 to July 1980, July 1981 to November 1982, and July 1990 to March 1991. Because the actual period of interest also includes the part of the expansionary phase when growth is still below average, the above listed periods do not perfectly correspond to periods of recessionary impact, but rather provide a basis for identifying years within which states might have been experiencing recession-induced fiscal stress.[13]

For expositional purposes, the recessions will be considered to be the fiscal years of 1974–1975, 1980–1983, and 1990–1991. Table 9.2 contains the annual

Table 9.2
Revenues, Expenditures, and Tax Changes during Recessions

Fiscal Year	Percentage Change in Real General Expenditures	Percentage Change in Real Tax Revenue	Tax Increases as a Percent of Taxes	Adjusted Growth Rate of Real Tax Revenues
1974	-0.2%	-1.8%	0.5%	-2.3%
1975	5.7%	-0.9%	2.0%	-2.9%
1980	0.3%	-3.3%	0.3%	-3.6%
1981	0.8%	-1.0%	2.5%	-3.5%
1982	0.1%	2.3%	1.8%	0.5%
1983	2.5%	2.1%	4.5%	-2.4%
1990	2.7%	0.4%	1.2%	-0.8%
1991	4.8%	-0.8%	3.0%	-3.8%
1992	7.1%	2.5%	6.5%	-4.0%
Average during recessions	2.6%	-0.1%	2.5%	-2.5%
Average 1980–1992	3.6%	3.0%	1.5%	1.5%

real percentage growth in state general expenditures and tax revenues, discretionary tax increases (either base broadening or rate changes) as a percentage of the previous fiscal year's tax revenues, and the adjusted growth in real tax revenues (taking out the revenue raised from discretionary tax increases) during the three recessionary periods listed above for all fifty states combined.[14]

From Table 9.2, it appears that state expenditure growth fared much better during the recession of 1990–1991 than it did during the other two recessions, falling below the 1980–1992 average only in 1990. The adjusted growth of tax revenues, which subtracts discretionary tax increases out of revenues, was impacted about as severely during the 1990-1991 recession as during the 1980-1982 recession, and worse in 1990–1991 than during the 1974–1975 recession.[15] The legislated tax increases, including both tax rate changes and base broadening, were more heavily relied on during the 1990–1991 recession, however. During fiscal year 1992 alone, states legislated about $20 billion in new taxes, the largest single year increase during any of the recessionary years considered here. Even though most states had saved relatively large surpluses during the 1980s, and most states had some type of rainy day fund by the 1990 downturn, tax increases were still relied upon to a great extent to compensate for revenue shortfalls. Additional data showing states' reliance on tax increases and stored surplus funds during and in the years before and after the 1990–1991 recession are given in Table 9.3.[16]

Table 9.3
Reliance on Tax Increases, Rainy Day Funds, and Other Balances during the 1989–1993 Period

Fiscal Year	Tax Increases	Change in Total Balances	Change in Rainy Day Fund Balances	Change in Other Fund Balances
1988	$ 892	$ 10690	$ 3364	$ 7326
1989	891	4547	592	3955
1990	3528	-2368	-35	-2332
1991	8880	-4803	-725	-4078
1992	20081	-1652	-326	-1326
1993	4061	8896	222	8674

Notes: All figures in millions of dollars. Change in total balances equals the sum of the change in rainy day fund balances plus the change in other fund balances. A negative entry indicates a net dissaving from fund balances.

Table 9.3 shows that during fiscal years 1988 and 1989 states not only increased taxes, but also increased the size of their rainy day and surplus general revenue funds. The savings channeled into general revenue surpluses during these two fiscal years were almost three times larger than the savings to rainy day funds. The tax increases during fiscal years 1988 and 1989 were used to build savings, rather than expand current expenditures, as Table 9.3 shows. During both years, saving was greater than the amount of revenue derived from discretionary tax increases. Beginning in 1990, the behavior of states changed drastically, with surplus balances being drawn down each year throughout the recession. During 1990, 1991, and 1992 states increased their reliance on tax increases to fund expenditures. During 1990 and 1991 alone, states raised almost $29 billion in new taxes. During 1990, states relied more heavily on previously saved general revenues, but with these balances running short, states turned to their rainy day funds in 1991.

The maximum reliance on rainy day funds was in 1991 when they were depleted by $725 million. There were thirty-eight states that had some type of rainy day fund in 1989 heading into the recession but only twenty-nine of them had positive balances. By the end of fiscal year 1991, eight of the states with positive balances in 1989 had completely depleted their rainy day funds, and another four had negligible balances. Of the forty-seven states with positive other balances in 1989, only thirty-six still had money remaining at the end of 1991. Five of the ten states that are allowed to carry over a deficit did so in either 1990 or 1991. In the latter half of fiscal 1991 and throughout fiscal 1992, with rainy day funds and other surpluses running low, states turned used tax increases to finance their expenditures.[17] When recessionary pressures eased in 1993, states still increased taxes but used this money to build back up their rainy day fund and other fund balances. Again, states placed more savings into other fund balances than into their rainy day fund balances.

The major tax increases instituted in fiscal 1991 and 1992 show that state rainy day funds and other surplus balances were insufficient to maintain state expenditures during this recession. The following section of this chapter calculates a measure of the degree of fiscal stress experienced by each state during the 1990–1991 recession. These results are then used to empirically investigate the impact of explicit state rainy day funds in easing state fiscal stress.

MEASURING STATE FISCAL STRESS DURING THE 1990–1991 RECESSION

The purpose of a rainy day fund is to help a state maintain its expenditure growth while reducing its need to raise taxes during a recession. Thus, a natural measure of fiscal stress for purposes of analyzing rainy day funds is the amount of discretionary tax increases plus the amount that expenditures were reduced from their long-run trend growth during a recession. Using this measure, a state that could maintain its long-run growth rate of expenditures without discretionary tax increases would have no fiscal stress. This measure of fiscal stress is used as a benchmark for analyzing the effectiveness of rainy day funds, but it is not intended to be a policy recommendation. States might desire to cut back on expenditures to some degree, or raise taxes, during recessions, for example. This measure is natural for the present purpose, however, because rainy day funds are intended to help states maintain their expenditures and reduce the pressures for increased taxes, which is exactly what is captured by this measure of fiscal stress.

Table 9.4 shows the amount of fiscal stress for each state between 1989 and 1992. The columns labeled expenditure shortfall (Exp. Short.) show the dollar amount by which each state's expenditures were below their real trend growth rate in that fiscal year.[18] A 0 in this column means that a state's expenditure growth was either equal to or above its real trend growth. The columns labeled tax increases (Tax Incr.) show the amount of legislated tax increases by fiscal year. These tax increase columns are cumulative, because an increase in the sales tax rate in 1990, for example, would be paid by citizens not only during the year in which it was implemented, but also during the subsequent years of 1991 and 1992. The final column of the table shows the total amount of tax increases and lower than average expenditure growth for each state as a percent of state general expenditures in 1988.

The numbers given in the final column of the table represent a measure of the degree of fiscal stress experienced by the state during the 1990–1991 recession, including fiscal years 1989 and 1992 when states also experienced below-average growth. Because the primary alternative to tax increases and expenditure reductions is to use previously accumulated surplus balances, these numbers also correspond to the amount by which surplus balances were insufficient to alleviate the fiscal stress of the recession. To see that accumulated balances can alleviate fiscal stress, look at Kansas, which has zeroes all the way across the Table. This means that Kansas had no tax increases, nor did its rate of expenditure growth ever fall below its 1984–1992 trend growth rate. Kansas did, however, draw down $230 million in previously accumulated fund balances to prevent fiscal stress, and enacted tax increases to take effect in 1993, a year beyond the data shown in the table.

In the total row, the total as a percentage of 1988 budget is the total fiscal stress divided by the total of all state 1988 budgets. The 1988 budget is used because that is the year in which states would have had to have accumulated surplus funds to carry them through the next four lean years. If states had tax cuts or above-average expenditure increases, they received zeroes in the table. If these funds had been entered as negative numbers in the table instead of zeroes, the total would have been $57,359.5 million, which is shown as the pooled total. This is only 13.27 percent of the 1988 budget, or less than half the 29.31 percent total that results from not pooling states with positive and negative fiscal stress.

The 29.31 percent total might be thought of as gross fiscal stress, which is the total fiscal stress felt by those states that were negatively impacted. If this gross fiscal stress were offset by the above-average expenditure growth that some states had in some years, the resulting 13.27 percent total could be thought of as net fiscal stress. This suggests that states could benefit from pooling their financial risks from recessions, a concept that is discussed further below. Given that many states created rainy day funds to reduce the impact of recessions after suffering through 1980–1982 recession, the next section of this chapter examines whether states that had rainy day funds in 1989 were more likely to have less fiscal stress, and whether the specific deposit and withdrawal provisions for these funds made a difference.

Table 9.4

Expenditure Shortfalls and Tax Increases during the 1990–1991 Recession (Dollar Figures in Millions of Current Dollars)

State	Fiscal Year 1989		Fiscal Year 1990		Fiscal Year 1991		Fiscal Year 1992		Total Fiscal Stress	Percentage of 1988 Budget
	Exp. Short	Tax Incr.	Exp. Short	Tax Incr.	Exp. Short	Tax Incr.	Exp. Short	Tax Incr.		
Alabama	48.0	0.0	0.0	0.0	0.0	34.2	0.0	206.2	288.4	4.58%
Alaska	185.9	0.0	487.8	242.0	762.2	242.0	935.3	243.0	3098.3	80.06%
Arizona	0.0	190.0	0.0	282.0	1248.9	497.0	951.6	506.1	3675.6	64.27%
Arkansas	65.2	0.0	91.4	9.0	89.2	37.7	0.0	302.4	594.9	18.04%
California	842.9	0.0	2845.9	0.0	5098.3	654.0	3580.9	7047.0	20069.0	33.63%
Colorado	193.3	0.0	102.9	71.0	62.5	71.0	36.9	117.7	655.2	13.40%
Connecticut	0.0	81.0	330.8	883.0	435.9	893.0	1307.2	1959.5	5890.5	85.47%
Delaware	9.2	0.0	13.2	0.0	48.3	9.2	144.2	83.6	307.7	18.73%
Florida	83.2	0.0	929.4	50.0	378.5	1135.4	1672.1	1186.5	5435.1	32.10%
Georgia	0.0	91.0	0.0	778.0	124.9	778.0	575.7	778.0	3125.6	34.31%
Hawaii	0.0	0.0	0.0	0.0	0.0	0.0	0.0	0.0	0.0	0.00%
Idaho	0.0	13.0	0.0	10.0	0.0	13.0	0.0	26.2	62.2	4.16%
Illinois	369.1	18.0	540.7	1096.0	22.9	1096.0	5.2	1828.0	4976.0	28.51%
Indiana	31.1	46.0	248.4	46.0	246.9	0.0	452.6	2.7	1073.8	12.78%
Iowa	0.0	59.0	67.3	52.0	55.6	46.3	121.2	49.4	450.8	9.06%
Kansas	0.0	0.0	0.0	0.0	0.0	0.0	0.0	0.0	0.0	0.00%
Kentucky	101.0	53.0	480.0	61.0	0.0	645.8	0.0	926.5	2267.3	35.69%
Louisiana	49.7	320.0	0.0	254.0	0.0	359.8	0.0	662.8	1646.3	22.57%
Maine	0.0	30.4	105.7	20.4	26.1	6.6	149.5	272.6	611.3	27.29%
Maryland	90.1	0.0	0.0	0.0	0.0	0.0	416.2	83.2	589.6	7.03%
Mass.	0.0	115.0	694.1	609.0	1083.0	1765.6	3063.5	3228.5	10558.8	74.06%
Michigan	773.8	0.0	1447.4	10.0	1717.9	39.0	1919.9	19.0	5927.0	32.80%
Minnesota	0.0	0.0	303.0	0.0	0.0	0.0	256.1	285.4	844.62	9.56%
Mississippi	0.0	0.0	93.7	17.0	148.1	17.0	0.0	17.0	292.8	7.78%
Missouri	388.1	11.0	684.1	110.0	687.0	110.0	390.9	264.1	2645.3	38.29%

Montana	0.0	0.0	87.3	19.0	0.0	18.0	92.9	13.3	230.5	16.20%
Nebraska	0.0	0.0	0.0	5.0	0.0	195.5	0.0	250.5	451.0	19.83%
Nevada	39.3	0.0	0.0	54.0	68.8	54.0	0.0	193.2	409.3	21.85%
N.H.	0.0	0.0	143.9	29.5	282.1	88.1	0.0	149.8	693.4	48.83%
New Jersey	229.1	0.0	2215.0	0.0	3014.2	2181.0	415.8	3461.0	11516.0	70.76%
N. Mexico	0.0	0.0	132.3	17.0	135.2	77.1	33.9	104.2	499.8	15.39%
New York	1158.6	0.0	2453.0	0.0	3315.9	680.0	1242.7	2076.0	10926.2	25.65%
N. Carolina	0.0	0.0	246.0	188.0	238.6	423.8	564.8	1029.5	2690.7	26.185%
N. Dakota	423.3	0.0	13.4	78.2	179.6	78.2	99.9	78.1	644.5	43.78%
Ohio	0.0	0.0	143.7	166.1	19.8	170.7	0.0	326.0	1249.6	7.22%
Oklahoma	0.0	0.0	186.8	5.3	0.0	208.7	0.0	208.7	609.5	12.40%
Oregon	600.5	0.0	0.0	57.0	0.0	63.4	0.0	156.0	276.4	6.05%
Penn.	0.0	0.0	1720.4	0.0	2388.1	0.0	0.0	3196.0	7905.0	42.42%
R.I.	131.5	0.0	38.3	78.0	204.4	218.3	433.1	379.6	919.1	41.99%
S. Carolina	0.0	0.0	0.0	20.0	0.0	7.3	0.0	17.9	609.8	11.16%
S. Dakota	70.2	41.4	15.9	32.7	32.7	0.0	171.1	0.0	48.6	4.50%
Tennessee	582.9	0.0	292.5	194.4	404.7	214.4	0.0	297.7	1686.4	25.46%
Texas	0.0	0.0	1400.6	0.0	298.4	233.5	0.0	1085.7	3601.1	17.43%
Utah	0.0	0.0	0.0	0.0	67.1	0.0	0.0	0.0	67.1	2.31%
Vermont	0.0	0.0	22.8	38.0	12.4	74.5	51.8	164.6	364.1	30.62%
Virginia	567.7	0.0	235.7	0.0	739.9	0.0	1412.0	0.0	2387.7	23.87%
Washington	243.6	31.0	35.9	101.4	0.0	236.4	0.0	276.8	1249.2	13.40%
W. Virginia	31.4	146.2	190.8	473.2	0.0	473.2	0.0	503.2	2030.2	63.88%
Wisconsin	0.0	0.0	59.9	0.0	0.0	0.0	0.0	0.0	37.3	0.41%
Wyoming	56.4	0.0	130.8	8.0	108.7	8.0	142.3	8.0	462.2	33.98%
Total	7365.2	1246.0	19294.0	6132.5	23747.2	14155.2	20639.2	34071.2	126650.5	29.31%
Pooled Total									57359.5	13.27%

THE IMPACT OF RAINY DAY FUNDS ON STATE
FISCAL STRESS

Because some states have explicit rainy day funds and others do not, and because the provisions for depositing and withdrawing rainy day funds differ substantially across states, it is natural to ask whether rainy day funds helped to minimize the degree of fiscal stress experienced by states during past recessions. This section of the chapter uses regression models to look at this question empirically. For the first regression, the dependent variable will be the measure of fiscal stress as a percentage of the state budget, as given in Table 9.4. A variable indicating whether the state had an explicit rainy day fund in 1989 (RDF), is included as an independent variable. RDF is a binary variable taking on a value of 1 for states with rainy day funds and 0 otherwise. Also included in the regression are specific provisions of state rainy day funds.[19] States that have explicit formulas or mandates for saving rainy day funds during the boom years are expected to have been better prepared for the recession than states whose saving to these funds is discretionary. The importance of these requirements was stressed by the National Conference of State Legislatures Fiscal Affairs and Oversight Committee.[20] The dummy variable, REQUIRED SAVINGS, is included in the regression and is expected to have a negative impact on the degree of fiscal stress experienced by the state. Often state rainy day fund balances are capped at a certain percentage of general fund expenditures or revenues. If this cap is binding, it might prevent a state from saving sufficiently in its rainy day fund.[21] A dummy variable, CAP, is included in the regression to capture the effect of these rainy day fund caps, and an additional variable, CAP%, denotes the percentage of the state budget at which the fund is capped. Additionally, states differ in terms of the provisions for withdrawal of funds from their rainy day accounts. A variable indicating that the state's rainy day fund cannot be accessed by regular legislative action, WITHDRAWAL REQ, is included and is expected to have a negative impact on the degree of fiscal stress.

In addition to these variables describing the characteristics of rainy day funds, a measure of the degree to which states were impacted by the recession is needed. By including this variable, it is possible to determine the impact of the other variables on states who were hit similarly by the recession. This is important because states that experienced little fiscal stress could have been that way because they were either hit hard by the recession but well prepared, or because they were not hit very hard by the recession. Including a variable reflecting the severity of the recession on a particular state also controls for any selection bias arising from states that are hit harder by recessions being more likely to have rainy day funds. SEVERITY is used in the regression model to calculate the impact on individual states due to reduced tax revenue growth. The rate of growth in state tax revenues during the recession, subtracting out any funds derived from discretionary tax increases, is used to calculate SEVERITY, under the assumption that states with slower revenue growth are the states that are more severely impacted by the recession. The sign is then reversed so that higher values of SEVERITY indicate a more severe impact. The result of this regression is given in the first column of Table 9.5.[22]

Table 9.5
Impact of Rainy Day Funds and Provisions on State Fiscal Stress during the 1990–1991 Recession

Independent Variable	Dependent Variable	
	Fiscal Stress	Share due to Expenditure Shortfalls
CONSTANT	39.34 (7.25)	31.58 (3.08)
RAINY DAY FUND	4.93 (0.75)	24.52 (1.98)
REQUIRED SAVINGS	-16.69 (2.60)	-10.47 (0.90)
CAP	-9.32 (0.83)	14.09 (0.69)
CAP%	-0.01 (0.01)	-2.30 (0.76)
WITHDRAWAL REQ	-2.62 (0.39)	8.28 (0.70)
SEVERITY	3.62 (5.85)	-1.78 (1.55)
R^2	0.52	0.16

Note: Absolute *t*-statistics are given in parentheses.

That regression, using fiscal stress as the dependent variable, shows that the mere existence of a rainy day fund does not alleviate fiscal stress, as shown by the insignificant coefficient on the RAINY DAY FUND variable. If, however, the rainy day fund has a legal requirement that money be deposited into the rainy day fund, fiscal stress is significantly reduced. The coefficient on REQUIRED SAVINGS shows that the presence of a deposit requirement reduced the fiscal stress experienced by the state by approximately 17 percent of the state budget. Data on state rainy day fund balances illustrates that states are not very disciplined with regard to saving money into their rainy day funds unless there is a legal requirement to do so, and the regression suggests that rainy day funds are likely to be ineffective without such a requirement. Of the thirty-eight states that had rainy day funds in 1989, twelve had REQUIRED SAVINGS.

The only other significant variable in the fiscal stress regression is SEVERITY, which measures the decline in tax revenues during the recession after removing any effects from rate increases. As expected, this variable indicates that greater tax revenue declines lead to greater fiscal stress. Although the variable reflecting the presence of a cap on the size of the rainy day fund is the expected sign, it is insignificant. There are two possible explanations for this. State surpluses could have been so small that the cap was not binding, or alternatively, states were able to offset the impact of the cap by saving funds as other surpluses. The WITHDRAWAL REQ variable is also insignificant, meaning that the presence of a withdrawal requirement does not significantly affect the degree of state fiscal stress. The regression implies that a requirement that money be put into the rainy day fund is much more important than a restriction on when funds can be withdrawn.

Another question of interest is how the division of fiscal stress between discretionary tax increases and expenditure reductions differed between states that had rainy day funds and those that did not. To answer this question, another regression was run with the same independent variables, but using the percent of the fiscal stress accounted for by expenditure shortfalls as the dependent variable. The only variable significant at the 5 percent level in that equation is the RAINY DAY FUND variable, meaning that states with rainy day funds are more likely to absorb fiscal stress through expenditure reductions than tax increases. The reason for this result is probably political. States that supported the creation of a rainy day fund are likely to be less supportive of tax increases, because rainy day funds were created, at least in part, to avoid tax increases.

States have implemented rainy day funds to try to reduce fiscal stress during recessionary times. This section finds that rainy day funds are successful in reducing fiscal stress only if they are accompanied by a provision that legally requires contributions into the rainy day fund. In addition, states with rainy day funds—whether or not they mandate contributions—are more likely to absorb fiscal stress through expenditure reductions than to react by increasing taxes.

STATE SURPLUSES AND FISCAL STRESS

The purpose of a rainy day fund is to reduce the need to legislate tax increases or reduce expenditure growth during recessions. This section calculates the level of fund balances that would have been needed prior to the 1990–91 recession to completely eliminate the need for any expenditure reductions or tax increases. The elimination of all fiscal stress, measured this way, may or may not be an appropriate policy goal, but it is a good benchmark for examining the effectiveness of state rainy day funds and other surplus balances. States may want to have some tax increases or expenditure growth reductions during recessions, in which case this measure of fiscal stress would overstate the optimal size of a rainy day fund. On the other hand, states might want spending to be countercyclical because of the increased demand for social welfare expenditures during recessions, in which case this benchmark might understate the optimal size of a rainy day fund. We take no stand on optimal state fiscal policy, but use this measure of fiscal stress only as a benchmark. Because the benchmark incorporates reductions in spending growth and increases in taxes, it captures exactly the effects that rainy day funds are designed to reduce.

The National Conference of State Legislatures Fiscal Affairs and Oversight Committee suggests that states hold balances equal to 5 percent of the state budget.[23] Steven Gold,[24] however, suggests that the volatility of the state's economy, as well as subjective views of the desirability of stability in tax rates, should be taken into account when deciding on the optimal size of state rainy day surpluses. When looking at historical data, Robert Crider suggests that it is important to consider the impact of a recession on how the actual budget differs from the potential budget (what the budget would have been in the absence of the recession).[25] Thus, there is some reason to consider differences among states when examining the performance of rainy day funds.

Table 9.6 calculates for each state the amount of funds the state would have had to have had on hand in 1988 to completely eliminate any fiscal stress over the next four years of below-average economic growth. Because this measure is derived from an ex post standpoint, it would give the exact amount states would have needed to have had on hand to mitigate the effects of the 1991 recession. An alternative measure, however, is to add to this amount the actual surplus the state had coming out of the recession, under the assumption that those states wanted to carry those balances as a cushion. These two measures will differ only for states that did not use all of their surplus balances, or for states that ran a deficit. State balances can be referred to as fully funded if the balances would have been sufficient to carry the state through 1989–1992 without any fiscal stress. Table 9.6 shows, for each state, the amount of surplus balances the state had going into the recession, their usage of these balances by fiscal year, and the two measures of fully funded balances. Fully funded size 1 represents the ex post amount just needed to eliminate all tax increases and reductions in expenditure growth, and fully funded size 2 represents the amount in fully funded size 1 plus enough to leave balances the same at the end of the recession as they actually were.

It is apparent from Table 9.6 that most states had balances well below what would have been needed to maintain expenditure growth without tax increases through the 1990–1991 recession. The surplus needed to fund a more severe recession, such as 1980–1982 would be larger than those given here. These estimates show that for most states a 5 percent balance is insufficient to cover average expenditure growth without tax increases during even the relatively mild 1990–1991 recession. The total row, second from the bottom in Table 9.6, shows that the average state would have had to have had rainy day funds equal to 34.18

Table 9.6
Actual and Fully Funded Surpluses during the 1990–1991 Recession
(Dollar Figures in Millions of Current Dollars)

State	Prior Balance	FY 1989 Bal. Used	FY 1990 Bal. Used	FY 1991 Bal. Used	FY 1992 Bal. Used	Total Bal. Used	Fully Funded Size 1	Percentage of 1988 Budget	Fully Funded Size 2	Percentage of 1988 Budget
Alabama	177	103	0	97	0	200	488.4	7.76%	465.4	7.40%
Alaska	224	61	0	0	0	61	3159.3	81.64%	3322.3	85.85%
Arizona	6	5	0	0	40	45	3720.6	65.06%	3681.6	64.38%
Arkansas	0	0	0	0	0	0	594.9	18.04%	594.9	18.04%
California	1109	0	564	3424	0	3988	24057.0	40.31%	21178.0	35.49%
Colorado	135	0	1	118	0	119	774.2	15.83%	790.2	16.16%
Connecticut	204	102	260	808	0	1170	7060.5	102.45%	6094.5	88.43%
Delaware	185	0	13	58	0	71	378.7	23.05%	492.7	29.99%
Florida	345	146	0	110	0	256	5691.1	33.61%	5780.1	34.14%
Georgia	433	0	376	22	0	398	3523.6	38.68%	3558.6	39.07%
Hawaii	629	0	173	110	0	283	283.0	11.01%	629.0	24.47%
Idaho	89	0	4	16	39	59	121.2	8.10%	151.2	10.11%
Illinois	541	0	146	295	0	441	5417.0	31.04%	5517.0	31.61%
Indiana	690	0	0	258	0	258	1331.8	15.86%	1763.8	21.00%
Iowa	95	0	23	61	9	93	543.8	10.93%	545.8	10.97%
Kansas	371	0	98	111	21	230	230.0	6.60%	371.0	10.64%
Kentucky	48	0	0	0	117	117	2384.3	37.54%	2315.3	36.45%
Louisiana	655	0	0	284	501	785	2431.3	33.33%	2301.3	31.55%
Maine	188	0	127	57	0	184	795.3	35.50%	799.3	35.68%
Maryland	482	0	307	175	56	538	1127.6	13.44%	1071.6	12.77%
Massachusetts	153	595	837	0	0	1432	11990.8	84.10%	10711.8	75.13%
Michigan	480	0	405	62	0	467	6394.0	35.39%	6407.0	35.46%
Minnesota	946	0	61	330	106	497	1341.6	15.18%	1790.6	20.27%
Mississippi	113	5	86	0	0	91	383.8	10.19%	405.8	10.78%
Missouri	110	0	53	17	0	70	2715.3	39.30%	2755.3	39.88%
Montana	67	0	0	30	35	65	295.5	20.77%	297.5	20.91%
Nebraska	340	0	41	16	55	112	563.0	24.76%	791.0	34.78%
Nevada	105	38	0	52	31	121	530.3	28.31%	514.3	27.46%
New Hampshire	40	5	46	14	0	65	758.4	53.41%	733.4	51.65%

New Jersey	1020	609	410	0	0	1019	12535.0	77.02%	12536.0	77.03%
New Mexico	155	42	5	45	0	92	591.8	18.22%	654.8	20.16%
New York	53	53	0	0	0	53	10979.2	25.78%	10979.2	25.78%
North Carolina	393	236	0	222	0	458	3148.7	30.64%	3083.7	30.01%
North Dakota	65	0	6	0	19	19	663.5	45.07%	709.5	48.20%
Ohio	815	0	11	374	344	724	1973.6	11.40%	2064.6	11.93%
Oklahoma	309	0	0	0	79	90	699.5	14.23%	918.5	18.68%
Oregon	296	0	0	0	0	0	276.4	6.05%	572.4	12.52%
Pennsylvania	497	0	234	715	0	949	8854.0	47.51%	8402.0	45.09%
Rhode Island	143	92	45	3	0	140	1059.1	48.38%	1062.1	48.52%
South Carolina	214	68	10	74	54	206	815.8	14.93%	823.8	15.08%
South Dakota	41	2	7	21	0	30	78.6	7.27%	89.6	8.29%
Tennessee	228	0	60	161	0	221	1907.4	28.79%	1914.4	28.90%
Texas	297	0	0	0	187	187	3788.1	18.33%	3893.1	18.87%
Utah	130	11	0	10	32	53	120.1	4.13%	197.1	6.78%
Vermont	82	58	14	67	8	147	511.1	42.98%	446.1	37.52%
Virginia	275	275	0	0	0	275	2662.7	26.62%	2662.7	26.62%
Washington	516	0	0	468	377	845	2094.2	22.46%	1765.2	18.94%
West Virginia	66	0	0	11	32	43	2073.2	65.24%	2096.2	65.96%
Wisconsin	375	0	68	193	40	301	338.3	3.73%	412.3	4.54%
Wyoming	127	15	17	14	3	49	511.2	37.59%	589.2	43.32%
Total	15057	2521	4508	8903	2185	18117	144767.5	34.18%	141707.5	32.79%
Pooled Total							75476.5	17.47%	72416.5	16.76%

175

percent of its 1988 budget to be fully funded according to one estimate, and 32.79 percent according to the other, to avoid any tax increases or expenditure growth reductions.

This measure of full funding in the total row adds all withdrawals from rainy day funds, but does not offset reductions of funds of some states by the increases of others. If the accumulated funds of those states with increases are used to offset decreases in others, the pooled total at the very bottom of Table 9.6 shows that states would have needed only from 16.76 percent to 17.47 percent of their 1988 budgets to be fully funded. If all states pooled their funds, they could have the same protection with a pooled rainy day fund of 17.47 percent of their budgets as would be produced with individual state funds averaging 34.18 percent of their budgets. For a multistate fund to work, many problems would have to be worked out, including provisions to overcome the common pool problem.[26] A comparison of the total with the pooled total is most useful for showing that individual states can suffer considerably more fiscal stress than all of the states in the aggregate. From Table 9.6, it is evident that states differ substantially in the amount of surplus balances that would be needed to carry them through a recession with no fiscal stress.

RAINY DAY FUNDS AND AVAILABLE SURPLUS BALANCES

Rainy day funds can help states save to alleviate fiscal stress during recessions, but accumulated general fund balances would serve them just as well. There is always the temptation to spend surplus general fund balances, however, so explicit rainy day funds have the potential to help states accumulate funds to be used during recessions. Keeping in mind that rainy day funds are close substitutes for surplus general fund balances, do rainy day funds actually add to surplus balances available to states to smooth spending during recessions? To answer that question, a regression was run using actual surplus balances (SB) in 1988 as the dependent variable, to see how rainy day funds affected total funds available prior to the 1990–1991 recession.

The actual surplus balances should be a function of the amount states would like to have, and the political and institutional constraints that could keep actual balances from equaling desired balances. Desired balances should be an increasing function of fully funded balances, calculated in the previous section, so fully funded balances (FFB) is included as an independent variable. The other independent variables are the institutional features of rainy day funds that vary among states. The regression was run on the 48 continental states for 1988, yielding

$$SB = 224.2 + 0.03FFB - 42.5RDF + 169.1REQSAV - 63.5WITHDR$$
$$ (3.03) \quad (4.58) \qquad (0.46) \qquad (1.88) \qquad\qquad (0.48)$$

$$ - 383.7CAP + 50.7CAP\% + \varepsilon,$$
$$ \;(2.57) \qquad\quad (2.15)$$

$R^2 = 0.43$ (*t*-values in parentheses).

The results of this regression lend additional insight into the regression results reported earlier, and show again that the most important feature for the effectiveness of rainy day funds is a provision requiring that money be put into them. The coefficient on FFB, fully funded balances, is significant and positive, providing the expected result that the larger a state's fully funded balance, as calculated in the previous section, the larger its surplus balances were going into the 1990–1991 recession. However, both SB and FFB are denominated in millions of dollars, so the coefficient shows that for each additional dollar of fully funded balances, actual surplus balances were larger by only three cents. The relationship is statistically significant, but small.

Both cap variables are significant at better than the .05 level. CAP is a binary variable showing that the existence of a cap on a rainy day fund lowers surplus balances by $384 million, whereas each percentage increase in CAP% increases surplus balances by $50 million. Thus, using these figures, a cap of 5 percent would lower surplus balances by $384 – $50 * 5 = $134 million. A cap of 7.62 percent would be the point at which the two effects would cancel each other. Of the sixteen states with caps, only four have caps above this level, suggesting that in most cases, a rainy day fund with a cap is detrimental to a state's readiness for a recession.

The required savings variable, REQSAV, is significant at the .07 level, and reinforces the earlier finding that having an explicit requirement that the state deposit money into the rainy day fund is the most important factor in creating an effective rainy day fund. REQSAV is a binary variable, so states with a saving requirement, on average, entered the recession with $169 million more in surplus balances. In contrast, the lack of explicit withdrawal requirements did not seem to reduce the effectiveness of rainy day funds.

CONCLUSION

This chapter has focused on fiscal stress caused by recessions because during recessions states face more serious fiscal problems than during nonrecessionary times. Rainy day funds provide a mechanism for easing the fiscal stress caused by economic fluctuations. States face other fiscal problems in addition to those brought on by business fluctuations, and those other problems may be more severe. The increased budgetary demands of Medicaid have strained state budgets, as have increased demands for expenditures in other areas such as prisons, law enforcement, and education. In addition, fiscal problems on the revenue side of the budget include uncertainties about federal assistance, and problems with tax bases such as general sales and motor fuels that have not kept up with income growth. This list is not meant to be exhaustive, but rather to illustrate that states face many other fiscal problems in addition to the cyclical variability of revenues, and a rainy day fund is only targeted at this one particular problem.

Rainy day funds are relatively recent as a nationwide phenomenon. Only twelve states had them in 1982, whereas forty-four states had them by 1994. Some form of saving over the business cycle is necessary for states if they do not want their expenditure growth rates to decline during recessions without raising taxes, because, unlike the federal government, states typically face some type of balanced budget requirement. Only by saving money ahead of time can states avoid fiscal stress caused by reduced revenue growth during economic downturns.

Despite the fact that most states had rainy day funds during the 1990–1991 recession, states still exhibited a significant amount of fiscal stress. After depleting the majority of their surpluses by the middle of fiscal year 1991, states turned to major tax increases to maintain their expenditures. Even with these tax increases, most states were unable to maintain expenditure growth at previous levels. This chapter computed a measure of state fiscal stress during the 1990–1991 recession as the amount of discretionary tax increases plus the amount by which expenditure growth fell below average. Then, an empirical model was used to see whether the presence of an explicit rainy day fund had an effect on the degree of fiscal stress experienced by a state.

The mere existence of a rainy day fund in a state had no measurable effect in limiting fiscal stress. However, rainy day funds were effective in reducing fiscal stress if they had mandatory requirements for making deposits. One might be concerned that once established, the funds would provide a source of revenue that could be raided by the legislature, rather than truly being saved for a rainy day. However, the empirical results indicate that rainy day funds are equally effective with or without a stringent requirement on the withdrawal of funds. The empirical results also show that for a given amount of fiscal stress, states that have rainy day funds are more likely to cope with that fiscal stress through spending reductions than through increases in taxes.

If states had wanted to maintain expenditure growth without tax increases during the 1991 recession, they would have needed rainy day (or other available) funds that were, on average, around 30 percent of their general expenditures. This is not intended as a recommendation that states have rainy day funds this large, but rather is an observation that if they do not, they are likely to have to rely on tax increases or declines in expenditure growth to cope with recessions. Many states created rainy day funds after the 1980–1982 recession to minimize future fiscal stress, but the degree to which they actually helped is an empirical question that has not been extensively analyzed. The conclusions of this chapter suggest that properly structured rainy day funds did ease the fiscal crises during the past recession, but that they still were insufficient to prevent major tax increases and expenditure reductions.

NOTES

1.   During the 1980–1982 recession, many states even instituted tax increases and spending cuts whose implementation was dependent on future budgetary or economic conditions, see Steven D. Gold, *Preparing for the Next Recession: Rainy Day Funds and Other Tools for the States*, Legislative Finance Paper No. 41 (Denver: National Conference of State Legislatures, 1983), and Cathy Daicoff Macsherry, "Assessing Revenue-Raising Ability: A Private-sector View of Changes," in *Measuring Fiscal Capacity*, ed., H. Clyde Reeves (Boston: Oelgeschlager, Gunn & Hain in association with the Lincoln Institute of Land Policy, 1986). These contingent taxes are often called "trigger taxes."

2.   Gold, *Preparing for the Next Recession*, discusses state strategies for dealing with the 1980–1982 recession.

3.   See Wallace E. Oates, *Fiscal Federalism* (New York: Harcourt Brace Jovanovich, 1972); Chapter 1, for the reasoning behind this neutrality view. Edward M. Gramlich, "The 1991 State and Local Fiscal Crises," *Brookings Papers on Economic Activity* 2 (1991): 249–87, describes the neutrality view, as well as two other possible types of state fiscal policy over the business cycle, perversity and stability. Under the perversity scenario, states balance their budgets annually by running procyclic fiscal policy, and under stability, they attempt to smooth the business cycle by running countercyclic fiscal policy.

4.   This policy also minimizes the excess burden of taxation over the business cycle, as argued by Robert J. Barro, "On the Determination of the Public Debt," *Journal of Political Economy* 87, no. 5 (October 1979): 940–71. Finn E. Kydland and Edward C. Prescott, "A Competitive Theory of Fluctuations and the Feasibility and Desirability of Stabilization Policy," in *Rational Expectations and Economic Policy*, ed. Stanley Fischer (Chicago: University of Chicago Press, 1980), and Robert E. Lucas and Nancy L. Stokey, "Optimal Fiscal and Monetary Policy in an Economic without Capital," *Journal of Monetary Economics* 12, no. 1 (January 1983): 55–94, also provide similar justification for smoothing tax rates. Chaipat Sahasakul, "The U.S. Evidence on Optimal Taxation Over Time," *Journal of Monetary Economics* 18, no. 3 (November 1986): 251–75, explains that the tax smoothing hypothesis is an application of the famous rule developed by Frank P. Ramsey, "A Contribution to the Theory of Taxation," *Economic Journal* 37 (1927): 47–61, to a multiperiod situation. Gold, *Preparing for the Next Recession*, mentions that the purpose of state rainy day funds is to minimize the disruptions in state expenditures and tax rates caused by economic fluctuations, and cites Adam Smith as proposing that certainty is one of the basic attributes of a good tax system.

5.   Data on stage budgetary constraints and the specific provisions of state rainy day funds are from U.S. Advisory Commission on Intergovernmental Relations, *Signified Features of Fescal Federalism* (Washington, D.C.: 1993).

6.   See Gramlich, "The 1991 State and Local Fiscal Crises."

7.   Tom Bryan and Dick Howard, "Michigan's Budget and Economic Stabilization Fund," *Innovations* (May 1979): 1–11 (Council of State Government), specifically discuss the establishment and operation of Michigan's rainy day fund.

8.   Gold, *Preparing for the Next Recession*, points out that states are more likely to adopt rainy day funds soon after a fiscal crisis.

9.   See Gold, *Preparing for the Next Recession*.

10.   Gold, *Preparing for the Next Recession*. William H. Oakland, "Proposition 13, Genesis and Consequences," *Review of the Federal Reserve Bank of San Francisco* (1979): 5–14, also makes this claim. Richard H. Mattoon and William A. Testa, "State and Local Government and the Business Cycle," in *Issues in State and Local Government Finance, Collected Works from the Federal Reserve Bank of Chicago*, ed. William A. Testa (Chicago: Federal Reserve Bank of Chicago, 1992), discuss a similar phenomenon in Alaska.

11.   The view that states are biased toward conservative revenue forecasts is widely accepted in the literature. However, provisions that states may use rainy day funds to cover unexpected revenue shortfalls may actually provide some incentive to underestimate revenues. Jon David Vasche and Brad Williams, "Optimal Government Budgeting Contingency Reserve Funds," *Public Budgeting and Finance* 7, no. 1 (spring 1987): 66–82, develop an idea of optimal funds to handle forecast errors in revenues.

12.   For a good discussion, see Helen F. Ladd, "State Responses to the TRA86 Revenue Windfalls: A New Test of the Flypaper Effect," *Journal of Policy Analysis and Management* 12, no. 1 (winter 1993): 82–103.

13.   Another complicating factor is that state fiscal years do not perfectly correspond to calendar years. All but four of the states have fiscal years running from the beginning of July to the end of June, Alabama and Michigan both have fiscal years running from the

beginning of October to the end of September, New York's fiscal year runs from the beginning of April to the end of March, and Texas's fiscal year runs from the beginning of September to the end of August. Fiscal years are named for the year in which they end so, for example, the contraction ending in November 1982 actually ended in fiscal year 1983 for all of the fifty states.

    14.   Data on tax increased for the period 1974–1983 are from Gold, *Preparing for the Next Recession*. These data were collected by the Tax Foundation and represents tax increases during a calendar year as a proportion of total tax revenues during the fiscal year that ends during that calendar year. The data for period 1990–1992 are calculated from the National Conference of State Legislatures, various years. They include actions taken in prior or preceding years and represents tax increases during a fiscal year as a proportion of total tax revenues during the previous fiscal year. Neither source includes accelerated tax collections.

    15.   Robert A. Crider, *The Impact of Recession on State and Local Finance*, Urban and Regional Development Series No. 6 (Columbus, Ohio: Academy for Contemporary Problems, 1978) more specifically discusses the impact of the 1974–1975 recession on state government finances. He finds that states whose unemployment rates were higher were more likely to increase taxes and have expenditure reductions, and that states in total were faced with a $26 billion decline in revenues. Paul R. Blackley and Larry DeBoer, "Explaining State Government Discretionary Revenue Increases in Fiscal Years 1991 and 1992," *National Tax Journal* 46, no. 1, (March 1993): 1–12, find that states with more severe recessions and higher average expenditure growth rates were more likely to increase taxes during fiscal years 1991 and 1992. Gramlich, "The 1991 State and Local Fiscal Crises," Mattoon and Testa "State and Local Government and the Business Cycle," and Mattoon and Testa, "State and Local Governments' Reaction to Recession," *Economic Perspectives* 16, no. 2 (March/April 1992): 19–27 (Federal Reserve Bank of Chicago), also discuss the impact of the 1990–1991 recession on state finance. Gold, *Preparing for the Next Recession*, discusses how Florida, whose rainy day fund was created in 1959, had to rely on tax increases during the late years of the 1980–1982 recession because its rainy day fund had been almost completely depleted. He also disculles the inadequacy of Michigan's rainy day fund, established in 1977, during this recession. Gold also discusses the impact of the 1980–1982 recession on state finances.

    16.   Data on balances in rainy day funds and other balances are from National Association of State Budget Officers, various years, data on tax increases are from National Conference of State Legislatures, various years. We are indebted to Stacey Mazer from the National Association of State Budget Officers and Corina Eckl from the National Conference of State Legislatures for their assistance in the data collection for this chapter.

    17.   Stephen D. Gold, "Changes in State Government Finances in the 1980s," *National Tax Journal* 44, no. 1 (March 1991): 1–19, gives specific details of the tax changes between 1987 and 1990. Blackley and DeBoer, "Explaining State Government Discretionary Revenue Increases in Fiscal Years 1991 and 1992," empirically find that states who were hit harder by the 1990–1991 recession wer more likely to increase taxes. Mattoon and Testa, "State and Local Government and the Business Cycle," and "State and Local Governments' Reaction to Recession," also discuss the impact of the recent recession in greater detail for the five states in the Seventh Federal Reserve District (Illinois, Indiana, Iowa, Michigan, and Wisconsin). State Policy Research, Inc., *State Policy Reports* 8, no. 8 (1991): 2–8, discusses the fact that state rainy dat funds were insufficient to cover needed expenditures because of the lack of funding put into them during the boom years of the mid 1980s, and Mattoon and Testa, "State and Local Government and the Business Cycle," also note that state rainy day funds were insufficiently small during the 1990–1991 recession.

    18.   The period used to calculate trend growth was 1984–1992. There are several reasons why this period was chosen to calculate the trend growth. First, Harold W. Elder, "Exploring the Tax Revolt: An Analysis of the Effects of State Tax and Expenditure

Limitation Laws," *Public Finance Quarterly* 20, no. 1 (January 1992): 47–63, finds that the expenditure limitations enacted during the tax revolt of the late 1970s and early 1980s did have a significant impact on the growth rate of state expenditures. If this is true, then the current long-term average growth rate would be different than that of the 1970s and early 1980s. Second, because it is an average growth rate over an entire business cycle, it represents the growth rate of expenditures during the post-1982 recession period that would have allowed states to save exactly enough surpluses before the 1990–1991 recession to cover the below average expenditure growth during the recession. Thus, it is the maximum sustainable constant growth rate of expenditures over the entire period, given the revenuws raised.

19. States that do not have rainy day funds are given 0s for all of these variables. Thus, these terms are in effect interacted with the rainy day fund variable.

20. Barbara A. Yondorf, *A Legislator's Guide to Budget Oversight After the Appropriations Act Has Passed* (Denver: National Conference of State Legislatures, 1983).

21. Gold, *Preparing for the Next Recession*, and Barbara A. Yondorf, *A Legislator's Guide to Budget Oversight After the Appropriations Act Has Passed*, cite these limitations as preventing sufficient savings to handle more severe recessions. They point out that at least twenty states had revenue shortfalls in fiscal year 1983 that exceeded the typical RDF cap of 5 percent.

22. The regressions were also performed using only the forty-eight continental states and the results were similar to those obtained on the full sample of fifty states.

23. See Yondorf, *A Legislator's Guide to Budget Oversight After the Appropriations Act Has Passed*. Sometimes this 5 percent figure is suggested as a percentage of general fund expenditures, whereas other times it is mentioned in the context of general expenditures. The difference is that general fund expenditures exclude earmarked funds and are thus only about one half the size of general expenditures. This analysis uses surpluses as a percentage of general expenditures, and one should keep this in mind when interpreting the results.

24. *Preparing for the Next Recession.*

25. Robert A. Crider, *The Impact of Recession on State and Local Finance*, Urban and Regional Development Series No. 6 (Columbus, Ohio: Academy for Contemporary Problems, 1978). Tom Supel and Bruce Litterman, "Using Vector Autoregressions to Measure the Uncertainty in Minnesota's Revenue Forecasts," *Quarterly Review* (Spring 1983): 10–22 (Federal Reserve Bank of Minneapolis), have designed a vector autoregression model that proposes to measure the probability of differing revenue losses. Estimates from this model were considered by Minnesota when it created its rainy day fund in 1983. It represents yet another possible way to calculate the optimal size of state surplus funds.

26. The federal countercyclical revenue sharing grants program created by Title II of the Public Works Employment Act of 1976 was a program designed to give states federal grants during recessions to keep states from having to increase taxes and reduce spending during recessions which would be offsetting to the countercyclic fiscal policy of the federal government (see Robert C. Vogel and Robert P. Trost, "The Response of State Government Receipts to Economic Fluctuations and the Allocation of Counter-Cyclical Revenue Sharing Grants," *Review of Economics and Statistics* 61, no. 3 [August 1979]: 389–400, and Crider, *The Impact of Recession on State and Local Finance*). Although this program was abandoned in the early 1980s, and was not exactly the same as a rainy day fund pool, it was an example of a national pool of recession oriented funds that could take advantage of the differing covariances of the states.

Chapter 10

Conclusion

In the last several decades of the twentieth century, state governments have faced increasing fiscal pressures. To a great extent these fiscal pressures are the result of changes in the role of state governments in the American economy. In 1950 state and local government expenditures made up 9 percent of GNP. By 1990 their share of the national economy had increased to 14.3 percent of GNP. Income grew substantially over that period as well, which further added to state and local government expenditures. After adjusting for inflation, real state and local government expenditures were 333 percent higher in 1990 than they were in 1950. As state and local government expenditures were increasing, the state share of state and local expenditures was increasing as well, placing increasing fiscal responsibilities on the states. When the economy has gone into a recession, these fiscal pressures have escalated to push many states into fiscal crises.

At the end of the twentieth century states face a substantial number of fiscal challenges, including trying to fund rapidly increasing entitlement programs like Medicaid, dealing with federal mandates that require state expenditures without providing revenues to the states, and responding to taxpayer demands that the growth in state taxation be stopped, or even reversed. These problems are distinct from the problem of fiscal crisis that has come with recessions, however. They are important problems, but they are not directly addressed here.[1] Those problems have to do with setting state priorities and facing up to the fact that states do have budget constraints. Money allocated to one purpose cannot be allocated to others, and state legislatures have to make the tough choices as to where they will allocate available resources. The recessionary fiscal crises that occur as a result of revenue slowdowns are a different type of problem and require a different type of solution.

Individuals face the same kind of budget constraints as state governments, and must allocate the resources they have available to the areas they view as most important. When individuals have temporary declines in their incomes, they often can make use of the public sector safety net that can provide them with unemployment compensation, food stamps, and other types of public assistance until they are able to get back on their feet. State governments have no safety net, so if they are to be able to insulate themselves from the impacts of temporary revenue declines, they must do so themselves. Unlike the federal government, and even individuals, states cannot effectively borrow to smooth their expenditure flows, closing off another possible channel of relief.

One often-used solution for overcoming state fiscal crises is increased taxes. Although increasing taxes will immediately generate more revenue, and will alleviate some fiscal stress in the short run, tax increases do not attack the fundamental problem that states overcommit resources during prosperous years, so that even after a tax increase, the next recession will bring with it another fiscal crisis. Tax increases may help to deal with other fiscal problems, such as providing revenues for unfunded mandates, but are not a solution for the fiscal crises that have periodically plagued the states. Periodic fiscal crises can be alleviated only by smoothing available resources over the revenue cycle through the use of a properly structured rainy day fund. We have arrived at this conclusion after a detailed examination of the facts behind state fiscal crises. We have examined the data on state budgets and concluded that the primary problems behind fiscal crises are not related to specific expenditure or revenue programs, but to revenue variability over the business cycle. We have examined in detail the data on state government revenue variability, and concluded that there is no good way to reduce it very much. Smoothing available resources over the revenue cycle by saving during healthy fiscal years and drawing on this during poor fiscal years is a straightforward and obvious solution. Because we have examined the data in detail throughout the book, this concluding chapter gives us the opportunity to step back and look at the big picture, supported by the work presented earlier in the book.

REVENUES AND EXPENDITURES

State government expenditures have grown because of increased demands for expenditures in some areas, and because of federal mandates that have made some expenditures less controllable. Coupled with taxpayer demands to hold the line on tax increases, expenditure demands have placed fiscal pressures on states. When looking at the big picture, however, the fundamental problem—that demands for state government expenditures exceed the supply of revenues to fund those demands—is a part of the institutional structure of the public sector. This problem always exists, and always should exist. States either give away their output or distribute it below cost to the consumers of government output. Interest groups approach state legislatures with ideas about how state revenues can be spent. State college students want expanded course offerings, smaller classes, and lower tuition. Businesses want more infrastructure, development incentives, and reduced taxes. Because all interests want the state to pay for something that benefits them, there will always be a greater demand for state government expenditures than there will be revenue to meet those demands. The role of the state legislature is to decide, given its revenue constraints, which of these demands most serves the public interest.

Following this line of reasoning, there will always be less revenue available to state governments than they would like to have to meet the demand for state government programs. That is the nature of the way that government works, rather than an indication of an impending fiscal crisis. Fiscal crises arise not because the demand for state government expenditures exceeds the supply, but because state governments have overcommitted on expenditure programs and do not have sufficient revenues to cover the expenditures they have pledged to undertake. This overcommittment occurs because during prosperous years, state governments spend as much money as they have available rather than saving some to make up for revenue shortfalls during recessions. Then, when a recession comes, no matter what the level of taxes, states experience a crisis because of insufficient revenues to meet their expenditure commitments.

Despite the force of this argument, we still wanted to examine the data on both revenues and expenditures to see if there were not some specific programs or revenue sources that were placing undue fiscal pressure on states. One reason for doing so is that other analyses of state fiscal crises have laid some of the blame on factors other than cyclical variability. Steven Gold distinguishes between short-run fiscal crises and long-run crises, and places the blame for short-run crisis situations primarily on recessions.[2] We concur with Gold's assessment. He goes on to look at components of what he calls the long-run fiscal crisis, and sees many additional problems related to state budgetary choices. We certainly agree with Gold that these are important fiscal issues, and that states must make difficult policy choices to deal with them. These ongoing fiscal issues are not crises, however, following the normal definition of the term. Rather, they are issues that must be dealt with as a part of the ongoing process of government.

We believe that the problems associated with fiscal crises can be separated from the ongoing issues of determining government priorities and designing revenue structures and expenditure programs to serve the continuing demands of government's constituents. We also believe it is important to separate these issues. It is important to recognize that even if the important long-run questions relating to state revenue and expenditure pressures are solved, states will still have fiscal crises unless they effectively deal with the cyclical variability of their revenue streams. Likewise, if they can deal with the cyclical variability of their revenues, they can prevent periodic fiscal crises, and so can deal with other fiscal issues more effectively.

We do not dismiss the idea that fiscal crises might be caused by longer-run revenue and expenditure trends out of hand, but rather analyze expenditures and revenues in Chapters 2 and 3. Several trends were noted that might increase the vulnerability of states to experience fiscal crises. First, over the years there has been a trend toward centralization. State government expenditures as a percentage of state and local expenditures have increased. When looking at the average of all states, in 1960 state government expenditures as a percentage of state and local expenditures was 57.7 percent, and by 1992 state expenditures were 66.4 percent of state and local expenditures. This indicates more responsibility taken on by states, but also indicates a turn toward relying on more cyclically variable tax bases. The largest source of tax revenue for local governments is the property tax, which is relatively stable over the business cycle, and so the move toward state rather than local expenditures is a factor that would lead to more fiscal stress.

Yet another factor is the dramatic decline in highway expenditures in state budgets. In the late 1950s and early 1960s, highway expenditures made up between 25 and 30 percent of state government expenditures, but by the early 1990s highway expenditures were less than 8 percent of state expenditures. Because roads are durable capital goods, most of the highways that exist in any one year are due to past construction, and current construction has relatively little impact on the current roadway system. Thus, during downturns, highway expenditures can be curtailed without creating much of an impact, making it easier for states to respond to fiscal stress. The decline in highway expenditures has been matched by an increase in state government welfare expenditures, which require current resources. Furthermore, the demand for welfare expenditures is countercyclical, further cutting the government's flexibility to respond to the demand, and further placing fiscal pressure on states.

Perhaps the most alarming component of welfare expenditures has been Medicaid which, even after adjusting for inflation, increased over 400 percent from 1970 to 1993, and in the early 1990s makes up about 75 percent of state welfare expenditures. The fiscal pressure created by this program alone has strained state government budgets, and during the 1991 recession some analysts argued that Medicaid was the most significant cause of fiscal crisis in many states. Surely states must take action to get Medicaid expenditures under control, and the task is made more difficult because, although much of the cost is borne by states, the federal government mandates many of the program's characteristics. Nevertheless, two facts illustrate that Medicaid has not caused fiscal crises, despite the fiscal problems that it presents. First, after the 1991 recession, states pulled out of their fiscal crises, but Medicaid remained intact. Second, Medicaid has been increasing as a state government expenditure in both crisis and noncrisis years.

State government expenditures on law enforcement and prisons have also been increasing as a share of state government expenditures, but in the early 1990s make up a small part of total state government expenditures. As welfare and criminal justice expenditures increase, they crowd out other areas of state government expenditures, such as education and highways. These changes signify legislative responses to the demands of citizens and interest groups, and one should expect the composition of expenditures to change over time. While states continue to feel budgetary pressures, state government expenditures continue to increase, however, and even the more serious fiscal challenges like those presented by Medicaid do not cause fiscal crises. Furthermore, Medicaid has had such a high growth rate that it is apparent that it cannot continue to grow this rapidly indefinitely. If the arrival of a fiscal crisis helps point out that Medicaid has an unsustainably high growth rate, the crisis might actually help states to take action sooner rather than later on a problem that must be addressed.

The substantial fiscal challenges that states face did not present themselves suddenly, but have been developing over the years. They require state legislatures to allocate their limited budgets to meet what they view as the most pressing needs, but because they have developed gradually, they have not been the cause of crisis. Our intention is not to minimize the fiscal challenges that states face, but rather to separate out the challenges of allocating limited budgetary resources to the many demands states face from the problems of fiscal crisis. Expenditures have grown in many areas, but they have not created the crises that states have periodically faced.

The problems associated specifically with fiscal crises lie on the revenue side of the budget. State tax bases have changed substantially over the years. In the mid-1950s motor fuels taxes were responsible for more than 20 percent of state tax revenues, but by the early 1990s they raised less than 7 percent. Meanwhile, state general sales and personal income taxes have increased dramatically. In 1993 state personal income taxes and general sales taxes raised about 32 percent each of total state tax revenues. In 1950 state income taxes raised only about 9 percent of state revenues, and general sales taxes raised 21 percent of state tax revenues. Since World War II there has been a continuing increase in the reliance on these two tax bases. Meanwhile, alcohol and tobacco taxes, which made up more than 10 percent of state tax revenues in 1950, have fallen to less than 3 percent. Historically, the most unstable source of revenues has been corporate income taxation, which has remained around about 7 percent of state tax revenues, although corporate income tax revenues did rise above 9 percent of tax revenues during the 1970s. The examination of state government revenues in Chapter 3 noted revenue trends, but did not find any factors that would lead to fiscal crises.

State government budgets have evolved over the years, to be sure, both on the expenditure and revenue sides of the ledger, but despite fiscal pressures brought on by demands for increased government expenditures, an analysis of those changes did not turn up any factors that would cause fiscal crises. Fiscal crises are caused by the cyclical variability in state government revenues.

THE 1950s AND 1960s VERSUS THE 1970s AND 1980s

State governments have grown substantially since World War II, but significant fiscal problems did not show up in states until that growth rate slowed. When examining the post–World War II data on state government finances, there is a clear difference between the decades of the 1950s and 1960s versus the 1970s and 1980s. The 1950s and 1960s were high-growth decades when compared to the 1970s and 1980s, and it was only when state government growth slowed down that state fiscal problems began to emerge. From 1950 through the early 1970s state government revenues expanded at an average annual rate of 7.7 percent. Since the early 1970s state revenues have averaged a 3.2 percent growth rate.

When state revenues were growing rapidly, as they were in the 1950s and 1960s, states could make expenditure commitments and then be able to follow through on most of them, even during recessionary years. When average revenue growth slowed during the 1970s and 1980s, if states committed all of their revenues during prosperous years, they found themselves overcommitted when recessions slowed their revenue growth below its long-term trend. Thus, state fiscal crises began appearing with more severity in the 1970s, 1980s, and 1990s.

Many other factors were at work to make state government finance after the early 1970s different from state government finance before that time. The overall increase in state government expenditures has already been noted, as has the relative decline in highway expenditures. Prior to the early 1970s, states increased their tax bases by introducing new taxes. From 1951 to 1969, sixteen states introduced general sales taxes. Since 1969 no state has added general sales taxation to its tax base. From 1961 to 1976, ten states introduced personal income taxation. Since that time one state (Connecticut, in 1991) has established a personal income tax, while one other (Alaska, 1979) has repealed personal income taxation. The opportunities for broadened tax bases helped ease state fiscal problems in the 1950s and 1960s, but those opportunities had almost all been exploited by the 1970s. Tax rates had been raised in states that did not introduce new taxes, also using up some opportunities for increasing state tax revenues. Thus, the 1970s saw a change in the state fiscal regime.

The late 1960s and early 1970s also saw a major change in the public perception of the role of both the federal and state governments. Lyndon Johnson's Great Society programs got the government more involved in income redistribution, and many of those programs, like Aid to Families with Dependent Children and Medicaid, brought state involvement with them. States began broadening their missions to include more redistributive activities, which increased fiscal pressure at the same time that two decades of rapid revenue growth were coming to an end. The initiatives to broaden expenditure programs in the 1960s were countered by a movement to limit taxes in the 1980s and 1990s, further putting fiscal pressure on states. When looking at state government finance, the 1950s and 1960s were different from the 1970s and 1980s, and the changes in budgetary priorities, the slowdown in revenue growth, and the popular demand to limit taxes have all played a role in the creation of fiscal crises in the 1970s, 1980s, and 1990s that did not exist in the prior decades.

State fiscal crises are relatively recent phenomena, having first raised widespread concern during the recessions in 1982 and in 1991. States had fiscal problems in the 1970s, but the 1970s was a difficult decade from an economic standpoint in many ways, so state government problems appeared to be a part of a larger economic slowdown. After the OPEC oil embargo in 1973, energy prices skyrocketed, the economy went into a prolonged slump, both inflation and unemployment increased, and the federal government began running increasing deficits. It was difficult to separate state government economic problems from the more general problems faced by the American economy.

The idea that states were in a crisis situation because of their fiscal problems first surfaced in earnest during the severe recession of 1982. A number of commentators identified these fiscal crises,[3] but the prosperity of the 1980s eliminated the crisis atmosphere until the next recession appeared in 1991. Along with that recession came renewed discussion of fiscal crises.[4] As the economy recovered during the middle 1990s the fiscal crises faced by states went away. The fiscal challenges of trying to meet increasing demands for expenditures with limited revenues remained, but the crises passed. The fiscal crisis phenomenon that we are analyzing is but one of many fiscal issues facing states, and we make no claim that it is the most important one. It is, however, a problem that is distinct from other fiscal issues facing states, and it calls for distinct measures to address it directly if the problem of periodic fiscal crises is to be solved.

At the root of the fiscal crisis problem is the fact that state governments have tended to spend as much revenue as they could during prosperous years, rather than setting some aside during the good years to provide a cushion for future recessions. Thus, states overcommitted their funds, and when the inevitable recession arrived, they found themselves short of resources to meet their commitments. Although additional taxes might temporarily help states to respond to more demands for government programs, no amount of additional tax bases or increases in tax rates will alleviate the problem of fiscal crises associated with recessions. Unless states can set aside funds to cope with upcoming economic downturns, or reduce the cyclical variability of their revenue flows, they will continue to face fiscal crises during recessions.

THE PROBLEM OF CYCLICAL VARIABILITY

The demand for state government expenditures tends to be countercyclical. During economic downturns, welfare case loads increase, and there is even an increased demand at state educational institutions, as people who have problems finding jobs decide to get more education instead. Meanwhile, revenues are procyclical, increasing during prosperous years and declining during recessions. So when a recession comes along, the demand for state expenditures increases, while state revenue growth declines. That, in a nutshell, is what causes state government fiscal crises.

The problems have become more severe over the past several decades as states have expanded their role in expenditure programs that are countercyclical, such as welfare programs, and contracted their role in programs that can more easily be delayed during economic downturns, such as highway construction. Another contributing factor to the increased severity of state fiscal crises has been the slowdown in the growth rate of state revenues since the early 1970s. Yet another factor is the increasing role of states relative to local governments, because states tend to have more cyclically variable revenue streams than local governments. There are many contributing factors, but the underlying problem leading to state government fiscal crises is cyclical variability in state revenues and expenditures.

The cyclical variability of expenditures could be reduced by reducing state expenditures in areas that are procyclical, like welfare, and shifting toward infrastructure production that can be put off during recessions. Obviously, decisions such as this should be made based on the overall priorities of state legislatures, that (hopefully) are more interested in undertaking expenditures to further the public interest rather than to reduce the cyclical variability of the expenditure flow. The expenditures side of the budget is determined for reasons other than cyclical variability, leaving little room for adjustments in the composition of the budget that might mitigate fiscal crises. That leaves the revenue side of the budget. Thus, we see that the way to mitigate state government fiscal crises might be to reduce the cyclical variability of the state government revenues that finance expenditures.

CAN CYCLICAL VARIABILITY OF STATE GOVERNMENT REVENUES BE REDUCED?

If state government fiscal crises are caused by cyclical variability, and if reducing expenditures in areas that have high cyclical variability is ruled out as a policy alternative, then one obvious avenue for reducing the severity of state fiscal crises would be to reduce the cyclical variability of state government revenues. Having identified cyclical variability in state government revenues as the fundamental problem that has caused state government fiscal crises, most of the material in this volume has been devoted to an analysis of the cyclical variability of revenues. That analysis has shown that there is no way to adjust state government revenues to produce a meaningful reduction in the cyclical variability of the revenue flow. Some changes in the structure of state funds, such as pooling together unstable revenue sources in the general fund and only earmarking unstable tax sources for expenditure programs that can more easily be cut during recessions (such as highway expenditures), might help to ease some of the fiscal stress experienced during recessions, but certainly not to a degree that would be meaningful.

In the 1990s the two major state government tax bases are general sales and personal income, which each make up more than 30 percent of state government revenues. Both tax bases fluctuate along with personal income in a state, which produce cyclically variable revenues. Although it makes sense that income and consumption would vary along with the business cycle, we analyzed these tax bases in some detail to see if there is not some way that states could manipulate their tax structures to reduce the cyclical variability of revenues. The main way in which cyclical variability could be reduced somewhat would be to include food in the general sales tax base in those states where food is now excluded. However, the issue of equity looms larger than the issue of cyclical variability in the food exemption, so we cannot offer this as a recommendation. The food exemption should be debated on more issues than just cyclical variability.

Even if state general sales taxes cover food, the tax base still varies with the business cycle, although not as much. On the issue of cyclical variability, neither personal income nor general sales has any significant advantage, so relying more on one or the other will not make an appreciable difference in the cyclical variability of state government revenues. Another avenue we explored was to see whether a combination of personal income and general sales taxes would be more stable than either tax by itself, which might be the case if the cycles in the two taxes were slightly out of phase with each other, but we found that combining the two tax bases would not make state revenues less cyclically variable. For the few states that have no personal income taxes or no general sales taxes, this means that adding the other tax base will not reduce the cyclical variability of the state's revenues, and for states with both, relying more heavily on one rather than the other will, likewise, make little difference.

Some tax bases are more cyclically variable than others. Corporate income is much more cyclically variable than either personal income or general sales, and makes up about 7 percent of total state tax revenues. Sin taxes, like those on alcohol and tobacco products, are less cyclically variable than other taxes, and in fact may be even slightly countercyclical. Alcohol and tobacco taxes, which were more than 10 percent of state tax revenues in 1950, are now less than 3 percent. Lower reliance on corporate income taxation coupled with greater reliance on sin taxes could produce a less cyclically variable stream of state tax revenues, but because they are relatively minor revenue sources, the potential to reduce cyclical variability by adjusting these taxes is limited.

Reducing the cyclical variability of state tax revenues is but one of many goals for state tax policy. Even if it were the only goal, it would be difficult to take the existing portfolio of state taxes and adjust it in such a way as to make an appreciable difference in the variability of state revenues over the business cycle. Furthermore, in some ways the procyclical revenue stream is desirable because it reduces the revenues taken from the private sector during downturns, helping the economy. Although we would not want to make too much of the concept of states using macroeconomic policy as a stabilizing device, the idea of automatic stabilizers in the tax system has been well accepted with regard to federal fiscal policy for decades. States will continue to have cyclically variable revenues, which has advantages as well as disadvantages, and because of this they must devise methods to deal with that variability. It cannot be eliminated.

MITIGATING STATE FISCAL CRISES

Having identified the cause of state fiscal crises as cyclical variability in state government revenues, and having concluded that it would not be possible to produce any meaningful decline in the degree of cyclical variability in state government revenues, the only remaining avenue for mitigating state fiscal crises is to smooth the flow of expenditures over the business cycle. States need to set aside revenues during prosperous years that they can then draw down during recessions to reduce their fiscal stress. Indeed, states have already picked up this message. In 1982, during the first clearly identified state fiscal crisis, only twelve states had rainy day funds. By 1994, forty-four states had them.

States could smooth their resources over the business cycle without rainy day funds by accumulating general fund surpluses during prosperous years and drawing them down during recessions, but several factors work against this strategy. First, it requires fiscal discipline to do so. Because there is an unlimited demand for government expenditure programs, it is too easy for states to look at surplus general revenues as a source of funds to undertake a few new programs and increase the funding levels of a few others. Part of the reason this temptation exists is that elected officials must always consider ways to get political support for upcoming elections. Thus, they have an incentive to spend now to get support, rather than to wait. It might be that if legislators are too frugal, any accumulated surpluses will be spent by their successors. There is also a "common pool" problem with surplus balances. If one legislator is restrained in trying to spend those funds for interests he supports, another legislator is likely to go after them for interests that she would prefer. Thus, legislators have an incentive to try to spend any surplus balances on causes they like rather than to leave them for potential raiding by other interests.

A second reason why the strategy of building up general fund surpluses might not work is that taxpayers might view the surplus balances as a potential source of tax cuts. If the government does not spend all the revenue it raises, why should taxpayers keep paying in to the government's coffers? This was one factor that led to California's Proposition 13 property tax limitation. California had substantial surplus general fund balances in 1978, when the measure passed.[5] A third reason weighing in favor of explicit rainy day funds is that it takes a more systematic approach by setting aside an explicit sum of money to mitigate the effects of future revenue downturns.

By looking at the experience of states with rainy day funds during the 1990–1991 recession, we found that just having a rainy day fund was not sufficient to ease fiscal crises. Only when these funds are governed by strict provisions for the depositing of money into the fund did they appear to be funded at a high enough level to be a meaningful aid to states. Based on our analysis, the establishment of a constitutional (not statutory) rainy day fund with explicit provisions for the deposit of money into the fund is the only way in which state fiscal crises can be significantly eased.

To completely offset the effects of recessionary downturns, however, states would have to maintain substantial rainy day funds, perhaps on the order of 30 percent of their budgets. We calculated this number in the previous chapter by looking at how much of a fund it would take for states to offset the effects of the 1991 recession. As a benchmark, we assumed that states would want to maintain their long-run rate of expenditure growth without implementing any new taxes or tax increases. Furthermore, because revenues began turning down in 1989, before the official recession set in, we looked at the amount of funds it would take to offset lower revenues in 1989, 1990, 1991, and 1992, and to smooth expenditures over those four years. The 1991 recession was not an overly severe recession (the one in 1982 was worse), so in one sense our estimate of the amount of funds necessary to mitigate the fiscal impact of a recession is conservative.

One reason the 30 percent figure may seem high is that funds have to be accumulated prior to revenue downturns, and must last throughout the entire period of below-average revenue increases. When that 30 percent figure is divided over four years, it comes out to about 7.5 percent per year. That figure also assumes that states do not want to increase taxes or reduce expenditures below their trend growth over the revenue downturn. We can see good reasons for avoiding tax increases during recessions. With the economy already slumping, tax increases place a bigger burden on taxpayers. Furthermore, tax increases may hinder an economic recovery, as already noted. The case for maintaining expenditure levels is less clear. Although many demands on the government's budget are pro-cyclical, fiscal stress may give governments an opportunity to look for areas in which government expenditures could be reduced, increasing the efficiency of government in both bad times and in good. In the public sector, just as in the private sector, no matter how efficient organizations might be at a particular point in time, they must continually work to reinvent themselves to maintain their efficiency.[6] Fiscal stress can provide the motivation to do so, thus improving the overall operation of government and, in the long run, helping government deal effectively with other fiscal issues.

The cyclical variability of revenues is explicitly a short-term problem that appears only during recessions, whereas the other fiscal problems faced by states are more long-term in nature. Smoothing available resources over the revenue cycle by using a rainy day fund will not directly solve many other major problems that states face, but it can help states cope with recessions. Because available revenues will be smoothed over the revenue cycle, it can also help states face up to their long-term budget constraints by preventing states from using temporary revenue gains during economic upswings to postpone dealing with longer term fiscal problems. Although rainy day funds are not the ultimate answer to most fiscal problems faced by states, they do deal directly with one clearly defined problem, and many states have established rainy day funds in order to try to ease the fiscal stress caused by recessions.

CONCLUSION

This study has covered a substantial amount of territory and has examined state fiscal data in detail to reach its conclusions, but the conclusions themselves can be stated very briefly. State government fiscal crises are caused by cyclical variability in state government revenues. When recessions reduce the growth in state government revenues, states tend to have fiscal crises. There is no good way to meaningfully reduce the cyclical variability of state government revenues. Therefore, the best way to minimize state government fiscal crises is to establish a properly structured rainy day fund. By setting aside some revenues during prosperous years for use during recessions, states can minimize their recession-induced fiscal stress and avoid fiscal crises.

As simple as this line of reasoning is, it is important from a policy perspective because during cyclical downturns analysts often confound the problems created by short-run declines in revenue growth and longer-run fiscal problems associated with expenditure demands. Revenue increases alone cannot solve the problem of state fiscal crises because the problem is cyclical in nature. Without a reserve of funds to draw on, fiscal crises will continue to reappear no matter now high revenues are. Conversely, during prosperous years revenues increase at an unsustainably high rate, perhaps misleading state legislators into thinking that their long-run fiscal situation is better than it actually is. By using a properly structured rainy day fund to reduce revenue availability during prosperous years, not only are states providing a cushion for the future, they are also providing a measure of fiscal discipline during the good years that might prevent excessive appropriations and unnecessary expenditures.

The periodic occurrence of fiscal crises created by the cyclical variability of state government revenues is not the most important fiscal issue that states face, but when a crisis occurs, it may appear to be. If states know what to expect, and can plan ahead to mitigate fiscal crises, they will also be better able to deal with the more important issues of designing expenditure programs and tax systems that enhance the long-run performance of the public sector.

NOTES

1.   Steven D. Gold, *The Fiscal Crisis of the States: Lessons for the Future* (Washington, D.C.: Georgetown University Press, 1995), ch. 2, considers state fiscal problems more broadly when discussing fiscal crises.

2.   Gold, *The Fiscal Crisis of the States*, 377.

3.   See, for examples, James A. Papke, "The Response of State-Local Government Taxation to Fiscal Crisis," *National Tax Journal* 36, no. 3 (September 1983): 401–05, and Steven D. Gold, "State Tax Increases of 1983: Prelude to Another Tax Revolt?" *National Tax Journal* 37, no. 1 (March 1984): 9–22.

4.   Edward M. Gramlich, "The 1991 State and Local Fiscal Crises," *Brookings Papers on Economic Activity* 2 (1991): 249–87, and Steven D. Gold, ed., *The Fiscal Crisis of the States: Lessons for the Future* (Washington, D.C.: Georgetown University Press, 1995).

5.   Randall G. Holcombe, *Public Finance: Government Revenues and Expenditures in the United States Economy* (Minneapolis/St. Paul: West Publishing Company, 1996), 328–29.

6.   David Osborne and Ted Gaebler, *Reinventing Government: How the Entrepreneurial Spirit is Transforming the Public Sector* (Reading, Mass.: Addison-Wesley, 1992).

Bibliography

Andrews, Donald W. K. "Tests for Parameter Instability and Structural Change with Unknown Change Point." *Econometrica* 61, no. 4 (July 1993): 821–56.

Bahl, Roy, and David L. Sjoquist. "The State and Local Fiscal Outlook: What Have We Learned and Where are We Headed?" *National Tax Journal* 43, no. 3 (September 1990): 321–42.

Barro, Robert J. "On the Determination of the Public Debt." *Journal of Political Economy* 87, no. 5 (October 1979): 940–71.

Becker, Gary S. "A Theory of Competition among Pressure Groups for Political Influence." *Quarterly Journal of Economics* 98 (August 1983): 371–400.

Bergstrom, Theodore C., and Robert Goodman. "Private Demand for Public Goods." *American Economic Review* 63 (June 1973): 280–96.

Blackley, Paul R., and Larry DeBoer. "Explaining State Government Discretionary Revenue Increases in Fiscal Years 1991 and 1992." *National Tax Journal* 46, no. 1 (March 1993): 1–12.

Borcherding, Thomas E., and Robert T. Deacon. "The Demand for Services of Non-Federal Governments." *American Economic Review* 62 (December 1972): 891–901.

Bryan, Tom, and Dick Howard. "Michigan's Budget and Economic Stabilization Fund." *Innovations* (May 1979): 1–11 (Council of State Governments).

Crider, Robert A. *The Impact of Recession on State and Local Finance.* Urban and Regional Development Series No. 6. Columbus, Ohio: Academy for Contemporary Problems, 1978.

Dickey, David A., and Wayne A. Fuller. "Distribution of the Estimators for Autoregressive Time Series with a Unit Root." *Journal of the American Statistical Association* 74, no. 366 (June 1979): 427–31.

Duncombe, William. "Economic Change and the Evolving State Tax Structure: The Case of the Sales Tax." *National Tax Journal* 45, no. 3 (September 1992): 299–313.

Dye, Richard F., and Therese J. McGuire. "Growth and Variability of State Individual Income and Sales Taxes." *National Tax Journal* 44, no. 1 (March 1991): 55–66.

Elder, Harold W. "Exploring the Tax Revolt: An Analysis of the Effects of State Tax and Expenditure Limitation Laws." *Public Finance Quarterly* 20, no. 1 (January 1992): 47–63.

Engle, Robert F., and Clive W. J. Granger. "Co-Integration and Error Correction: Representation, Estimation, and Testing." *Econometrica* 55, no. 2 (March 1987): 251–76.

Feenberg, Daniel R., William Gentry, David Gilroy, and Harvey S. Rosen. "Testing the Rationality of State Revenue Forecasts." *Review of Economics and Statistics* 71, no. 2 (May 1989): 300–308.

Flowers, Marilyn R. "Shared Tax Sources in a Leviathan Model of Federalism." *Public Finance Quarterly* 16, no. 1 (January 1988): 67–77.

Fox, William F., and Charles Campbell. "Stability of the State Sales Tax Income Elasticity." *National Tax Journal* 37, no. 2 (June 1984): 201–12.

Friedlaender, Ann F., Gerald J. Swanson, and John F. Due. "Estimating Sales Tax Revenue Changes in Response to Changes in Personal Income and Sales Tax Rates." *National Tax Journal* 26, no. 1 (March 1973): 103–13.

Friedman, Milton. *A Theory of the Consumption Function.* Princeton, N.J.: Princeton University Press, 1957.

———. "Do Old Fallacies Ever Die?" *Journal of Economic Literature* 30, no. 4 (December 1992): 2129–32.

Fuller, Wayne A. *Introduction to Statistical Time Series.* New York: John Wiley & Sons, 1976.

Gentry, William M. "Do State Revenue Forecasters Utilize Available Information?" *National Tax Journal* 42, no. 4 (December 1989): 429–39.

Geweke, J., R. Meese, and W. Dent, "Comparing Alternative Tests of Causality in Temporal Systems," *Journal of Econometrics* 21 (1982), pp. 161– 94.

Gold, Steven D. *Preparing for the Next Recession: Rainy Day Funds and Other Tools for the States.* Legislative Finance Paper No. 41. Denver: National Conference of State Legislatures, 1983.

———. "State Tax Increases of 1983: Prelude to Another Tax Revolt?" *National Tax Journal* 37, no. 1 (March 1984): 9–22.

———. "Changes in State Government Finances in the 1980s." *National Tax Journal* 44, no. 1 (March 1991): 1–19.

———, ed. *The Fiscal Crisis of the States: Lessons for the Future.* Washington, D.C.: Georgetown University Press, 1995.

Gramlich, Edward M. "Alternative Federal Policies for Stimulating State and Local Expenditures: A Comparison of Their Effects." *National Tax Journal* 21, no. 2 (June 1968): 119–29.

———. "The 1991 State and Local Fiscal Crises." *Brookings Papers on Economic Activity* 2 (1991): 249–87.

Granger, C.W.J., and P. Newbold. "Spurious Regressions in Econometrics." *Journal of Econometrics* 2 (1974): 111–20.

Groves, Harold M., and C. Harry Kahn. "The Stability of State and Local Tax Yields," *American Economic Review* 42, no. 1 (March 1952): 87–102.

Hamilton, James D. *Time Series Analysis.* Princeton, N.J.: Princeton University Press, 1994.

Hellerstein, Walter. "Florida's Sales Tax on Services." *National Tax Journal* 41, no. 1 (March 1988): 1–18.

Holcombe, Randall G. *An Economic Analysis of Democracy.* Carbondale: Southern Illinois University Press, 1985.

———. *Public Finance: Government Revenues and Expenditures in the United States Economy.* Minneapolis/St. Paul: West Publishing Company, 1996.

Holcombe, Randall G., and Russell S. Sobel. "The Relative Variability of State Income and Sales Taxes Over the Revenue Cycle." *Atlantic Economic Journal* 23, no. 2 (June 1995): 97–112.

Hulten, Charles R. "Productivity Changes in State and Local Governments." *Review of Economics and Statistics* 66, no. 2 (May 1984): 256–66.

Johansen, Soren. "Statistical Analysis of Cointegrating Vectors." *Journal of Economic Dynamics and Control* 12, no. 2/3 (June/September 1988): 231–54.

———. "Estimation and Hypothesis Testing of Cointegration Vectors in Gaussian Vector Autoregressive Models." *Econometrica* 59, no. 6 (November 1991): 1551–80.

———. "Cointegration in Partial Systems and the Efficiency of Single-Equation Analysis." *Journal of Econometrics* 52, no. 3 (June 1992): 389–402.

Kydland, Finn E., and Edward C. Prescott. "A Competitive Theory of Fluctuations and the Feasibility and Desirability of Stabilization Policy." In *Rational Expectations and Economic Policy,* edited by Stanley Fischer. Chicago: University of Chicago Press, 1980.

Ladd, Helen F. "State Responses to the TRA86 Revenue Windfalls: A New Test of the Flypaper Effect." *Journal of Policy Analysis and Management* 12, no. 1 (Winter 1993): 82–103.

Legler, John B., and Perry Shapiro. "The Responsiveness of State Tax Revenue to Economic Growth." *National Tax Journal* 21, no. 1 (March 1968): 46–56.

Lucas, Robert E., and Nancy L. Stokey. "Optimal Fiscal and Monetary Policy in an Economy without Capital." *Journal of Monetary Economics* 12, no. 1 (January 1983): 55–94.

MacKinnon, James G. "Critical Values for Cointegration Tests." In *Long-Run Economic Relationships: Readings in Cointegration,* edited by R. F. Engle and C. W. J. Granger. Oxford: Oxford University Press, 1990. 267–76.

Macsherry, Cathy Daicoff, "Assessing Revenue-raising Ability: A Private-sector View of Changes." In *Measuring Fiscal Capacity,* edited by H. Clyde Reeves. Boston: Oelgeschlager, Gunn & Hain in association with the Lincoln Institute of Land Policy, 1986.

Mattoon, Richard H., and William A. Testa. "State and Local Government and the Business Cycle." In *Issues in State and Local Government Finance, Collected Works From the Federal Reserve Bank of Chicago,* edited by William A. Testa. Federal Reserve Bank of Chicago, 1992.

———. "State and Local Governments' Reaction to Recession." *Economic Perspectives* 16, no. 2 (March/April 1992): 19–27 (Federal Reserve Bank of Chicago).

Mikesell, John L. "Income Elasticities of State Sales Tax Base Components." *Quarterly Review of Economics and Business* 17, no. 1 (Spring 1977): 83–94.

———. "Election Periods and State Tax Policy Cycles." *Public Choice* 33, no. 3 (1978): 99–106.

Mills, Terence C. *Time Series Techniques for Economists.* Cambridge: Cambridge University Press, 1990.

Misiolek, Walter S., and D. Grady Perdue. "The Portfolio Approach to State and Local Tax Structures." *National Tax Journal* 40, no. 1 (March 1987): 111–14.

National Association of State Budget Officers. *Fiscal Survey of the States* (various issues). Washington, D.C.: National Governors' Association.

National Conference of State Legislatures. *State Budget and Tax Actions.* (various years). Denver, Colorado.

Nelson, Charles R., and Charles I. Plosser. "Trends and Random Walks in Macroeconomic Time Series: Some Evidence and Implications." *Journal of Monetary Economics* 10, no. 2 (September 1982): 139–62.

Newey, Whitney K., and Kenneth D. West. A Simple, Positive Semi-Definite, Heteroskedasticity and Autocorrelation Consistent Covariance Matrix." *Econometrica* 55, no. 3 (May 1987): 703–8.

Oakland, William H. "Proposition 13, Genesis and Consequences." *Review of the Federal Reserve Bank of San Francisco* (1979): 5–14.

Oates, Wallace E. *Fiscal Federalism.* New York: Harcourt Brace Jovanovich, 1972.

Ogaki, Masao. "Unit Roots in Macroeconomics: A Survey." *Bank of Japan Monetary and Economic Studies* 11, no. 2 (November 1993): 131–54.

Osborne, David. *Laboratories of Democracy.* Boston: Harvard Business School Press, 1988.

Osborne, David, and Ted Gaebler. *Reinventing Government: How the Entrepreneurial Spirit Is Transforming the Public Sector.* Reading, Mass.: Addison-Wesley, 1992.

Papke, James A. "The Response of State-Local Government Taxation to Fiscal Crisis." *National Tax Journal* 36, no. 3 (September 1983): 401–5.

Park, Joon Y. "Canonical Cointegrating Regressions." *Econometrica* 60, no. 1 (January 1992): 119–43.

Peltzman, Sam. "Toward a More General Theory of Regulation." *Journal of Law & Economics* 19 (August 1976): 211–40.

Phillips, Peter C. B. "Understanding Spurious Regressions in Econometrics." *Journal of Econometrics* 33 (December 1986): 311–40.

Phillips, Peter C. B., and Mico Loretan. "Estimating Long-Run Economic Equilibria." *Review of Economic Studies* 58, No. 3 (May 1991), pp. 407–36.

Ramsey, Frank P. "A Contribution to the Theory of Taxation." *Economic Journal* 37 (1927): 47–61.

Ring, Raymond J., Jr. "The Proportion of Consumers' and Producers' Goods in the General Sales Tax." *National Tax Journal* 42, no. 2 (June 1989): 167–79.

Sahasakul, Chaipat. "The U.S. Evidence on Optimal Taxation Over Time." *Journal of Monetary Economics* 18, no. 3 (November 1986): 251–75.

Said, Said E., and David A. Dickey. "Testing for Unit Roots in Autoregressive-Moving Average Models of Unknown Order." *Biometrica* 71 (1984): 599–607.

Saikkonen, Pentti. "Asymptotically Efficient Estimation of Cointegrating Regressions." *Econometric Theory* 7, no.1 (March 1991): 1–21.

Sobel, Russell S. "Optimal Taxation in a Federal System of Governments." *Southern Economic Journal* (October 1997), forthcoming.

———, "West Virginia's Tax Structure and Rainy Day Fund." *West Virginia Public Affairs Reporter* 13, no. 1 (Winter 1996).

Sobel, Russell S., and Randall G. Holcombe, "The Impact of State Rainy Day Funds in Easing State Fiscal Crises During the 1990-91 Recession." *Public Budgeting & Finance* 16, no. 3 (Fall 1996): 28–48.

———, and ———. "Measuring the Growth and Variability of Tax Bases Over the Business Cycle." *National Tax Journal* 49, no. 4 (December 1996): 535–52.

Solon, Gary R. "Intergenerational Income Mobility in the United States." *American Economic Review* 82, no. 3 (June 1992): 393–408.

State Policy Research, Inc. *State Policy Reports* 8, no. 8 (1991): 2–8.

Stock, James H. "Asymptotic Properties of Least Squares Estimators of Cointegrating Vectors." *Econometrica* 55 (1987): 1035–56.

Stock, James H., and Mark W. Watson. "A Simple Estimator of Cointegrating Vectors in Higher Order Integrated Systems." *Econometrica* 61, no. 4 (July 1993): 783–820.

Supel, Tom, and Bruce Litterman. "Using Vector Autoregressions to Measure the Uncertainty in Minnesota's Revenue Forecasts." *Quarterly Review* (Spring 1983): 10–22 (Federal Reserve Bank of Minneapolis).

Suyderhoud, Jack P. "State-Local Revenue Diversification, Balance, and Fiscal Performance." *Public Finance Quarterly* 22, no. 2 (April 1994): 168–94.

U.S. Advisory Commission on Intergovernmental Relations. *Significant Features of Fiscal Federalism.* Washington, D.C. (various years).

Vasche, Jon David, and Brad Williams. "Optimal Government Budgeting Contingency Reserve Funds." *Public Budgeting and Finance* 7, no. 1 (Spring 1987): 66–82.

Vickrey, William. "Some Limits to the Income Elasticity of Income Tax Yields." *Review of Economics and Statistics* 31, no. 2 (May 1949): 140–44.

Vogel, Robert C., and Robert P. Trost. "The Response of State Government Receipts to Economic Fluctuations and the Allocation of Counter-Cyclical Revenue Sharing Grants." *Review of Economics and Statistics* 61, no. 3 (August 1979): 389–400.

Wagoner, Charles B. "Local Fiscal Competition: An Intraregional Perspective." *Public Finance Quarterly* 23, no. 1 (January 1995): 95–114.

Walton, Terry Wilford. "State Tax Stability Criteria and the Revenue-Income Elasticity Coefficient Reconsidered." *National Tax Journal* 18, no. 3 (September 1965): 304–12.

Weingast, Barry R., Kenneth A. Shepsle, and Christopher Johnsen. "The Political Economy of Benefits and Costs: A Neoclassical Approach to Distributive Politics." *Journal of Political Economy* 89, no. 4 (August 1981): 642–64.

West, Kenneth D. "The Insensitivity of Consumption to News About Income." *Journal of Monetary Economics* 21, no. 1 (January 1988): 17–33.

West Virginia Tax Expenditure Study: Expenditures for Consumer Sales Tax and Use Tax, West Virginia Department of Tax and Revenue, January 1995.

White, Fred C. "Trade-Off in Growth and Stability in State Taxes." *National Tax Journal* 36, no. 1 (March 1983): 103–14.

Wilford, W. T. "State Tax Stability Criteria and the Revenue-Income Coefficient Reconsidered." *National Tax Journal* 18, no. 3 (September 1965): 304–12.

———. "A Comment on 'The Stability, Growth, and Stabilizing Influence of State Taxes.'" *National Tax Journal* 28, no. 4 (December 1975): 452–58.

Williams, William V., Robert M. Anderson, David O. Froehle, and Kaye L. Lamb. "The Stability, Growth, and Stabilizing Influence of State Taxes." *National Tax Journal* 26, no. 2 (June 1973): 267–74.

Yondorf, Barbara A. *A Legislator's Guide to Budget Oversight After the Appropriations Act Has Passed.* Denver: National Conference of State Legislatures, 1983.

Zimmerman, David J. "Regression Toward Mediocrity in Economic Stature." *American Economic Review* 82, no. 3 (June 1992): 409–29.

Index

About the Authors

RANDALL G. HOLCOMBE is DeVoe Moore Professor of Economics at Florida State University. He is also chairman of the Research Advisory Council at the James Madison Institute for Public Policy Studies, a Tallahassee-based think-tank that specializes in issues facing state governments. He is the author of seven books, including *Public Policy and Quality of Life* (Greenwood, 1995). His primary research areas are public finance and the economic analysis of public policy issues.

RUSSELL S. SOBEL is Assistant Professor of Economics at West Virginia University and a faculty research associate with the Bureau of Business and Economic Research at West Virginia University. He is the author of several articles.

ISBN 0-313-30423-8

EAN

9 780313 304231

HARDCOVER BAR CODE